A Modern Approach to Computer Vision

A Modern Approach to Computer Vision

Aria Anderson

Larsen & Keller
www.larsen-keller.com

A Modern Approach to Computer Vision
Aria Anderson
ISBN: 978-1-64172-382-4 (Hardback)

 Larsen & Keller

Published by Larsen and Keller Education,
5 Penn Plaza,
19th Floor,
New York, NY 10001, USA

Cataloging-in-Publication Data

A modern approach to computer vision / Aria Anderson.
    p. cm.
Includes bibliographical references and index.
ISBN 978-1-64172-382-4
1. Computer vision. 2. Artificial intelligence. 3. Image processing.
4. Computer science. I. Anderson, Aria.
TA1634 .M63 2020
006.37--dc23

For more information regarding Larsen and Keller Education and its products, please visit the publisher's website www.larsen-keller.com

TABLE OF CONTENTS

This book is a culmination of my many years of practice in this field. I attribute the success of this book to my support group. I would like to thank my parents who have showered me with unconditional love and support and my peers and professors for their constant guidance.

The scientific field which is concerned with how computers can be made to gain high-level understanding from videos or digital images, is known as computer vision. Some of the common tasks of computer vision include acquiring, analyzing, processing and understanding digital images as well as the extraction of high-dimensional data from real world to produce numerical or symbolic information. There are various sub-domains of computer vision such as event detection, scene reconstruction, video tracking, 3D pose estimation, image restoring, motion estimation and object recognition. Signal processing, solid-state physics and information engineering are some of the related fields of computer vision. This book presents the complex subject of computer vision in the most comprehensible and easy to understand language. The topics covered herein deal with the core aspects of this field. This textbook is appropriate for students seeking detailed information in this area as well as for experts.

The details of chapters are provided below for a progressive learning:

Chapter – What is Computer Vision?

An inter-disciplinary field that deals with usage of computer in gaining high-level knowledge, by the means of images, audios and videos, is referred to as computer vision. Some of its aspects include deep learning for computer vision, computer stereo vision, underwater computer vision, etc. This is an introductory chapter which will briefly introduce all these significant aspects of computer vision.

Chapter – Digital Image Processing

An ordinary image that can be represented as a set of numbers or pixels, which can be processed by digital computer is defined as digital image. The algorithm used for processing digital images is called digital image processing. This chapter has been carefully written to provide an easy understanding of the varied facets of digital image processing.

Chapter – Color Vision

The capability of differentiating lights of various wavelengths and frequencies by the means of computer machines is termed as color vision. Color management, color space, color mapping, color constancy, visual perception, color appearance model, etc. are some of its concepts. These diverse concepts of color vision have been thoroughly discussed in this chapter.

Chapter – Geometry in Computer Vision

Geometry has numerous uses in terms of computer vision. Projective geometry, epipolar geometry, etc. are some of its types. Some of its aspects are bundle adjustment, fundamental matrix of computer vision, essential matrix, camera matrix, camera resectioning, structure from motion and image rectification. The topics elaborated in this chapter will help in gaining a better perspective about the use of geometry in computer vision.

Chapter – Applications

Computer vision is a vast subject that has an array of applications. Some of them are facial recognition system, gesture recognition, 3D single-object recognition, face detection, handwriting recognition, machine vision, self-driving car, remote sensing, etc. This chapter closely examines these applications of computer vision to provide an extensive understanding of the subject.

Aria Anderson

What is Computer Vision?

An inter-disciplinary field that deals with usage of computer in gaining high-level knowledge, by the means of images, audios and videos, is referred to as computer vision. Some of its aspects include deep learning for computer vision, computer stereo vision, underwater computer vision, etc. This is an introductory chapter which will briefly introduce all these significant aspects of computer vision.

Computer Vision is the process of using machines to understand and analyze imagery (both photos and videos). While these types of algorithms have been around in various forms since the 1960's, recent advances in Machine Learning, as well as leaps forward in data storage, computing capabilities, and cheap high-quality input devices, have driven major improvements in how well our software can explore this kind of content.

Computer Vision is the broad parent name for any computations involving visual content – that means images, videos, icons, and anything else with pixels involved. But within this parent idea, there are a few specific tasks that are core building blocks:

- In object classification, you train a model on a dataset of specific objects, and the model classifies new objects as belonging to one or more of your training categories.

- For object identification, your model will recognize a specific instance of an object – for example, parsing two faces in an image and tagging one as Tom Cruise and one as Katie Holmes.

A classical application of computer vision is handwriting recognition for digitizing handwritten content. Outside of just recognition, other methods of analysis include:

- Video motion analysis uses computer vision to estimate the velocity of objects in a video, or the camera itself.

- In image segmentation, algorithms partition images into multiple sets of views.

- Scene reconstruction creates a 3D model of a scene inputted through images or video.

- In image restoration, noise such as blurring is removed from photos using Machine Learning based filters.

Any other application that involves understanding pixels through software can safely be labeled as computer vision.

Working of Computer Vision

One of the major open questions in both Neuroscience and Machine Learning is: how exactly do our brains work, and how can we approximate that with our own algorithms? The reality is that there are very few working and comprehensive theories of brain computation; so despite the fact that Neural Nets are supposed to "mimic the way the brain works," nobody is quite sure if that's actually true.

The same paradox holds true for computer vision – since we're not decided on how the brain and eyes process images, it's difficult to say how well the algorithms used in production approximate our own internal mental processes. For example, studies have shown that some functions that we thought happen in the brain of frogs actually take place in the eyes. We're a far cry from amphibians, but similar uncertainty exists in human cognition.

Machines interpret images very simply: as a series of pixels, each with their own set of color values. Consider the simplified image below, and how grayscale values are converted into a simple array of numbers:

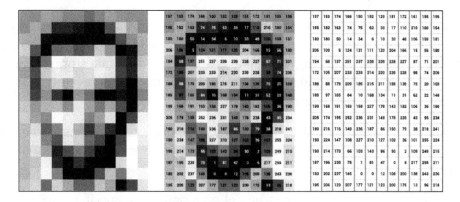

Think of an image as a giant grid of different squares, or pixels (this image is a very simplified version of what looks like either Abraham Lincoln or a Dementor). Each pixel in an image can be represented by a number, usually from 0 – 255. The series of numbers on the right is what software sees when you input an image. For our image, there are 12 columns and 16 rows, which mean there are 192 input values for this image.

When we start to add in color, things get more complicated. Computers usually read color as a series of 3 values – red, green, and blue (RGB) – on that same 0 – 255 scale. Now, each pixel actually has 3 values for the computer to store in addition to its position. If we were to colorize President Lincoln (or Harry Potter's worst fear), that would lead to 12 x 16 x 3 values, or 576 numbers.

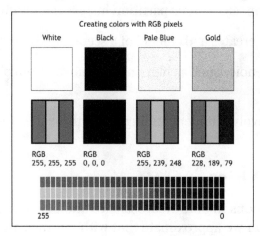

For some perspective on how computationally expensive this is, consider this tree:

- Each color value is stored in 8 bits.

- 8 bits x 3 colors per pixel = 24 bits per pixel.

- A normal sized 1024 x 768 image x 24 bits per pixel = almost 19M bits, or about 2.36 megabytes.

That's a lot of memory to require for one image, and a lot of pixels for an algorithm to iterate over. But to train a model with meaningful accuracy – especially when you're talking about Deep Learning – you'd usually need tens of thousands of images, and the more the merrier. Even if you were to use Transfer Learning to use the insights of an already trained model, you'd still need a few thousand images to train yours on.

With the sheer amount of computing power and storage required just to train deep learning models for computer vision, it's not hard to understand why advances in those two fields have driven Machine Learning forward to such a degree.

Business use Cases for Computer Vision

Computer vision is one of the areas in Machine Learning where core concepts are already being integrated into major products that we use every day. Google is using maps to leverage their image data and identify street names, businesses, and office buildings. Facebook is using computer vision to identify people in photos, and do a number of things with that information.

> Face Recognition   •••
>
> **Introducing Face Recognition For More Features**
> Hi Justin, we're always working to make Facebook better, so we're adding more ways to use face recognition besides just suggesting tags. For example, face recognition technology can do things like:
>
> • Find photos you're in but haven't been tagged
> • Help protect you from strangers using your photo
> • Tell people with visual impairments who's in your photo or video
>
> You control face recognition. This setting is on, but you can turn it off any time, which applies to features we may add later.
>
> -The Facebook Team

But it's not just tech companies that are leverage Machine Learning for image applications. Ford, the American car manufacturer that has been around literally since the early 1900's, is investing heavily in autonomous vehicles (AVs). Much of the underlying technology in AVs relies on analyzing the multiple video feeds coming into the car and using computer vision to analyze and pick a path of action.

Another major area where computer vision can help is in the medical field. Much of diagnosis is image processing, like reading x-rays, MRI scans, and other types of diagnostics. Google has been working with medical research teams to explore how deep learning can help medical workflows, and have made significant progress in terms of accuracy.

Advantages of Computer Vision

- Faster and simpler process: Computer vision systems can carry out monotonous, repetitive tasks at a faster rate, making the entire process simpler.

- Accurate outcome: It's no secret that machines never make any mistake. Likewise, computer vision systems with image-processing capabilities will commit zero mistakes, unlike humans. Ultimately, products or services provided will not only be quick but also of high quality.

- Cost-reduction: With machines taking up responsibilities of performing cumbersome tasks, errors will be minimized, leaving no room for faulty products or services. As a result, companies can save a lot of money that would be otherwise spent on fixing flawed processes and products.

Disadvantages of Computer Vision

- Lack of specialists: Computer vision technology involves the use of AI and ML. To train a computer vision system powered by AI and ML, companies need to have a team of professionals with technical expertise. Without them, building a system that can analyze and process the possible surrounding details is not possible.

- Need for regular monitoring: What if a computer vision system breaks down or has a technical glitch? To ensure that doesn't happen, companies have to get a dedicated team onboard for regular monitoring and evaluation.

DEEP LEARNING FOR COMPUTER VISION

Deep learning has several uses in helping to achieve computer vision and overcoming its challenges - here are five of them.

Facial Recognition

Probably the computer vision capability familiar to most people is facial recognition, which is a common feature in today's smartphones and cameras. Modern facial recognition systems at large enterprises are powered by deep learning networks and algorithms.

Facebook's DeepFace identifies human faces in digital images using a nine-layer neural network. The system has 97 percent accuracy, which is famously better than the FBI's facial recognition system. Google also developed its own highly accurate facial recognition system named FaceNet.

Object Classification and Localization

Classification with localization means identifying objects of a certain class in images and videos and highlighting their location, typically by drawing a box around the object. This particular computer vision use case is more challenging than simple object classification, which assigns labels to entire images (e.g. cat, bird, and dog).

Classification with localization is particularly helpful in the medical field because healthcare organizations can train neural networks to rapidly identify cancerous regions of the body based on x-rays and other diagnostic medical images.

An extension of object classification and localization is object detection, in which the model can identify many objects of different types in images.

Semantic Segmentation

Semantic segmentation is a more advanced form of image classification and localization made possible by neural networks. With semantic segmentation, a model can classify and locate all of the pixels in an image or video.

The most exciting potential use for this computer vision function is real-time semantic segmentation used by self-driving cars. Identifying and localizing objects accurately can improve the safety and reliability of autonomous vehicles.

Colorization

Colorization is the process of converting grayscale images to full-color images. The excitement of this use case comes from its aesthetic appeal. Colorization with deep learning can give new context and vibrancy to old black and white movies and photos.

Reconstructing Images

Technology giant Nvidia sent the Internet into frenzy in 2018 when it announced a new technique that can reconstruct corrupted images. Wear and tear on old printed photographs can lead to holes, blurring, and other damage to the image. Digital images can get damaged and lose some of their pixels due to corrupt memory cards.

The technique uses deep learning to fill in the missing parts of images. According to the research paper, the deep learning model used by Nvidia can "robustly handle holes of any shape, size, location, or distance from the image borders".

COMPUTER STEREO VISION

Stereo Vision is an area of study in the field of Machine Vision that attempts to recreate the human vision system by using two or more 2D views of the same scene to derive 3D depth information about the scene.

Depth information can be used to track moving objects in 3D space, gather distance information for scene features, or to construct a 3D spatial model of a scene.

The binocular (two-eyed) human vision system captures two different views of a scene. The human brain processes each view and matches similarities. Most of the information captured in each a particular view is congruent with the information captured in the other, however, some information is not. The differences allow the human brain to build depth information.

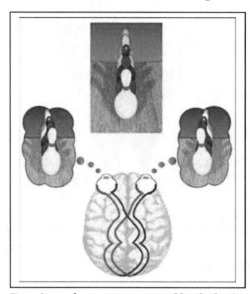

Two views of a scene as captured by the brain.

The ability of a machine to capture 3D information from the real world in a similar fashion to a human being is of great interest to science and industry. Research is being conducted in Stereo Vision to unlock the visual real world environment for intelligent machine participation.

The manufacturing industry has maintained an interest in automating production roles, and researches are being done into Stereo Vision to automate spatially-perceptive manufacturing processes in the automotive, aircraft, and shipbuilding industries.

Stereo Vision systems are being developed to inspect infrastructure in human-inaccessible tunnels and pipes, and long sections of road and bridges.

The medical procedures involved with anthropometry and plastic surgery may be augmented by new systems capable of capturing and reproducing 3D information about the human body.

Stereo Vision is of particular interest to robotics. Several major projects have been undertaken by European automobile manufacturers to automate driving and navigation of road vehicles. Robots are being developed to build and flesh-out accurate three-dimensional maps of both indoor and outdoor areas.

Applications

Autonomous Road Vehicle Navigation

Autonomous vehicles (or robots) employing Stereo Vision techniques must operate in real time, and thus are driving research for faster and more efficient Stereo Vision algorithms, whilst retaining enough accuracy to build a navigable 3D map, track moving obstacles, and eliminate a reasonable volume of noise.

Autonomous vehicles are primarily interested in identifying, classifying, and tracking the movement of obstacles, in order to plan paths of movement that avoid collision. Betrozzi et al. give us a breakdown of the common obstacle recognition model.

Road vehicle vision systems and algorithms, if they are to be broadly applicable, must be robust enough to handle changes to:

- Road

- Traffic

- Illumination

- Weather

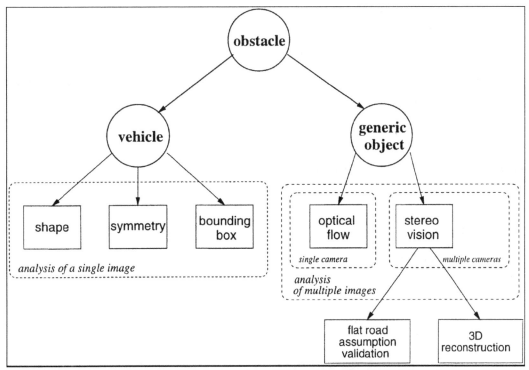

Machine Vision techniques used for different classifications of obstacle.

We can see that different subsets of Machine Vision algorithms are used for analysing different types of obstacles. Betrozzi gives us the abstract model used in autonomous road vehicles in figure. Moving obstacles are positioned in the conceptual 3D space created by the Stereo Vision system, and given simplified dimensions by surrounding the object with a bounding box. The autonomous vehicle then requires minimum calculation to plan a path that will avoid collision with the obstacle. Other obstacles are tracked using optical flow, and compared to the velocity vector of the car to determine if they are moving or stationary obstacles. Additionally, we can see that road vehicles perform some simple 3D reconstruction of the road ahead to assist forward-thinking path planning features of the navigation system.

The VaMP prototype autonomous road vehicle.

Many researches with autonomous road vehicles have been conducted by various universities, automobile manufacturers and military contractors, however very few have produced more than ponderous results. Some autonomous road vehicles (or Smart Cars), have successfully driven over long distances, and produced very promising experimental results, driving in real traffic conditions at high speed. The following experimental vehicles are amongst the most successful:

- The VaMP prototype was driven from Munich, Germany to Odense, Denmark in 1995

- The RALPH system was tested using the NavLab 5 Stereo Vision sytem over a journey from Pittsburgh, PA to San Diego, CA in 1995.

- The ARGO experimental vehicle was driven by the GOLD system for nearly 2000 km throughout Italy during the MilleMiglia in Automatico Tour in 1998.

Betrozzi et al. tell us from experience with the ARGO vehicle that the Stereo Vision systems of autonomous road vehicles must meet a number of different challenges, and so several subsystems, with specially designed algorithms, must be created to provide:

- Lane markings detection,

- Traffic signs recognition,

- Obstacle identification,

- Filter out shadows on the road,

- Adapt if other road vehicles that obscure visibility.

Typical result for (a) Lane detection, (b) Obstacle detection, (c) Vehicle detection, and (d) Pedestrians detection.

Several of the Stereo Vision sub-systems used in the ARGO road vehicle.

All-terrain Robot Navigation

Until now NASA moon rovers have been tele-operated from Earth. There is an enormous time delay between communications to and from Earth, which presents a major problem to NASA. Autonomous robot rovers are being designed at Carnegie Mellon University to fully automate small rover journeys over lunar terrain using a Stereo Vision-based approach. The CMU team has adopted a very simple navigation algorithm for their lunar rover:

- Analyse images of area directly in front of rover,

- Identify obstacles,

- Identify terrain type (e.g loose, hard rock),

- Determine 3D positions, and put in a small grid,

- Choose the best of 8 possible paths through grid.

The Stereo Vision system of the CMU lunar rover analyses terrain immediately ahead of the vehicle, and tries to identify obstacle features. Each obstacle triangulated in 3D space, and awarded a terrain roughness score (by an undisclosed filtering/classification system). The obstacles are then plotted on a simple grid, representing the area in front of the rover. The darker squares in figure represent those obstacles with higher terrain roughness ratings.

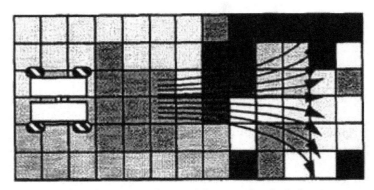

Plotting obstacles on a grid map of the area ahead of a lunar rover.

Again, with reference to figure, the rover navigation system sums the scores of every cell in the grid passed, for each of nine hard-coded paths. The system then selects the path with the lowest total score through the grid. Presumably an additional system would be required to ensure the long-term path of the rover was valid, and that the rover would be able to reverse or turn on the spot, should all possible paths be obstructed.

Method

Triangulation

The same method that is used in navigation and surveying is used to calculate depth. Basic triangulation uses the known distance of two separated points looking at the same scene point. From these parameters the distance to the scene point can be calculated. This same basic idea is used in stereo vision to find depth information from two images. Figure graphically shows the geometry.

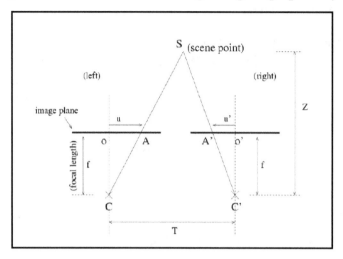

Triangulation in a Stereo Vision system.

In the previous arrangement, two cameras (C, C') see the same feature point (S). The location of the point in the two image planes is denoted by A and A'. When the cameras are separated by a distance T, the location of A and A' from the cameras normal axis will differ (denoted by U, U'). Using these differences, the distance (Z) to the point can be calculated from the following formula:

$$Z = f \frac{T}{U - U'}$$

In order to calculate depth however, the difference of U and U' need to be established.

Disparity

Differences between two images give depth information. These differences are known as disparities. The key step to obtaining accurate depth information is therefore finding a detailed and accurate disparity map. Disparity maps can be visualised in greyscale. Close objects result in a large disparity value. This is translated into light greyscale values. Objects further away will appear darker.

Obtaining depth information is achieved through a process of four steps. Firstly the cameras need to be calibrated. After calibrating the cameras the assumption is made that the differences in the images are on the same horizontal or epipolar line. The secondly step is the decision as to which method is going to be used to find the differences between the two images. Once this decision is made, an algorithm to obtain the disparity map needs to be designed or decided on. The third step is to implement the algorithm to obtain the disparity information. The final step is to use the disparity information, along with the camera calibration set in step one, to obtain a detailed three dimensional view of the world.

This report focuses on the basic ideas behind the algorithms used to obtain disparity information. The other steps are relatively straight forward in their operation and implementation. It should be noted that even within the algorithms; there is ongoing research and therefore many different implementations.

There are many algorithms used to find the disparity between the left and right images. Additionally, there is a large amount of ongoing research into finding quicker and more accurate algorithms. However there are two commonly used algorithms that are currently used to find disparity. The first method is feature-based. The second method is an area-based statistical method. Because they are widely used, we will focus on these two methods in this report.

Feature based Disparity

This method looks at features in one image and tries to find the corresponding feature in the other. The features can be edges, lines, circles and curves. Nasrabadi applies a curve segment based matching algorithm. Curve segments are used as the building block in the matching process. Curve segments are extracted from the edge points detected. The centre of each extracted curve is used as the feature in the matching process.

Medioni and Nevatia uses segments of connected edge points as matching primitives. Stereo correspondence is achieved through minimising the differential disparity measure for global matching, by taking into account things such as end points and segment orientation.

For each feature in the left hand image (QL) there needs to be a similar feature in the right hand image (QR). A measure of similarity is needed to associate the two features. This measure is given by the following formula adapted from Candocia and Adjouadi.

$$\psi(L \rightarrow R) = \frac{1}{N_L} \sum_{q=1}^{h} \frac{1}{(D_q - 1)}$$

Where NL = total number of features in the left image. $\frac{1}{N_L}$ is the weight associated with a matched feature. h is the minimum number of features found in either image, i.e. h = min(NL,NR). D_q is the minimum distance between a matched feature in the left and right images.

The features in the right image, within a constrained search area, with the highest similarity coefficient over a threshold are associated. These are then compared globally to other associated features to check for consistency. The difference in location of these features gives the disparity.

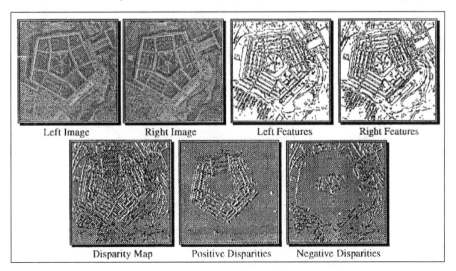

Left Image   Right Image   Left Features   Right Features

Disparity Map   Positive Disparities   Negative Disparities

Table: Results of the stereo feature matching technique.

Scene	Features	Features Matched	% Matched	Features Corrected	% Corrected	Time
Pentagon	13491	10928	81.0%	1223	11.2%	4h 9m 36s
Fruit	7525	6159	84.9%	655	10.6	3h 37m 40s
Renault	2459	2093	85.1%	226	10.8	1h 48m 20s
Stereogram	6800	6257	92.0%	0	0	15m 56s

Area based Disparity

There are two techniques that are used in this algorithm. In both these methods a window is placed on one image. The other image is scanned using the same size window. The pixels in each window are compared and operated on. These are then summed to give a coefficient for the centre pixel. These techniques have been developed by Okutomi and Kanade.

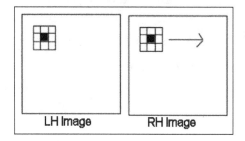

The first operation described is correlation. The output of the scanning window is convolved with the first and the location that gives the highest convolution coefficient is deemed to be the corresponding area. The correlation coefficient is given by:

$$C_{LR} = \sum_{[i,j] \in Window} L(i,j)R(i,j)$$

The second method uses the same window principle, but uses the sum of squared differences (SSD). This examines the pixel values in both windows and estimates the disparity by calculating the SSD coefficients. In this method the SSD coefficient needs to be minimised. The formula for SSD is:

$$SSD = \sum_{[i,j] \in Window} [L(i,j) - R(i,j)]^2$$

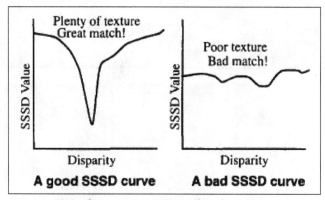

SSD values over scan area taken from Ross.

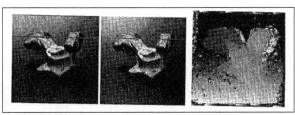

LH Image.   RH Image.   Disparity Map.

OpenCV Implementation

OpenCV has a predefined library that includes a method of obtaining disparity maps for a given stereo pair. The following result was obtained.

LH Image.   RH Image.

Disparity Map.

After trying many different options this is the best result that was obtained.

The disparity map shows streaking errors. This is attributed to the fact that OpenCV, misses important disparity jumps at the edges of objects and therefore assume the wrong disparities in later search stages.

Each algorithm has distinct advantages and disadvantages. These generally relate to speed and accuracy. There are also a few considerations and assumptions that are made in all stereo vision algorithms.

UNDERWATER COMPUTER VISION

Underwater object recognition using computer vision is rather difficult due to the lighting condition of such environment. Kim et al. present a vision-based object detection method based on template matching and tracking for underwater robots using artificial objects. All the tests are performed in a swimming pool. Several works perform object detection by segmenting the scene according to color and, then, by performing a more accurate assessment on the found region of interest. Bazeille et al. discuss the color modification occuring in underwater environments and experimentally assess the performance of object detection based on color. Since underwater imaging suffers from short range, low contrast and non-uniform illumination, simple color segmentation is one of the few viable approaches. In the underwater stereo vision system used in Trident European project is described. Object detection is performed by constructing a color histogram in HSV space of the target object. In the performed experiments, there is an intermediate step between inspection and intervention where real images of the site to manipulate are available and used for acquiring the underwater target object appearance.

Object Detection

The aim of object detection is the identification of a region in the image containing the target object in order to estimate its pose. The input data of the algorithm consist of a set of image pairs acquired by an underwater stereo vision system. If the pose estimation is based on dense stereo estimation, then the convenient output of the detection algorithm is a selection mask computed on the stereo reference image (usually the left one). Otherwise, the detection procedure may also extract the features required for a sparse stereo matching from both stereo images, for example the straight object contours.

Two main properties typical of humanmade artifacts are used: the relative color uniformity and the regular shape. The underwater lighting conditions make it difficult to fully exploit the first hypothesis. The water medium distorts colors so that even with a priori information about the target color, color segmentation is often unreliable. Moreover, the object contours are often ambiguous due to the fading luminance. Taking advantage from the regular shape condition, the target contours are searched by fitting lines. In our experiment, the object to be found is a pipe, although this information is not explicitly used until pose estimation. Two detection algorithms have been proposed to take advantage of these properties. PFC algorithm performs clustering on the pixels of the image according to local pixel features and next selects the connected components according to the shape. MGS algorithm belongs to the popular graph-cut approach representing the image as a grid graph. It first exploits color uniformity to enable better partitioning of the image into homogeneous regions, and then finds the shape searching for regular contours.

The image processing pipeline includes pre-processing, object detection and poses estimation. Pre-processing consists of image rectification and color restoration. Next, object detection and recognition are performed according to MFC or CFC methods.

Pre-processing

Pre-processing consists of two main operations related to the effect of light propagation in water. The first one is the dedistortion and rectification of the input images acquired by the stereo. While this is a standard operation, it has to be carefully performed to achieve accurate line extraction.

The values of intrinsic parameters of a camera are affected by the water medium and have to be computed accordingly. The second relevant operation is the restoration of the color modified by water. Figure shows an example of underwater image with altered color. The pixel color shift is apparent in all images, but it is most noticeable for the grey pipe that appears in cyan shades. In order to facilitate detection, it would be convenient to restore the color shades to their original color in air. Several approaches have been proposed for color restoration. In our case, a color constancy method based on grey-world hypothesis, which assumes the average edge difference in the scene to be achromatic, sufficed. The results are illustrated by the example in figure.

An example of color restoration: the originally acquired image from the dataset (left) and after color restoration according to grey world hypothesis (right).

Pixel-feature Clustering

The PFC algorithm extracts a vector of local features from each pixel like the HSV color values and the response to an edge extraction filter. The input image can be rescaled to a lower size to remove unnecessary details and to reduce the computational complexity of object detection. The scaling operation also acts as a low-pass filter in the image. The initial classification of each pixel p_i is independent from the classification of other pixels. In particular, the feature vector computed for p_i consists of the color channels of HSV space, respectively hue h_i, saturation s_i and value v_i, and of the gradient response to a Sobel filter g_i. Next, the item vectors $f_i = [h_i, s_i, v_i, g_i] >$ are clustered according to k-means algorithm. The number of clusters used in the experiments is k = 3 and is independent from the number of objects in the scene.

The connected regions of each cluster are classified according to the corresponding angular histogram computed on its contour. The angular histogram of artifacts is concentrated on one or few peaks, while the histograms corresponding to the blobs extracted from natural seabed elements are usually more distributed. Hence, a set of segments is extracted from the contour. Each segment j is described by its length l_j and by its supporting line with equation $x \cos \alpha_j + y \sin \alpha_j = r_j$ (coordinates are expressed w.r.t. the image origin). Detection of line direction is allowed by an angular histogram H with bin counters $h_s \in N$ and intervals $[s\Delta\theta, (s + 1)\Delta\theta[s = 0, \ldots, n_h - 1$ and $\Delta\theta = \pi/(2n_h)$. In particular, the segment j increments the corresponding angle bin h_k with a contribution proportional to the square of its length l_j as:

$$s = \left\lceil \frac{(\alpha_j + \pi) \bmod \frac{\pi}{2}}{\Delta\theta} \right\rceil$$

$$h_s \leftarrow h_s + \left(\frac{l_j}{\max_i l_i} \right)^2$$

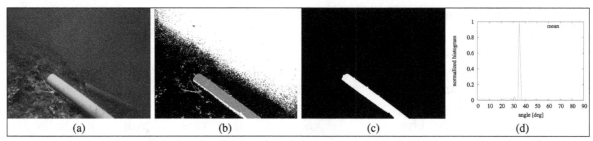

An image with a uniformly colored object from (a), the output of the initial k-mean clustering (b), one connected component of a k-mean cluster (c) and its corresponding angular histogram (d).

The square of the normalized length reduces the influence of the smaller segments resulting from the potential over-segmentation of the contour. Finally, a cluster is classified as an object with regular shape if the histogram is "peaked", i.e. it is distributed along few principal directions. In particular, the validation condition of clusters is:

$$\overline{h} = \frac{1}{n_h} \sum_{s=0}^{n_h-1} h_s < \sigma_{th} \max_{0 \le s \le n_h} h_s$$

The condition of previous equation is satisfied when there is a dominant orientation in the histogram w.r.t. the average bin value $\overline{h}$. This occurs for objects with regular shapes and segment contours like the pipe considered.

Multiscale Graph-based Segmentation

The MGS method combines the detection of uniform color regions and the multiscale paradigm to identify the stable image partitions. The MGS method, like all graphcut algorithms, enables to find contiguous regions of the image with homogeneous features. The borders of such regions correspond to high luminance or color gradients. Hence, unlike the segmentation achieved by PFC, the partitions computed with MGS consist of contiguous pixels by construction at each scale. Algorithm illustrates the steps of MGS that are presented in the following.

Let I^s be the images at different scales $s = 0, \dots, n_s$ with I^0 is the input image with size $w^0 \times h^0$. Each image I^s at scale $s > 0$ is obtained by successively applying a Gaussian blur filter and down sampling I^{s-1}. The scale factor of I^s w.r.t. I^{s-1} is equal to $1 : 2$. The multi-scale operations are shown at lines 2-7 of algorithm: the segmentation algorithm MinForestSegmentation and the edge extraction.

Data: $\mathcal{I}^0$: input image. Parameters: n_s maximum scale; K_τ initial connection threshold; s_{min} minimum size of partition; d_{th} distance threshold; γ_{th} histogram ratio threshold.

Result: $\mathcal{O}$: image mask corresponding to the image.

1   $\mathcal{E} \leftarrow \{black\}$;
2   **for** $s = 0, \dots, n_s$ **do**
3      $sm \leftarrow \min\{1, s_{min} \, 2^{-s}\}$;
4      $\{\mathcal{S}_i^s\}_{i=1,\dots,k_s} \leftarrow MinForestSegmentation(\mathcal{I}^s, K_\tau, sm)$;
5      $\mathcal{E} \leftarrow \mathcal{E} + Contour(\cup_{i=1}^{k_s} \mathcal{S}_i^s)$;
6      $\mathcal{I}^{s+1} \leftarrow Downscale(\mathcal{I}^s)$;
7   **end**
8   $l = (\theta_l, \rho_l) \leftarrow FindDominantLine(RosinThres(\mathcal{E}))$;

9 $\mathcal{U}_l \leftarrow \{black\}, \mathcal{D}_l \leftarrow \{black\};$
10 for $s = 0, \ldots, n_s$ **do**
11   **for** $i = 0, \ldots, k_s$ **do**
12 $c \leftarrow Mean(\mathcal{S}_i^s, l);$
13 $d \leftarrow \min_{p \in \mathcal{S}_i^s} \|p_x \cos\theta_l + p_y \sin\theta_l - \rho_l\|;$
14   **if** $d < d_{th}$ **and** $c_x \cos\theta_l + c_y \sin\theta_l - \rho_l \geq 0$ **then**
15 $\mathcal{U}_l \leftarrow \mathcal{U}_l + Mask(\mathcal{S}_i^s);$
16   **else if** $d < d_{th}$ **and** $c_x \cos\theta_l + c_y \sin\theta_l - \rho_l < 0$ **then**
17 $\mathcal{D}_l \leftarrow \mathcal{D}_l + Mask(\mathcal{S}_i^s);$
18   **end**
19   **end**
20 end
21 $\mathcal{H}_U \leftarrow HoughSpetrum(Contour(RosinThres(\mathcal{U}_l))),$
    $\gamma_U \leftarrow \frac{\text{mean}\mathcal{H}_U}{\max \mathcal{H}_U};$
22 $\mathcal{H}_D \leftarrow HoughSpetrum(Contour(RosinThres(\mathcal{D}_l))),$
    $\gamma_D \leftarrow \frac{\text{mean}\mathcal{H}_D}{\max \mathcal{H}_D};$
23 if $\gamma_U \leq \gamma_D$ **and** $\gamma_U < \gamma_{th}$ **then**
24 $\mathcal{O} \leftarrow \mathcal{H}_U;$
25 else if $\gamma_U > \gamma_D$ **and** $\gamma_D < \gamma_{th}$ **then**
26 $\mathcal{O} \leftarrow \mathcal{H}_D;$
27 else
28 $\mathcal{O} \leftarrow \{black\};$
29 end

The unsupervised graph-cut algorithm MinForestSegmentation proposed is used to partition each image I^s. The method is closely related to Kruskal algorithm for the construction of minimum spanning tree. The algorithm handles each pixel $p_i^s \in I^s$ as a node of a weighted undirected grid graph connected to its 8-neighbors. The weights of the edges are computed as the color distance between adjacent pixels. In particular, the weight w_{ij}^s between two adjacent pixels p_i^s and p_j^s is computed as Manhattan norm of RGB component vectors of p_i^s and p_j^s. Hence after, the apex ^{s} is omitted when the scale s is clear from the context. Initially, the image I^s is partitioned into segment regions $S_{l_i}^s \subset I^s$, each consisting of exactly one pixel. All the edges are sorted in increasing order according to their weights. At each iteration, the algorithm visits each edge (p_i, p_j) with weight w_{ij}. If (p_i, p_j) connects two pixels belonging to different regions, i.e. $p_i \in S_{l_i}^s$ and $p_j \in S_{l_j}^s$ with $S_{l_i}^s \cap S_{l_j}^s = \emptyset$, then the segments $S_{l_i}^s$ and $S_{l_j}^s$ could be joined in a unique segment. Such decision depends on the thresholds τl_i and τl_j associated respectively to $S_{l_i}^s$ and $S_{l_j}^s$: the two segments are joined into segment $S_{\bar{l}} = S_{l_i}^s \cup S_{l_j}^s$, if $w_{ij} \leq \tau_{l_i}$ and $w_{ij} \leq \tau_{l_j}$. The threshold of the joined segment is equal to:

$$\tau_{\bar{l}} = w_{ij} + \frac{K_\tau}{|S_{\bar{l}}|}$$

Where, K_τ is a parameter of the algorithm. The thresholds $\tau_{\bar{l}}$ represent the sum of the minimal internal difference of segment $S_{\bar{l}}^s$ and of a tolerance dependent on K_τ and decreasing with the size of the segment. The parameter K_τ is the most critical for the resulting segmentation, since it affects the size and the number of segments. If K_τ is too low, the result is an over segmented graph due to the local color and luminance changes. Otherwise, if it is too high, the contour of the object may be lost. To overcome this problem, segmentation is repeated on downscaled versions of the input image.

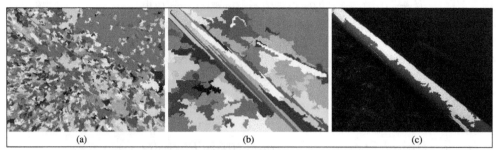

Graph-based segmentation of image in previous figure at the original resolution (a), at the 3-times rescaled version (b) and the detected region (c).

Scaling enables removal of the ephemeral image details associated to light propagation in water and highlighting of the object shapes. Object shape recognition is easier on images with a coarser segmentation. Figure shows the segmentation output at two different scales. The overdetails at the lowest scale are limited and the general shape is easier to find. The target object used in the experiments is recognizable from its longer borders. Thus, the contours of segment regions S_l^s are extracted and accumulated into an edge image ε (line 5), which is used to find the dominant line l (line 8). The dominant line l is a peculiar feature that enables to find the segment regions corresponding to the target object. Such dominant line divides the object area from the background, but without further analysis it is unclear which one of the two half-planes defined by l contains the object. Thus, two candidates ROIs U_l and D_l are built using the segment regions. In lines 10-20, each segment region S_i^s, which is close to l (i.e. with distance d less than threshold d_{th}), is associated either to the ROI U_l above the line or to the ROI D_l below the line according to the position of its centroid c. The two candidates ROIs U_l and D_l are binarized using Rosin threshold. The contour of the binarized regions is used to build their Hough Spectrum histograms H_U and H_D. The two histograms provide the same information of the angular histogram in equation ($h_s \leftarrow h_s + \left(\dfrac{l_j}{\max_i l_i} \right)^2$). Thus, the target object is detected if either H_U or H_D satisfies the "peak" test in equation ($\bar{h} = \dfrac{1}{n_h} \displaystyle\sum_{s=0}^{n_h-1} h_s < \sigma_{th} \; \max_{0 \le s \le n_h} h_s$), after changing the respective histogram and by using threshold γ_{th} instead of σ_{th}. This operation is illustrated at lines 21-29 of Algorithm table and figure (c) shows an example of algorithm output.

Pose Estimation

The pose estimation of an object is possible once the geometry of the object is known. Its pose is defined by a reference frame conveniently placed on the object. The frame coordinates are extracted from its recognizable parts in the image. In our case, the target object has a cylindrical shape identified by a pair of straight contour lines. The target may completely lie inside the field-of-view (FoV) or be only partially visible. In particular, one or both far ends of the cylinder may be occluded. Due to the symmetry of the cylinder, when no end-point is visible, the information is insufficient to properly estimate the reference frame.

Pose computation of the cylinder can be performed from a single frame or from two frames acquired by the stereo vision system. In the first case, the radius of the cylinder must be known in order to correctly find the cylinder symmetry axis. If the length of the cylinder c_l is also known, then the cylinder position is know completely. In particular, a cylinder is defined given the radius c_r and its axis, a line in the form $c(t) = c_p + c_d t$. In the image plane, the cylinder contour is delimited by two lines with equations $l_i^T u = 0$, where $u = [u_x, u_y, 1]^T$ is the pixel coordinate vector and l_1, l_2 are the line coefficients. The sign of each line coefficient vector l_i is conventionally chosen s.t. the cylinder lies in the positive half-plane $l_i^T u > 0$. Let Pc be the projection matrix which projects 3D points in the camera coordinate frame to 2D pixel coordinates using intrinsic and distortion camera parameters. Each contour line is projected in the 3D space as a plane πi with equation $n_i^T p + c_i = 0$ where $[n_i^T | c_i]^T = P_c^T l_i$ and p a generic point in camera reference frame coordinates. Since n_i points orthogonally through the center of the cylinder, the axis line can be obtained by intersecting both translated planes of the radius c_r in $\hat{n}_i$ direction, where, $\hat{n}i = n_i / \|n_i\|$. Thus, the direction of the cylinder axis is given by direction vector $c_d = \hat{n}_1 \times \hat{n}_2$. Let π_{ep} be the plane $n_{ep}^T p + c_{ep} = 0$ passing through one of the cylinder end-point with normal vector n_{ep} parallel to c_d. The cylinder center point c_c is computed as:

$$\begin{bmatrix} n_1^T \\ n_2^T \\ n_3^T \end{bmatrix} \cdot p_{ep} = \begin{bmatrix} -c_1 \\ -c_2 \\ -c_{ep} \end{bmatrix}$$

$$c_c = p_{ep} + \hat{n}_{ep} \frac{c_1}{2}$$

The accuracy of this approach entirely depends on the detection of object edges in the image and on the camera calibration parameters.

Stereo processing can be exploited in different ways. For example, a dense point cloud can be obtained by computing the disparity image from the two frames and the cylinder could be found through shape fitting techniques. Although this approach is rather general and can be applied to arbitrary shapes, it has several drawbacks. First, the point cloud density depends on the availability of reliable homologous points and, thus, on the color and pattern of the scene. Color uniformity facilitates the detection of target object, in particular due to the blurred and poor light conditions of underwater environments, but it may result into empty regions in the disparity image. Second, the accuracy of stereo 3D estimation depends on the accuracy of camera calibration. An approach similar to the single-frame method can be performed on a stereo image pair. The same cylindrical contour is projected in two different image planes resulting in four major contour lines. Each line is then reprojected in the 3D space resulting in four planes tangent to the cylinder. Let P_L and P_R be the projection matrices of the left and the right cameras respectively, π_{Li} and π_{Ri} the planes tangent to the cylinder obtained projecting in the 3D space the lines contour computed in both stereo images. Matrices P_L and P_R are referred to the same reference frame. The direction of the cylinder axis vector cd must be orthogonal to each plane normal vectors $\hat{n}_{Li}$ and $\hat{n}_{Ri}$ respectively. Let N be the matrix whose rows are the normal vectors of planes through the cylinder axis:

$$N = \begin{bmatrix} n_{L1}^T \\ n_{L2}^T \\ n_{R1}^T \\ n_{R2}^T \end{bmatrix}$$

The cylinder axis direction c_d is estimated as the normalized vector that satisfies homogeneous linear equation:

$$N \cdot c_d = 0$$

Clearly, this method is consistent with the single frame case which requires just a cross product to compute the cylinder axis vector. Moreover, solving is more robust in presence of noisy data as can be the projection of lines in 3D space. This method does not require all the projected planes.

If there are only two planes with normals $\hat{n}_1$ and $\hat{n}_2$, the cylinder axis is estimated as in the single frame case without loss of generality. As for the single frame method, let πep be the plane passing through one of the cylinder end-point detected in one of the stereo images. Then, the cylinder center point is obtained as:

$$\begin{bmatrix} n_{L1}^T \\ n_{L2}^T \\ n_{R1}^T \\ n_{R2}^T \\ n_{ep}^T \end{bmatrix} \cdot P_{ep} = \begin{bmatrix} -c_{L1} \\ -c_{L2} \\ -c_{R1} \\ -c_{R2} \\ -c_{ep} \end{bmatrix}$$

$$c_c = p_{ep} + \hat{n}_{ep} \frac{c_1}{2}$$

The cylinder reference frame cannot be estimated without ambiguity due to the intrinsic symmetry of the cylinder.

Experiments

The performance of MGS object detection has been compared with the PFC algorithm on a dataset acquired using a stereo vision system near Portofino (Italy). The underwater stereo vision system was submerged at a depth of 10 m together with a set of cylindrical pipes of different colors. The dataset provides pairs of camera frames acquired by stereo cameras, but the proposed object detection algorithms operate on a single frame. Hence, a subset of 305 frames acquired by the left camera has been selected and manually annotated. The chosen frames may contain one or two cylindrical objects, but there is always only one object in the foreground that is considered as target object. For example, in figure (a) there are two pipes, but the orange one is in the background. The proposed detection algorithms have been designed to search exactly one target object and, when multiple candidate objects appear in the frame, it selects the one with prominent features (image area, regular borders, etc.).

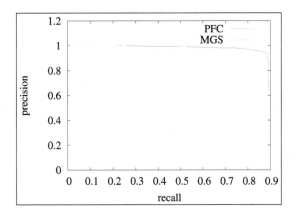

PR curves of PFC and MGS algorithms for Portofino dataset.

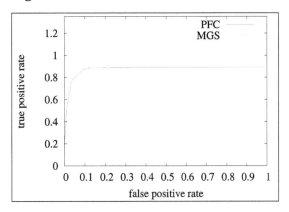

ROC of PFC and MGS algorithms for Portofino dataset.

Table: Detection results for pfc and mgs algorithms on the dataset.

	PFC	MGS
Frame number	305	
Threshold	$\sigma_{th} = 0.04$	$\gamma_{th} = 0.48$
TP	179	177
TN	91	94
FP	11	7
FN	24	27
Precision	94.2%	96.2%
Recall	88.2%	86.8%
Accuracy	88.5%	88.9%
I-FPRate	89.2%	93.1%
F-Measure	91.1%	91.2%

The detection algorithm output and the annotated groundtruth consist of binary images: the white color pixels correspond to the positive region (i.e. occupied by the target object) and the black ones to the negative. The aim of the detection algorithms is the identification of the image region containing a significant part of the target object. Let D be the pixel sets classified as target object and G the groundtruth. A correct detection occurs if $|D \cap G|/|D| > 0.5$.

Figures show the precision-recall (PR) and receiving operating curve (ROC) for the two proposed algorithms PFC and MGS. Table illustrates the classification values obtained for a specific value of acceptance thresholds σ_{th} and γ_{th}. Observe that the recall value of PFC and MGS never reaches the 100% due to the filtering in the segmentation phase: even after increasing the thresholds σ_{th} and γ_{th}, clearly negative images are not classified as positive and the precision is not compromised. An alteration of the initial algorithm steps would be required for an indiscriminate acceptance of all input images as positive. Although the PR and the ROC curves of PFC and MGS tend to overlap, MGS achieves slightly better results. In particular, the precision of MGS is higher than PFC: the regions obtained from graph cut better fit the object than those based on color. The values in table confirm the previous observation: performance parameters, in general, are better for MGS than for PFC. The only exception is the recall value, which is slightly better for PCF. Both proposed algorithms exhibit detection performance suitable for the execution of manipulation tasks, which usually allow the repeated observation of the object to be grasped.

The pose estimation method has not been quantitatively assessed. The qualitative assessment showed that the robustness and stability of pose estimation highly depends on object detection.

We have presented a novel object detection algorithm for underwater environments relying on multiscale graph-based segmentation. The algorithm exploits the refined image segmentation obtained from the graph-based approach and which consists of connected regions. The segmentation procedure is applied at different scales to capture both the accurate contour in high resolution images and the general shape of the object at higher scales. High scale images are free from ephemeral image details, since they are obtained by iteratively blurring and downsampling the original image. The candidate ROI containing the object is computed by merging the overlapping image segments at different scales. The ROI is classified as target object according to a shape regularity test.

The proposed MGS algorithm has been compared with a pixel-feature clustering algorithm. The detection performances of both algorithms are comparable w.r.t. both precision and recall values with a slight advantage for the multiscale graph-based segmentation. Both algorithms achieve performance suitable for the execution of manipulation tasks.

References

- Introduction-to-computer-vision: algorithmia.com, Retrieved 05 January, 2019

- Understanding-computer-vision-its-advantages-and-limitations: allerin.com, Retrieved 28 August, 2019

- Deep-learning-for-computer-vision-a-beginners-guid: dzone.com, Retrieved 14 May, 2019

- Computer-Vision-in-Underwater-Environments-a-Multiscale-Graph-Segmentation-Approach- 275207420: researchgate.net, Retrieved 18 April, 2019

- "A Real-Time Large Disparity Range Stereo-System using FPGAs," icvs, p. 13, Fourth IEEE International Conference on Computer Vision Systems (ICVS'06), 2006

Digital Image Processing

An ordinary image that can be represented as a set of numbers or pixels, which can be processed by digital computer is defined as digital image. The algorithm used for processing digital images is called digital image processing. This chapter has been carefully written to provide an easy understanding of the varied facets of digital image processing.

DIGITAL IMAGE

A digital image is a representation of a real image as a set of numbers that can be stored and handled by a digital computer. In order to translate the image into numbers, it is divided into small areas called pixels (picture elements). For each pixel, the imaging device records a number, or a small set of numbers, that describe some property of this pixel, such as its brightness (the intensity of the light) or its color. The numbers are arranged in an array of rows and columns that correspond to the vertical and horizontal positions of the pixels in the image.

Digital images have several basic characteristics. One is the type of the image. For example, a black and white image records only the intensity of the light falling on the pixels. A color image can have three colors, normally RGB (Red, Green, and Blue) or four colors, CMYK (Cyan, Magenta, Yellow, blacK). RGB images are usually used in computer monitors and scanners, while CMYK images are used in color printers. There are also non-optical images such as ultrasound or X-ray in which the intensity of sound or X-rays is recorded. In range images, the distance of the pixel from the observer is recorded. Resolution is expressed in the number of pixels per inch (ppi). A higher resolution gives a more detailed image. A computer monitor typically has a resolution of 100 ppi, while a printer has a resolution ranging from 300 ppi to more than 1440 ppi. This is why an image looks much better in print than on a monitor.

The color depth (of a color image) or "bits per pixel" is the number of bits in the numbers that describe the brightness or the color. More bits make it possible to record more shades of gray or more colors. For example, an RGB image with 8 bits per color has a total of 24 bits per pixel ("true color"). Each bit can represent two possible colors so we get a total of 16,777,216 possible colors. A typical GIF image on a web page has 8 bits for all colors combined for a total of 256 colors. However, it is a much smaller image than a 24 bit one so it downloads more quickly. A fax image has only one bit or two "colors," black and white. The format of the image gives more details about how the numbers are arranged in the image file, including what kind of compression is used, if any. Among the most popular of the dozens of formats available are TIFF, GIF, JPEG, PNG, and Post-Script.

Digital images tend to produce big files and are often compressed to make the files smaller. Compression takes advantage of the fact that many nearby pixels in the image have similar colors or brightness. Instead of recording each pixel separately, one can record that, for example, "the 100 pixels around a certain position are all white." Compression methods vary in their efficiency and speed. The GIF method has good compression for 8 bit pictures, while the JPEG is lossy, i.e. it causes some image degradation. JPEG's advantage is speed, so it is suitable for motion pictures.

One of the advantages of digital images over traditional ones is the ability to transfer them electronically almost instantaneously and convert them easily from one medium to another such as from a web page to a computer screen to a printer. A bigger advantage is the ability to change them according to one's needs. There are several programs available now which give a user the ability to do that, including Photoshop, Photopaint, and the Gimp. With such a program, a user can change the colors and brightness of an image, delete unwanted visible objects, move others, and merge objects from several images, among many other operations. In this way a user can retouch family photos or even create new images. Other software, such as word processors and desktop publishing programs, can easily combine digital images with text to produce books or magazines much more efficiently than with traditional methods.

A very promising use of digital images is automatic object recognition. In this application, a computer can automatically recognize an object shown in the image and identify it by name. One of the most important uses of this is in robotics. A robot can be equipped with digital cameras that can serve as its "eyes" and produce images. If the robot could recognize an object in these images, then it could make use of it. For instance, in a factory environment, the robot could use a screwdriver in the assembly of products. For this task, it has to recognize both the screwdriver and the various parts of the product. At home a robot could recognize objects to be cleaned. Other promising applications are in medicine, for example, in finding tumors in X-ray images. Security equipment could recognize the faces of people approaching a building. Automated drivers could drive a car without human intervention or drive a vehicle in inhospitable environments such as on the planet Mars or in a battlefield.

To recognize an object, the computer has to compare the image to a database of objects in its memory. This is a simple task for humans but it has proven to be very difficult to do automatically. One reason is that an object rarely produces the same image of itself. An object can be seen from many different viewpoints and under different lighting conditions and each such variation will produce an image that looks different to the computer. The object itself can also change; for instance, a smiling face looks different from a serious face of the same person. Because of these difficulties, research in this field has been rather slow, but there are already successes in limited areas such as inspection of products on assembly lines, fingerprint identification by the FBI, and optical character recognition (OCR). OCR is now used by the U.S. Postal Service to read printed addresses and automatically direct the letters to their destination, and by scanning software to convert printed text to computer readable text.

DIGITAL IMAGE PROCESSING

In computer science, digital image processing is the use of a digital computer to process digital images through an algorithm. As a subcategory or field of digital signal processing, digital image processing has many advantages over analog image processing. It allows a much wider range of algorithms to be applied to the input data and can avoid problems such as the build-up of noise and distortion during processing. Since images are defined over two dimensions (perhaps more) digital image processing may be modeled in the form of multidimensional systems.

Image Sensor

An image sensor or imager is a sensor that detects and conveys information used to make an image. It does so by converting the variable attenuation of light waves (as they pass through or reflect off objects) into signals, small bursts of current that convey the information. The waves can be light or other electromagnetic radiation. Image sensors are used in electronic imaging devices of both analog and digital types, which include digital cameras, camera modules, camera phones, optical mouse devices, medical imaging equipment, night vision equipment such as thermal imaging devices, radar, sonar, and others. As technology changes, electronic and digital imaging tends to replace chemical and analog imaging.

A CCD image sensor on a flexible circuit board.

The two main types of electronic image sensors are the charge-coupled device (CCD) and the active-pixel sensor (CMOS sensor). Both CCD and CMOS sensors are based on metal–oxide–semiconductor (MOS) technology, with CCDs based on MOS capacitors and CMOS sensors based on MOSFET (MOS field-effect transistor) amplifiers. Analog sensors for invisible radiation tend to involve vacuum tubes of various kinds. Digital sensors include flat-panel detectors.

An American Microsystems, Inc., (AMI) 1-kilobit DRAM chip (center chip with glass window) used as an image sensor on the Cromemco Cyclops.

CCD vs. CMOS Sensors

The two main types of digital image sensors are the charge-coupled device (CCD) and the active-pixel sensor (CMOS sensor), fabricated in complementary MOS (CMOS) or N-type MOS (NMOS or Live MOS) technologies. Both CCD and CMOS sensors are based on MOS technology, with MOS capacitors being the building blocks of a CCD, and MOSFET amplifiers being the building blocks of a CMOS sensor.

A micrograph of the corner of the photosensor array of a webcam digital camera.

Cameras integrated in small consumer products generally use CMOS sensors, which are usually cheaper and have lower power consumption in battery powered devices than CCDs. CCD sensors are used for high end broadcast quality video cameras, and (C)MOS sensors dominate in still photography and consumer goods where overall cost is a major concern. Both types of sensor accomplish the same task of capturing light and converting it into electrical signals.

Image sensor (upper left) on the motherboard of a Nikon Coolpix L2 6 MP.

Each cell of a CCD image sensor is an analog device. When light strikes the chip it is held as a small electrical charge in each photo sensor. The charges in the line of pixels nearest to the (one or more) output amplifiers are amplified and output, then each line of pixels shifts its charges one line closer to the amplifiers, filling the empty line closest to the amplifierss. This process is then repeated until all the lines of pixels have had their charge amplified and output.

A CMOS image sensor has an amplifier for each pixel compared to the few amplifiers of a CCD. This results in less area for the capture of photons than a CCD, but this problem has been overcome by using microlenses in front of each photodiode, which focus light into the photodiode that would have otherwise hit the amplifier and not been detected. Some CMOS imaging sensors also use Back-side illumination to increase the number of photons that hit the photodiode. CMOS sensors can potentially be implemented with fewer components, use less power, and provide faster readout than CCD sensors. They are also less vulnerable to static electricity discharges.

Another design, a hybrid CCD/CMOS architecture (sold under the name "sCMOS") consists of CMOS readout integrated circuits (ROICs) that are bump bonded to a CCD imaging substrate – a technology that was developed for infrared staring arrays and has been adapted to silicon-based detector technology. Another approach is to utilize the very fine dimensions available in modern CMOS technology to implement a CCD like structure entirely in CMOS technology: such structures can be achieved by separating individual poly-silicon gates by a very small gap; though still a product of research hybrid sensors can potentially harness the benefits of both CCD and CMOS imagers.

Performance

There are many parameters that can be used to evaluate the performance of an image sensor, including dynamic range, signal-to-noise ratio, and low-light sensitivity. For sensors of comparable types, the signal-to-noise ratio and dynamic range improve as the size increases.

Exposure-time Control

Exposure time of image sensors is generally controlled by either a conventional mechanical shutter, as in film cameras, or by an electronic shutter. Electronic shuttering can be "global", in which case the entire image sensor area's accumulation of photoelectrons starts and stops simultaneously, or "rolling" in which case the exposure interval of each row immediate precedes that row's readout, in a process that "rolls" across the image frame (typically from top to bottom in landscape format). Global electronic shuttering is less common, as it requires "storage" circuits to hold charge from the end of the exposure interval until the readout process gets there, typically a few milliseconds later.

Color Separation

There are several main types of color image sensors, differing by the type of color-separation mechanism:

- Bayer-filter sensor, low-cost and most common, using a color filter array that passes red, green, and blue light to selected pixel sensors. Each individual sensor element is made sensitive to red, green, or blue by means of a color gel made of chemical dyes patterned over the elements. The most common filter matrix, the Bayer pattern, uses two green pixels for each red and blue. This results in less resolution for red and blue colors. The missing color samples may interpolated using a demosaicing algorithm, or ignored altogether by lossy compression. In order to improve color information, techniques like color co-site sampling use a piezo mechanism to shift the color sensor in pixel steps.

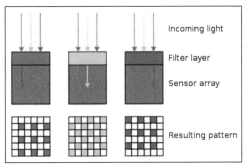

Bayer pattern on sensor.

- Foveon X3 sensor, using an array of layered pixel sensors, separating light via the inherent wavelength-dependent absorption property of silicon, such that every location senses all three color channels. This method is similar to how color film for photography works.

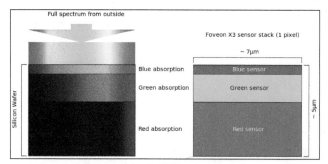

Foveon's scheme of vertical filtering for color sensing.

- 3CCD, using three discrete image sensors, with the color separation done by a dichroic prism. The dichroic elements provide a sharper color separation, thus improving color quality. Because each sensor is equally sensitive within its passband, and at full resolution, 3-CCD sensors produce better color quality and better low light performance. 3-CCD sensors produce a full 4:4:4 signal, which is preferred in television broadcasting, video editing and chroma key visual effects.

Specialty Sensors

Special sensors are used in various applications such as thermography, creation of multi-spectral images, video laryngoscopes, gamma cameras, sensor arrays for x-rays, and other highly sensitive arrays for astronomy.

Infrared view of the Orion Nebula taken by ESO's HAWK-I, a cryogenic wide-field imager.

While in general digital cameras use a flat sensor, Sony prototyped a curved sensor in 2014 to reduce/eliminate Petzval field curvature that occurs with a flat sensor. Use of a curved sensor allows a shorter and smaller diameter of the lens with reduced elements and components with greater aperture and reduced light fall-off at the edge of the photo.

Image Compression

Image compression is a type of data compression applied to digital images, to reduce their cost for storage or transmission. Algorithms may take advantage of visual perception and the statistical properties of image data to provide superior results compared with generic data compression methods which are used for other digital data.

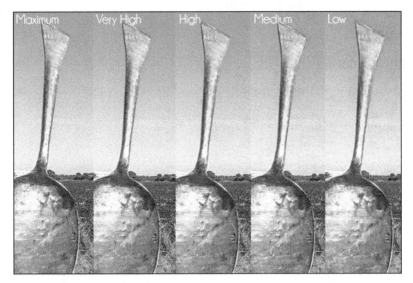

Comparison of JPEG images saved by Adobe Photoshop at different quality
levels and with or without "save for web".

Lossy and Lossless Image Compression

Image compression may be lossy or lossless. Lossless compression is preferred for archival purposes and often for medical imaging, technical drawings, clip art, or comics. Lossy compression methods, especially when used at low bit rates, introduce compression artifacts. Lossy methods are especially suitable for natural images such as photographs in applications where minor (sometimes imperceptible) loss of fidelity is acceptable to achieve a substantial reduction in bit rate. Lossy compression that produces negligible differences may be called visually lossless.

Methods for lossy compression:

- Transform coding: This is the most commonly used method.

  ○ Discrete Cosine Transform (DCT): The most widely used form of lossy compression. It is a type of Fourier-related transform, and was originally developed by Nasir Ahmed, T. Natarajan and K. R. Rao in 1974. The DCT is sometimes referred to as "DCT-II" in the context of a family of discrete cosine transforms. It is generally the most efficient form of image compression.

  ○ DCT is used in JPEG, the most popular lossy format, and the more recent HEIF.

- The more recently developed wavelet transform is also used extensively, followed by quantization and entropy coding.

- Reducing the color space to the most common colors in the image. The selected colors are specified in the color palette in the header of the compressed image. Each pixel just references the index of a color in the color palette; this method can be combined with dithering to avoid posterization.

- Chroma subsampling: This takes advantage of the fact that the human eye perceives spatial changes of brightness more sharply than those of color, by averaging or dropping some of the chrominance information in the image.

- Fractal compression.

Methods for lossless compression:

- Run-length encoding: Used in default method in PCX and as one of possible in BMP, TGA, TIFF;

- Area image compression;

- Predictive coding: Used in DPCM;

- Entropy encoding: The two most common entropy encoding techniques are arithmetic coding and Huffman coding;

- Adaptive dictionary algorithms such as LZW: Used in GIF and TIFF;

- DEFLATE: Used in PNG, MNG, and TIFF;

- Chain codes.

Other Properties

The best image quality at a given compression rate (or bit rate) is the main goal of image compression; however, there are other important properties of image compression schemes:

- Scalability generally refers to a quality reduction achieved by manipulation of the bitstream or file (without decompression and re-compression). Other names for scalability are progressive coding or embedded bitstreams. Despite its contrary nature, scalability also may be found in lossless codecs, usually in form of coarse-to-fine pixel scans. Scalability is especially useful for previewing images while downloading them (e.g., in a web browser) or for providing variable quality access to e.g., databases. There are several types of scalability:

  - Quality progressive or layer progressive: The bitstream successively refines the reconstructed image.

  - Resolution progressive: First encode a lower image resolution; then encode the difference to higher resolutions.

  - Component progressive: First encode grey-scale version; then adding full color.

- Region of interest coding: Certain parts of the image are encoded with higher quality than others. This may be combined with scalability (encode these parts first, others later).

- Meta information: Compressed data may contain information about the image which may be used to categorize, search, or browse images. Such information may include color and texture statistics, small preview images, and author or copyright information.

- Processing power: Compression algorithms require different amounts of processing power to encode and decode. Some high compression algorithms require high processing power.

The quality of a compression method often is measured by the peak signal-to-noise ratio. It measures the amount of noise introduced through a lossy compression of the image, however, the subjective judgment of the viewer also is regarded as an important measure, perhaps, being the most important measure.

Digital Signal Processor

A digital signal processor (DSP) is a specialized microprocessor (or a SIP block) chip, with its architecture optimized for the operational needs of digital signal processing. DSPs are fabricated on MOS integrated circuit chips. They are widely used in audio signal processing, telecommunications, digital image processing, radar, sonar and speech recognition systems, and in common consumer electronic devices such as mobile phones, disk drives and high-definition television (HDTV) products.

The goal of a DSP is usually to measure, filter or compress continuous real-world analog signals. Most general-purpose microprocessors can also execute digital signal processing algorithms successfully, but may not be able to keep up with such processing continuously in real-time. Also, dedicated DSPs usually have better power efficiency, thus they are more suitable in portable devices such as mobile phones because of power consumption constraints. DSPs often use special memory architectures that are able to fetch multiple data or instructions at the same time. DSPs often also implement data compression technology, with the discrete cosine transform (DCT) in particular being a widely used compression technology in DSPs.

A digital signal processor chip found in a guitar effects unit. A crystal oscillator may be seen above.

Digital signal processing algorithms typically require a large number of mathematical operations to be performed quickly and repeatedly on a series of data samples. Signals (perhaps from audio or video sensors) are constantly converted from analog to digital, manipulated digitally, and then converted back to analog form. Many DSP applications have constraints on latency; that is, for the system to work, the DSP operation must be completed within some fixed time, and deferred (or batch) processing is not viable.

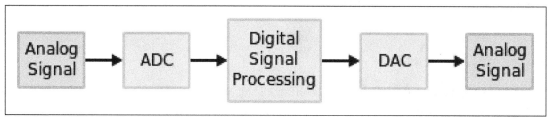

A typical digital processing system.

Most general-purpose microprocessors and operating systems can execute DSP algorithms successfully, but are not suitable for use in portable devices such as mobile phones and PDAs because of power efficiency constraints. A specialized DSP, however, will tend to provide a lower-cost solution, with better performance, lower latency, and no requirements for specialised cooling or large batteries.

Such performance improvements have led to the introduction of digital signal processing in commercial communications satellites where hundreds or even thousands of analog filters, switches, frequency converters and so on are required to receive and process the uplinked signals and ready them for downlinking, and can be replaced with specialised DSPs with significant benefits to the satellites' weight, power consumption, complexity/cost of construction, reliability and flexibility of operation. For example, the SES-12 and SES-14 satellites from operator SES launched in 2018, were both built by Airbus Defence and Space with 25% of capacity using DSP.

The architecture of a DSP is optimized specifically for digital signal processing. Most also support some of the features as an applications processor or microcontroller, since signal processing is rarely the only task of a system. Some useful features for optimizing DSP algorithms are outlined below.

Architecture

Software Architecture

By the standards of general-purpose processors, DSP instruction sets are often highly irregular; while traditional instruction sets are made up of more general instructions that allow them to perform a wider variety of operations; instruction sets optimized for digital signal processing contain instructions for common mathematical operations that occur frequently in DSP calculations. Both traditional and DSP-optimized instruction sets are able to compute any arbitrary operation but an operation that might require multiple ARM or x86 instructions to compute might require only one instruction in a DSP optimized instruction set.

One implication for software architecture is that hand-optimized assembly-code routines (assembly programs) are commonly packaged into libraries for re-use, instead of relying on advanced compiler technologies to handle essential algorithms. Even with modern compiler optimizations hand-optimized assembly code is more efficient and many common algorithms involved in DSP calculations are hand-written in order to take full advantage of the architectural optimizations.

Instruction Sets

- Multiply–accumulates (macs, including fused multiply–add, FMA) operations.

  ○ Used extensively in all kinds of matrix operations:

    ▪ Convolution for filtering

    ▪ Dot product

    ▪ Polynomial evaluation

  ○ Fundamental DSP algorithms depend heavily on multiply–accumulate performance:

    ▪ FIR filters

    ▪ Fast Fourier transform (FFT)

- Related ISA and instructions:

  ○ SIMD

  ○ VLIW

  ○ Superscalar architecture

- Specialized instructions for modulo addressing in ring buffers and bit-reversed addressing mode for FFT cross-referencing.

- Dsps sometimes use time-stationary encoding to simplify hardware and increase coding efficiency.

- Multiple arithmetic units may require memory architectures to support several accesses per instruction cycle.

- Special loop controls, such as architectural support for executing a few instruction words in a very tight loop without overhead for instruction fetches or exit testing.

Data Instructions

- Saturation arithmetic, in which operations that produce overflows will accumulate at the maximum (or minimum) values that the register can hold rather than wrapping around (maximum+1 doesn't overflow to minimum as in many general-purpose CPUs, instead it stays at maximum). Sometimes various sticky bits operation modes are available.

- Fixed-point arithmetic is often used to speed up arithmetic processing.

- Single-cycle operations to increase the benefits of pipelining.

Program Flow

- Floating-point unit integrated directly into the datapath.

- Pipelined architecture.

- Highly parallel multiplier–accumulators (MAC units).

- Hardware-controlled looping, to reduce or eliminate the overhead required for looping operations.

Hardware Architecture

In engineering, hardware architecture refers to the identification of a system's physical components and their interrelationships. This description, often called a hardware design model, allows hardware designers to understand how their components fit into system architecture and provides to software component designers important information needed for software development and integration. Clear definition of a hardware architecture allows the various traditional engineering disciplines (e.g., electrical and mechanical engineering) to work more effectively together to develop and manufacture new machines, devices and components.

Hardware is also an expression used within the computer engineering industry to explicitly distinguish the (electronic computer) hardware from the software that runs on it. But hardware, within the automation and software engineering disciplines, need not simply be a computer of some sort. A modern automobile runs vastly more software than the Apollo spacecraft. Also, modern aircraft cannot function without running tens of millions of computer instructions embedded and distributed throughout the aircraft and resident in both standard computer hardware and in specialized hardware components such as IC wired logic gates, analog and hybrid devices, and other digital components. The need to effectively model how separate physical components combine to form complex systems is important over a wide range of applications, including computers, personal digital assistants (PDAs), cell phones, surgical instrumentation, satellites, and submarines.

Memory Architecture

DSPs are usually optimized for streaming data and use special memory architectures that are able to fetch multiple data or instructions at the same time, such as the Harvard architecture or Modified von Neumann architecture, which use separate program and data memories (sometimes even concurrent access on multiple data buses).

DSPs can sometimes rely on supporting code to know about cache hierarchies and the associated delays. This is a tradeoff that allows for better performance. In addition, extensive use of DMA is employed.

Addressing and Virtual Memory

DSPs frequently use multi-tasking operating systems, but have no support for virtual memory or memory protection. Operating systems that use virtual memory require more time for context switching among processes, which increases latency.

- Hardware modulo addressing:

  ◦ Allows circular buffers to be implemented without having to test for wrapping.

- Bit-reversed addressing, a special addressing mode:
    - Useful for calculating FFTs.
- Exclusion of a memory management unit.
- Address generation unit.

Modern DSPs

Modern signal processors yield greater performance; this is due in part to both technological and architectural advancements like lower design rules, fast-access two-level cache, (E)DMA circuitry and a wider bus system. Not all DSPs provide the same speed and many kinds of signal processors exist, each one of them being better suited for a specific task, ranging in price from about US$1.50 to US$300.

Texas Instruments produces the C6000 series DSPs, which have clock speeds of 1.2 GHz and implement separate instruction and data caches. They also have an 8 MiB 2nd level cache and 64 EDMA channels. The top models are capable of as many as 8000 MIPS (millions of instructions per second), use VLIW (very long instruction word), perform eight operations per clock-cycle and are compatible with a broad range of external peripherals and various buses (PCI/serial/etc). TMS320C6474 chips each have three such DSPs, and the newest generation C6000 chips support floating point as well as fixed point processing.

Freescale produces a multi-core DSP family, the MSC81xx. The MSC81xx is based on StarCore Architecture processors and the latest MSC8144 DSP combines four programmable SC3400 StarCore DSP cores. Each SC3400 StarCore DSP core has a clock speed of 1 GHz.

XMOS produces a multi-core multi-threaded line of processor well suited to DSP operations, They come in various speeds ranging from 400 to 1600 MIPS. The processors have a multi-threaded architecture that allows up to 8 real-time threads per core, meaning that a 4 core device would support up to 32 real time threads. Threads communicate between each other with buffered channels that are capable of up to 80 Mbit/s. The devices are easily programmable in C and aim at bridging the gap between conventional micro-controllers and FPGAs

CEVA, Inc. produces and licenses three distinct families of DSPs. Perhaps the best known and most widely deployed is the CEVA-TeakLite DSP family, a classic memory-based architecture, with 16-bit or 32-bit word-widths and single or dual MACs. The CEVA-X DSP family offers a combination of VLIW and SIMD architectures, with different members of the family offering dual or quad 16-bit MACs. The CEVA-XC DSP family target Software-defined Radio (SDR) modem designs and leverages a unique combination of VLIW and Vector architectures with 32 16-bit MACs.

Analog Devices produce the SHARC-based DSP and range in performance from 66 MHz/198 MFLOPS (million floating-point operations per second) to 400 MHz/2400 MFLOPS. Some models support multiple multipliers and ALUs, SIMD instructions and audio processing-specific components and peripherals. The Blackfin family of embedded digital signal processors combine the features of a DSP with those of a general use processor. As a result, these processors can run simple operating systems like µCLinux, velocity and Nucleus RTOS while operating on real-time data.

NXP Semiconductors produce DSPs based on TriMedia VLIW technology, optimized for audio and video processing. In some products the DSP core is hidden as a fixed-function block into a SoC, but NXP also provides a range of flexible single core media processors. The TriMedia media processors support both fixed-point arithmetic as well as floating-point arithmetic, and have specific instructions to deal with complex filters and entropy coding.

CSR produces the Quatro family of SoCs that contain one or more custom Imaging DSPs optimized for processing document image data for scanner and copier applications.

Microchip Technology produces the PIC24 based dsPIC line of DSPs. Introduced in 2004, the dsPIC is designed for applications needing a true DSP as well as a true microcontroller, such as motor control and in power supplies. The dsPIC runs at up to 40MIPS, and has support for 16 bit fixed point MAC, bit reverse and modulo addressing, as well as DMA.

Most DSPs use fixed-point arithmetic, because in real world signal processing the additional range provided by floating point is not needed, and there is a large speed benefit and cost benefit due to reduced hardware complexity. Floating point DSPs may be invaluable in applications where a wide dynamic range is required. Product developers might also use floating point DSPs to reduce the cost and complexity of software development in exchange for more expensive hardware, since it is generally easier to implement algorithms in floating point.

Generally, DSPs are dedicated integrated circuits; however DSP functionality can also be produced by using field-programmable gate array chips (FPGAs).

Embedded general-purpose RISC processors are becoming increasingly DSP like in functionality. For example, the OMAP3 processors include an ARM Cortex-A8 and C6000 DSP.

In Communications a new breed of DSPs offering the fusion of both DSP functions and H/W acceleration function is making its way into the mainstream. Such Modem processors include ASOCS ModemX and CEVA's XC4000.

In May 2018, Huarui-2 designed by Nanjing Research Institute of Electronics Technology passed acceptance. With a processing speed of 0.4 TFLOPS, the chip can achieve better performance than current mainstream DSP chips. The design team has begun to create Huarui-3, which has a processing speed in TFLOPS level and a support for artificial intelligence.

IMAGE ENHANCEMENT

Image enhancement is the process of digitally manipulating a stored image using software. The tools used for image enhancement include many different kinds of software such as filters, image editors and other tools for changing various properties of an entire image or parts of an image.

Some of the most basic types of image enhancement tools simply change the contrast or brightness of an image or manipulate the grayscale or the red-green-blue color patterns of an image. Some types of basic filters also allow changing a color image to black and white, or to a sepia-tone image, or adding visual effects.

More sophisticated types of image enhancement tools can apply changes more specifically to certain parts of an image. Professional packages like those offered by Adobe allow designers to do a more specialized or professional kind of image enhancement or to pursue results for graphic design projects where the actual image is changed into a stylized or otherwise embellished version of itself. More advanced types of image enhancement tools also include features like Wiener filters for actual de-blurring of images and other complex resources for restoring or clarifying images that may be in poor condition, due to sub-optimal image capture conditions, aging or other causes.

Image Denoising

Digital images plays very significant role in our daily routine like they are used in satellite television, Intelligent traffic monitoring, handwriting recognition on checks, signature validation, computer resonance imaging and in area of research and technology such as geographical information systems and astronomy. In digital imaging, the acquisition techniques and systems introduce various types of noises and artifacts. Denoising is more significant than any other tasks in image processing, analysis and applications. Reserving the details of an image and removing the random noise as far as possible is the goal of image denoising approaches. Besides the noisy image produces undesirable visual quality, it also lowers the visibility of low contrast objects. Hence noise removal is essential in digital imaging applications in order to enhance and recover fine details that are hidden in the data. In many occasions, noise in digital images is found to be additive in nature with uniform power in the whole bandwidth and with Gaussian probability distribution. Such a noise is referred to as Additive White Gaussian Noise (AWGN). It is difficult to Suppress AWGN since it corrupts almost all pixels in an image. In denoising there is always a tradeoff between noise suppression and preserving actual image discontinuities. To remove noise without excessive smoothing of important details, a denoising technique needs to be spatially adaptive. Different techniques are used depending on the noise model. Due to properties like sparsity, an edge detection and multiresolution, the wavelet naturally facilitates such spatially adaptive noise filtering.

Evolution of Image Denoising Techniques

Image denoising is the fundamental problem in Image processing. Wavelet gives the excellent performance in field of image denoising because of sparsity and multiresolution structure. With the popularity of Wavelet Transform for the last two decades, several algorithms have been developed in wavelet domain. The focus was shifted to Wavelet domain from spatial and Fourier domain. Ever since the Donoho's wavelet based thresholding approach was published in 2003, there was surge in the image denoising papers being published. Although his approach was not revolutionary, it did not require tracking and correlation of the wavelet maxima and minima across the different scales as proposed by Mallat .Thus there was renewed interest in wavelet approach since Donoho's demonstrated a simple solution to difficult problem domain. Researchers published different approaches to compute the simulation parameters for wavelet coefficients. To achieve optimum threshold value, data adaptive thresholds were introduced. Substantial improvements in perceptual quality could be obtained by translation invariant method based on thresholding of an Undecimated Wavelet transform. Much effort has been devoted to Bayesian denoising in wavelet domain. Gaussian scale mixtures and hidden markov models have also become popular and more research is continued to be published and Independent component analyses (ICA) have been explored in data adaptive components. Different statistical models are focused to model the statistical properties of wavelet coefficients and its neighbours. Future trend will be to find more probabilistic model for non-orthogonal wavelet coefficients distribution.

There has been a significant amount of work done on image denoising techniques. Existing methods are able to produce good results in many practical scenarios. The various denoising techniques are as follows:

1. Spatial Filtering: A traditional way to remove noise from image data is to employ spatial filters. Spatial filtering is commonly used to clean up the output of lasers, removing aberrations in the beam due to imperfect, dirty or damaged optics. Spatial filters can be further classified into non-linear and linear filters.

2. Linear Filters: Linear filters process time-varying input signals to produce output signals, subject to constraint of linearity. A mean filter is the optimal linear filter for Gaussian noise in the sense of mean square error. Linear filters too tend to blur sharp edges, destroy lines and other fine image details, and perform poorly in the presence of signal-dependent noise. The wiener filtering method requires the information about the spectra of the noise and the original signal and it works well only if the underlying signal is smooth. Wiener method implements spatial smoothing and its model complexity control correspond to choosing the window size. To overcome the weakness of the Wiener filtering, Donoho and Johnstone proposed the wavelet based denoising scheme in.

3. Mean Filter: A mean filter acts on an image by smoothing it; that is, it reduces the intensity variation between adjacent pixels. The mean filter is nothing but a simple sliding window spatial filter that replaces the center value in the window with the average of all the neighboring pixel values including it. Image corrupted with salt and pepper noise is subjected to mean filtering and it can be observed that the noise dominating is reduced. The white and dark pixel values of the noise are changed to be closer to the pixel values of the surrounding ones. Also, the brightness of the input image remains unchanged because of the use of the mask, whose coefficients sum up to the value one.The mean filter is used in applications where the noise in certain regions of the image needs to be removed. In other words, the mean filter is useful when only a part of the image needs to be processed.

4. LMS Adaptive Filter: Adaptive filters are capable of denoising non-stationary images, that is, images that have abrupt changes in intensity. Such filters are known for their ability in automatically tracking an unknown circumstance or when a signal is variable with little a priori knowledge about the signal to be processed .An adaptive filter does a better job of denoising images compared to the averaging filter as the Least Mean Square (LMS) adaptive filter is known for its simplicity in computation and implementation. The LMS adaptive filter works well for images corrupted with salt and pepper type noise. But this filter does a better denoising job compared to the mean filter.

5. Non-linear filters: Non-linear filters have many applications, especially in removal of certain types of noise that are not additive. Generally spatial filters remove noise to a reasonable extent but at the cost of blurring images which in turn makes the edges in pictures invisible. In recent years, a variety of nonlinear median type filters such as weighted median, rank conditioned rank selection, and relaxed median have been developed to overcome this drawback.

6. Median Filter: The median filter also follows the moving window principle similar to the mean filter. A 3×3, 5×5, or 7×7 kernel of pixels is scanned over pixel matrix of the entire image. The

median of the pixel values in the window is computed, and the center pixel of the window is replaced with the computed median. The median is more robust compared to the mean. Thus, a single very unrepresentative pixel in a neighborhood will not affect the median value significantly. Since the median value must actually be the value of one of the pixels in the neighborhood, the median filter does not create new unrealistic pixel values when the filter straddles an edge. For this reason the median filter is much better at preserving sharp edges than the mean filter. These advantages aid median filters in denoising uniform noise as well from an image.

7. Spatial Median Filter: The spatial median filter is also noise removal filter where the spatial median is calculated by calculating the spatial depth between a point and a set of point. In this filter after finding out the spatial depth of each point lying within the filtering mask, this information is used to decide whether the central pixel of window is corrupted or not, If central pixel is uncorrupted then it will not be changed. We then find out the spatial depth of each pixel within the mask and then sort these spatial depths in descending order .The point with largest spatial depth represent the spatial median of the set.

8. Weighted Median Filter (WMF): The centre weighted median filter is an extension of the weighted median filter. The weighted median filter previously designed gives more weight to some values within the window whereas centre weighted median filter gives more weight to the central value of a window thus easier to design and implement than other weighted median filter.

9. Wavelet Transforms: Wavelets are mathematical functions that analyze data according to scale or resolution. They aid in studying a signal in different windows or at different resolutions. For instance, if the signal is viewed in a large window, gross features can be noticed, but if viewed in a small window, only small features can be noticed. Wavelets provide some advantages over Fourier transforms. For example, they do a good job in approximating signals with sharp spikes or signals having discontinuities. The wavelet equation produces different wavelet families like Daubechies, Haar, Coiflets, etc.

10. Mallat's Algorithm: Mallat's algorithm is a computationally efficient method of implementing the wavelet transform. It calculates DWT wavelet coefficients for a finite set of input data, which is a power of 2. This input data is passed through two convolution functions, each of which creates an output stream that is half the length of the original input. This procedure is referred to as down sampling. Once the processing is done, the data vector is built back from the coefficients. This process of reconstruction is referred to as the inverse Mallat's algorithm.

Tables shows the SNR (signal to noise ratio) of the input and output images for the filtering approach. It shows how SNR varies with different type of noise and filters used.

Table: SNR values for filtering approach.

Method	SNR of input image	SNR of output image	Noise type and variance, σ
Mean filter	18.88	27.43	Salt and pepper, 0.05
Mean filter	13.39	21.24	Gaussian, 0.05
LMS adaptive filter	18.88	28.01	Salt and pepper, 0.05
LMS adaptive filter	13.39	22.40	Gaussian, 0.05
Median filter	18.88	47.97	Salt and pepper, 0.05
Median filter	13.39	22.79	Gaussian, 0.05

11. Wavelet Thresholding: Donoho and Johnstone pioneered the work on filtering of additive Gaussian noise using wavelet thresholding. Wavelet coefficients calculated by a wavelet transform represent change in the time series at a particular resolution. By considering the time series at various resolutions, it is then possible to filter out noise.The term wavelet thresholding is explained as decomposition of the data or the image into wavelet coefficients, comparing the detail coefficients with a given threshold value, and shrinking these coefficients close to zero to take away the effect of noise in the data. The image is reconstructed from the modified coefficients. There are various thresholding techniques. Some of these are discussed below:

12. VisuShrink: VisuShrink was introduced by Donoho . It uses a threshold value t that is proportional to the standard deviation of the noise. It follows the hard thresholding rule. It is also referred to as universal threshold and is defined as $t = \sigma \sqrt{2\log n}$

VisuShrink does not deal with minimizing the mean squared error. It can be viewed as general-purpose threshold selectors that exhibit near optimal minimax error properties and ensures with high probability that the estimates are as smooth as the true underlying functions. However, VisuShrink is known to yield recovered images that are overly smoothed. This is because VisuShrink removes too many coefficients. Another disadvantage is that it cannot remove speckle noise. It can only deal with an additive noise. VisuShrink follows the global thresholding scheme where there is a single value of threshold applied globally to all the wavelet coefficients.

13. SureShrink: A threshold chooser based on Stein's Unbiased Risk Estimator (SURE) was proposed by Donoho and Johnstone and is called as SureShrink. It is a combination of the universal threshold and the SURE threshold. The SureShrink threshold t^* is defined as $t^* = \min(t, \sigma \sqrt{2\log n})$.

Where, t denotes the value that minimizes Stein's Unbiased Risk Estimator, σ is the noise variance and n is the size of the image.

SureShrink follows the soft thresholding rule. SureShrink suppresses noise by thresholding the empirical wavelet coefficients. SureShrink produces the best SNR as compared to VisuShrink and BayesShrink.

14. BayesShrink: BayesShrink was proposed by Chang, Yu and Vetterli . The goal of this method is to minimize the Bayesian risk, and hence its name, BayesShrink. It uses soft thresholding and is subband-dependent, which means that thresholding is done at each band of resolution in the wavelet decomposition. Like the SureShrink procedure, it is smoothness adaptive. The Bayes threshold, tB, is defined as $t_B = \sigma^2 / \sigma_s$.

Where, σ^2 is the noise variance and σ^2 is the signal variance without noise.

The output from BayesShrink method is much closer to the high quality image and there is no blurring in the output image unlike the other two methods.

Image Histogram

An image histogram is a type of histogram that acts as a graphical representation of the tonal distribution in a digital image. It plots the number of pixels for each tonal value. By looking at the histogram for a specific image a viewer will be able to judge the entire tonal distribution at a glance.

Sunflower image.

Image histograms are present on many modern digital cameras. Photographers can use them as an aid to show the distribution of tones captured, and whether image detail has been lost to blown-out highlights or blacked-out shadows. This is less useful when using a raw image format, as the dynamic range of the displayed image may only be an approximation to that in the raw file.

The horizontal axis of the graph represents the tonal variations, while the vertical axis represents the total number of pixels in that particular tone.

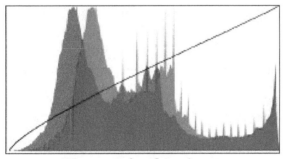

Histogram of sunflower image.

The left side of the horizontal axis represents the dark areas, the middle represents mid-tone values and the right hand side represents light areas. The vertical axis represents the size of the area (total number of pixels) that is captured in each one of these zones.

Thus, the histogram for a very dark image will have most of its data points on the left side and center of the graph.

Conversely, the histogram for a very bright image with few dark areas and shadows will have most of its data points on the right side and center of the graph.

Image Manipulation and Histograms

Image editors typically create a histogram of the image being edited. The histogram plots the number of pixels in the image (vertical axis) with a particular brightness or tonal value (horizontal axis). Algorithms in the digital editor allow the user to visually adjust the brightness value of each pixel and to dynamically display the results as adjustments are made. Histogram equalization is a popular example of these algorithms. Improvements in picture brightness and contrast can thus be obtained.

In the field of computer vision, image histograms can be useful tools for thresholding. Because the information contained in the graph is a representation of pixel distribution as a function of tonal variation, image histograms can be analyzed for peaks and valleys. This threshold value can then be used for edge detection, image segmentation, and co-occurrence matrices.

Color Histogram

In image processing and photography, a color histogram is a representation of the distribution of colors in an image. For digital images, a color histogram represents the number of pixels that have colors in each of a fixed list of color ranges that span the image's color space, the set of all possible colors.

The color histogram can be built for any kind of color space, although the term is more often used for three-dimensional spaces like RGB or HSV. For monochromatic images, the term intensity histogram may be used instead. For multi-spectral images, where each pixel is represented by an arbitrary number of measurements (for example, beyond the three measurements in RGB), the color histogram is N-dimensional, with N being the number of measurements taken. Each measurement has its own wavelength range of the light spectrum, some of which may be outside the visible spectrum.

If the set of possible color values is sufficiently small, each of those colors may be placed on a range by itself; then the histogram is merely the count of pixels that have each possible color. Most often, the space is divided into an appropriate number of ranges, often arranged as a regular grid, each containing many similar color values. The color histogram may also be represented and displayed as a smooth function defined over the color space that approximates the pixel counts.

Like other kinds of histograms, the color histogram is a statistic that can be viewed as an approximation of an underlying continuous distribution of colors values.

Color histograms are flexible constructs that can be built from images in various color spaces, whether RGB, rg chromaticity or any other color space of any dimension. A histogram of an image is produced first by discretization of the colors in the image into a number of bins, and counting the number of image pixels in each bin. For example, a Red–Blue chromaticity histogram can be formed by first normalizing color pixel values by dividing RGB values by R+G+B, then quantizing the normalized R and B coordinates into N bins each. A two-dimensional histogram of Red-Blue chromaticity divided into four bins (N=4) might yield a histogram that looks like this table:

	0-63	red			
		6 4 - 127	128-191	192-255	
blue	0-63	43	78	18	0
	64-127	45	67	33	2
	128-191	127	58	25	8
	192-255	140	47	47	13

A histogram can be N-dimensional. Although harder to display, a three-dimensional color histogram for the above example could be thought of as four separate Red-Blue histograms, where each of the four histograms contains the Red-Blue values for a bin of green (0-63, 64-127, 128-191, and 192-255).

The histogram provides a compact summarization of the distribution of data in an image. The color histogram of an image is relatively invariant with translation and rotation about the viewing axis, and varies only slowly with the angle of view. By comparing histograms signatures of two images and matching the color content of one image with the other, the color histogram is particularly well suited for the problem of recognizing an object of unknown position and rotation within a scene. Importantly, translation of an RGB image into the illumination invariant rg-chromaticity space allows the histogram to operate well in varying light levels.

Histogram

A histogram is a graphical representation of the number of pixels in an image. In a more simple way to explain, a histogram is a bar graph, whose X-axis represents the tonal scale (black at the left and white at the right), and Y-axis represents the number of pixels in an image in a certain area of the tonal scale. For example, the graph of a luminance histogram shows the number of pixels for each brightness level (from black to white), and when there are more pixels, the peak at the certain luminance level is higher.

A color histogram of an image represents the distribution of the composition of colors in the image. It shows different types of colors appeared and the number of pixels in each type of the colors appeared. The relation between a color histogram and a luminance histogram is that a color histogram can be also expressed as "Three Luminance Histograms", each of which shows the brightness distribution of each individual Red/Green/Blue color channel.

Characteristics of a Color Histogram

A color histogram focuses only on the proportion of the number of different types of colors, regardless of the spatial location of the colors. The values of a color histogram are from statistics. They show the statistical distribution of colors and the essential tone of an image.

In general, as the color distributions of the foreground and background in an image are different, there might be a bimodal distribution in the histogram.

For the luminance histogram alone, there is no perfect histogram and in general, the histogram can tell whether it is over exposure or not, but there are times when you might think the image is over exposed by viewing the histogram; however, in reality it is not.

Principles of the Formation of a Color Histogram

The formation of a color histogram is rather simple. From the definition above, we can simply count the number of pixels for each 256 scales in each of the 3 RGB channel, and plot them on 3 individual bar graphs.

In general, a color histogram is based on a certain color space, such as RGB or HSV. When we compute the pixels of different colors in an image, if the color space is large, then we can first divide the color space into certain numbers of small intervals. Each of the intervals is called a bin. This process is called color quantization. Then, by counting the number of pixels in each of the bins, we get the color histogram of the image.

Drawbacks and other Approaches

The main drawback of histograms for classification is that the representation is dependent of the color of the object being studied, ignoring its shape and texture. Color histograms can potentially be identical for two images with different object content which happens to share color information. Conversely, without spatial or shape information, similar objects of different color may be indistinguishable based solely on color histogram comparisons. There is no way to distinguish a red and white cup from a red and white plate. Put another way, histogram-based algorithms have no concept of a generic 'cup', and a model of a red and white cup is no use when given an otherwise identical blue and white cup. Another problem is that color histograms have high sensitivity to noisy interference such as lighting intensity changes and quantization errors. High dimensionality (bins) color histograms are also another issue. Some color histogram feature spaces often occupy more than one hundred dimensions.

Some of the proposed solutions have been color histogram intersection, color constant indexing, cumulative color histogram, quadratic distance, and color correlograms. Although there are drawbacks of using histograms for indexing and classification, using color in a real-time system has several advantages. One is that color information is faster to compute compared to other invariants. It has been shown in some cases that color can be an efficient method for identifying objects of known location and appearance.

Further research into the relationship between color histogram data to the physical properties of the objects in an image has shown they can represent not only object color and illumination but relate to surface roughness and image geometry and provide an improved estimate of illumination and object color.

Usually, Euclidean distance, histogram intersection, or cosine or quadratic distances are used for the calculation of image similarity ratings. Any of these values do not reflect the similarity rate of two images in itself; it is useful only when used in comparison to other similar values. This is the reason that all the practical implementations of content-based image retrieval must complete computation of all images from the database, and is the main disadvantage of these implementations.

Another approach to representative color image content is two-dimensional color histogram. A two-dimensional color histogram considers the relation between the pixel pair colors (not only the lighting component). A two-dimensional color histogram is a two-dimensional array. The size of each dimension is the number of colors that were used in the phase of color quantization. These arrays are treated as matrices, each element of which stores a normalized count of pixel pairs, with each color corresponding to the index of an element in each pixel neighborhood. For comparison of two-dimensional color histograms it is suggested calculating their correlation, because constructed as described above, is a random vector (in other words, a multi-dimensional random value). While creating a set of final images, the images should be arranged in decreasing order of the correlation coefficient.

The correlation coefficient may also be used for color histogram comparison. Retrieval results with correlation coefficient are better than with other metrics.

Histogram Equalization

Histogram equalization is a method in image processing of contrast adjustment using the image's histogram.

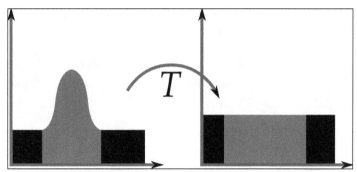

Histograms of an image before and after equalization.

This method usually increases the global contrast of many images, especially when the usable data of the image is represented by close contrast values. Through this adjustment, the intensities can be better distributed on the histogram. This allows for areas of lower local contrast to gain a higher contrast. Histogram equalization accomplishes this by effectively spreading out the most frequent intensity values.

The method is useful in images with backgrounds and foregrounds that are both bright or both dark. In particular, the method can lead to better views of bone structure in x-ray images, and to better detail in photographs that are over or under-exposed. A key advantage of the method is that it is a fairly straightforward technique and an invertible operator. So in theory, if the histogram equalization function is known, then the original histogram can be recovered. The calculation is not computationally intensive. A disadvantage of the method is that it is indiscriminate. It may increase the contrast of background noise, while decreasing the usable signal.

In scientific imaging where spatial correlation is more important than intensity of signal (such as separating DNA fragments of quantized length), the small signal to noise ratio usually hampers visual detection.

Histogram equalization often produces unrealistic effects in photographs; however it is very useful for scientific images like thermal, satellite or x-ray images, often the same class of images to which one would apply false-color. Also histogram equalization can produce undesirable effects (like visible image gradient) when applied to images with low color depth. For example, if applied to 8-bit image displayed with 8-bit gray-scale palette it will further reduce color depth (number of unique shades of gray) of the image. Histogram equalization will work the best when applied to images with much higher color depth than palette size, like continuous data or 16-bit gray-scale images.

There are two ways to think about and implement histogram equalization, either as image change or as palette change. The operation can be expressed as P(M(I)) where I is the original image, M is histogram equalization mapping operation and P is a palette. If we define a new palette as P'=P(M) and leave image I unchanged then histogram equalization is implemented as palette change. On the other hand, if palette P remains unchanged and image is modified to I'=M(I) then the implementation is by image change. In most cases palette change is better as it preserves the original data.

Modifications of this method use multiple histograms, called subhistograms, to emphasize local contrast, rather than overall contrast. Examples of such methods include adaptive histogram equalization, contrast limiting adaptive histogram equalization or CLAHE, multipeak histogram equalization (MPHE), and multipurpose beta optimized bihistogram equalization (MBOBHE).

The goal of these methods, especially MBOBHE, is to improve the contrast without producing brightness mean-shift and detail loss artifacts by modifying the HE algorithm.

A signal transform equivalent to histogram equalization also seems to happen in biological neural networks so as to maximize the output firing rate of the neuron as a function of the input statistics. This has been proved in particular in the fly retina.

Histogram equalization is a specific case of the more general class of histogram remapping methods. These methods seek to adjust the image to make it easier to analyze or improve visual quality (e.g., retinex).

Back Projection

The back projection (or "project") of a histogrammed image is the re-application of the modified histogram to the original image, functioning as a look-up table for pixel brightness values.

For each group of pixels taken from the same position from all input single-channel images, the function puts the histogram bin value to the destination image, where the coordinates of the bin are determined by the values of pixels in this input group. In terms of statistics, the value of each output image pixel characterizes the probability that the corresponding input pixel group belongs to the object whose histogram is used.

Implementation

Consider a discrete grayscale image $\{x\}$ and let n_i be the number of occurrences of gray level i. The probability of an occurrence of a pixel of level i in the image is:

$$p_x(i) = p(x = i) = \frac{n_i}{n}, \quad 0 \le i < L$$

L being the total number of gray levels in the image (typically 256), n being the total number of pixels in the image, and $p_x(i)$ being in fact the image's histogram for pixel value i, normalized to [0,1].

Let us also define the cumulative distribution function corresponding to p_x as:

$$cdf_x(i) = \sum_{j=0}^{i} p_x(j)$$

Which is also the image's accumulated normalized histogram.

We would like to create a transformation of the form y = T(x) to produce a new image $\{y\}$, with a flat histogram. Such an image would have a linearized cumulative distribution function (CDF) across the value range, i.e.

$$cdf_y(i) = iK$$

For some constant K. The properties of the CDF allow us to perform such a transform; it is defined as:

$$cdf_y(y') = cdf_y(T(k)) = cdf_x(k)$$

Where, k is in the range [0,L]). Notice that T maps the levels into the range [0,1], since we used a normalized histogram of {x}. In order to map the values back into their original range, the following simple transformation needs to be applied on the result:

$$y' = y \cdot (\max\{x\} - \min\{x\}) + \min\{x\}$$

Of Color Images

The above describes histogram equalization on a grayscale image. However it can also be used on color images by applying the same method separately to the Red, Green and Blue components of the RGB color values of the image. However, applying the same method on the Red, Green, and Blue components of an RGB image may yield dramatic changes in the image's color balance since the relative distributions of the color channels change as a result of applying the algorithm. However, if the image is first converted to another color space, Lab color space, or HSL/HSV color space in particular, then the algorithm can be applied to the luminance or value channel without resulting in changes to the hue and saturation of the image. There are several histogram equalization methods in 3D space. Trahanias and Venetsanopoulos applied histogram equalization in 3D color space However, it results in "whitening" where the probability of bright pixels are higher than that of dark ones. Han et al. proposed to use a new cdf defined by the iso-luminance plane, which results in uniform gray distribution.

Adaptive Histogram Equalization

Adaptive histogram equalization (AHE) is a computer image processing technique used to improve contrast in images. It differs from ordinary histogram equalization in the respect that the adaptive method computes several histograms, each corresponding to a distinct section of the image, and uses them to redistribute the lightness values of the image. It is therefore suitable for improving the local contrast and enhancing the definitions of edges in each region of an image.

However, AHE has a tendency to overamplify noise in relatively homogeneous regions of an image. A variant of adaptive histogram equalization called contrast limited adaptive histogram equalization (CLAHE) prevents this by limiting the amplification.

Motivation and Explanation of the Method

Ordinary histogram equalization uses the same transformation derived from the image histogram to transform all pixels. This works well when the distribution of pixel values is similar throughout the image. However, when the image contains regions that are significantly lighter or darker than most of the image, the contrast in those regions will not be sufficiently enhanced.

Adaptive histogram equalization (AHE) improves on this by transforming each pixel with a transformation function derived from a neighbourhood region. It was first developed for use in aircraft cockpit displays. cited in In its simplest form, each pixel is transformed based on the histogram of a square surrounding the pixel, as in the figure. The derivation of the transformation functions from the histograms is exactly the same as for ordinary histogram equalization: The transformation function is proportional to the cumulative distribution function (CDF) of pixel values in the neighbourhood.

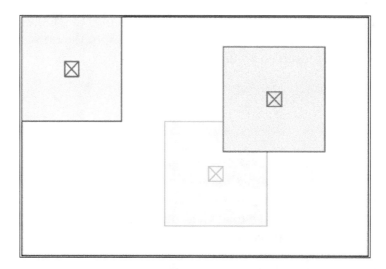

Pixels near the image boundary have to be treated specially, because their neighbourhood would not lie completely within the image. This applies for example to the pixels to the left or above the blue pixel in the figure. This can be solved by extending the image by mirroring pixel lines and columns with respect to the image boundary. Simply copying the pixel lines on the border is not appropriate, as it would lead to a highly peaked neighbourhood histogram.

Properties of AHE

- The size of the neighbourhood region is a parameter of the method. It constitutes a characteristic length scale: contrast at smaller scales is enhanced, while contrast at larger scales is reduced.

- Due to the nature of histogram equalization, the result value of a pixel under AHE is proportional to its rank among the pixels in its neighbourhood. This allows an efficient implementation on specialist hardware that can compare the center pixel with all other pixels in the neighbourhood. An unnormalized result value can be computed by adding 2 for each pixel with a smaller value than the center pixel, and adding 1 for each pixel with equal value.

- When the image region containing a pixel's neighbourhood is fairly homogeneous regarding to intensities, its histogram will be strongly peaked, and the transformation function will map a narrow range of pixel values to the whole range of the result image. This causes AHE to overamplify small amounts of noise in largely homogeneous regions of the image.

Contrast Limited AHE

Ordinary AHE tends to overamplify the contrast in near-constant regions of the image, since the histogram in such regions is highly concentrated. As a result, AHE may cause noise to be amplified in near-constant regions. Contrast Limited AHE (CLAHE) is a variant of adaptive histogram equalization in which the contrast amplification is limited, so as to reduce this problem of noise amplification.

In CLAHE, the contrast amplification in the vicinity of a given pixel value is given by the slope of the transformation function. This is proportional to the slope of the neighbourhood cumulative distribution function (CDF) and therefore to the value of the histogram at that pixel value. CLAHE limits the amplification by clipping the histogram at a predefined value before computing the CDF. This limits the slope of the CDF and therefore of the transformation function. The value at which the histogram is clipped, the so-called clip limit, depends on the normalization of the histogram and thereby on the size of the neighbourhood region. Common values limit the resulting amplification to between 3 and 4.

It is advantageous not to discard the part of the histogram that exceeds the clip limit but to redistribute it equally among all histogram bins.

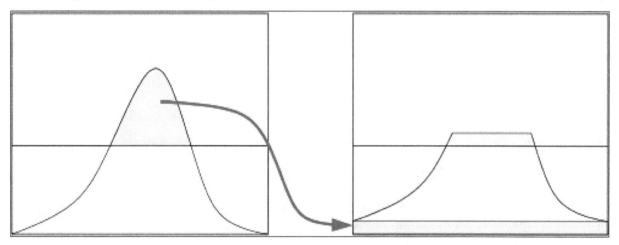

The redistribution will push some bins over the clip limit again (region shaded green in the figure), resulting in an effective clip limit that is larger than the prescribed limit and the exact value of which depends on the image. If this is undesirable, the redistribution procedure can be repeated recursively until the excess is negligible.

Efficient Computation by Interpolation

Adaptive histogram equalization in its straightforward form presented above, both with and without contrast limiting, requires the computation of a different neighbourhood histogram and transformation function for each pixel in the image. This makes the method very expensive computationally.

Interpolation allows a significant improvement in efficiency without compromising the quality of the result. The image is partitioned into equally sized rectangular tiles as shown in the right part of the figure. (64 tiles in 8 columns and 8 rows is a common choice.) A histogram, CDF and transformation function is then computed for each of the tiles. The transformation functions are appropriate for the tile center pixels, black squares in the left part of the figure. All other pixels are transformed with up to four transformation functions of the tiles with center pixels closest to them, and are assigned interpolated values. Pixels in the bulk of the image (shaded blue) are bilinearly interpolated, pixels close to the boundary (shaded green) are linearly interpolated, and pixels near corners (shaded red) are transformed with the transformation function of the corner tile. The interpolation coefficients reflect the location of pixels between the closest tile center pixels, so that the result is continuous as the pixel approaches a tile center.

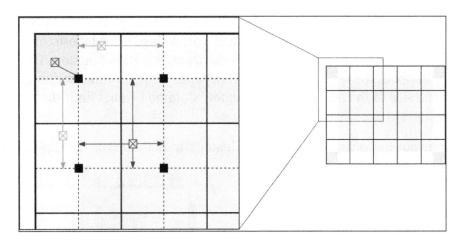

This procedure reduces the number of transformation functions to be computed dramatically and only imposes the small additional cost of linear interpolation.

Efficient Computation by Incremental Update of Histogram

An alternative to tiling the image is to "slide" the rectangle one pixel at a time, and only incrementally update the histogram for each pixel, by adding the new pixel row and subtracting the row left behind. The algorithm is denoted SWAHE (Sliding Window Adaptive Histogram Equalization) by the original authors. The computational complexity of histogram calculation is then reduced from $O(N^2)$ to $O(N)$ (with N = pixel width of the surrounding rectangle); and since there is no tiling a final interpolation step is not required.

Histogram Matching

In image processing, histogram matching or histogram specification is the transformation of an image so that its histogram matches a specified histogram. The well-known histogram equalization method is a special case in which the specified histogram is uniformly distributed.

It is possible to use histogram matching to balance detector responses as a relative detector calibration technique. It can be used to normalize two images, when the images were acquired at the same local illumination (such as shadows) over the same location, but by different sensors, atmospheric conditions or global illumination.

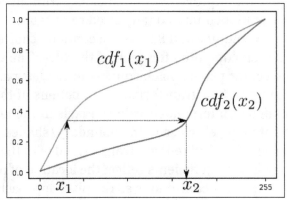

An example of histogram matching.

Implementation

Consider a grayscale input image X. It has a probability density function $p_r(r)$, where r is a grayscale value, and $p_r(r)$ is the probability of that value. This probability can easily be computed from the histogram of the image by:

$$p_r(r_j) = \frac{n_j}{n}$$

Where n_j is the frequency of the grayscale value r_j, and n is the total number of pixels in the image.

Now consider a desired output probability density function $p_z(z)$. A transformation of $p_r(r)$ is needed to convert it to $p_z(z)$.

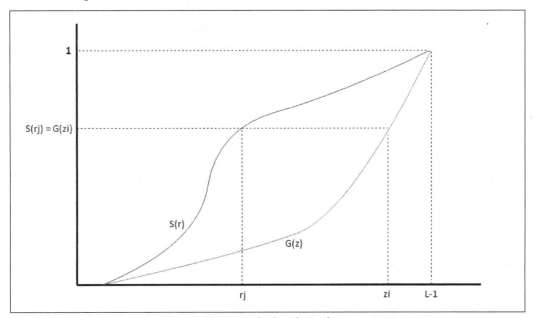

Input image CDF matched to desired output CDF.

Each pdf (probability density function) can easily be mapped to its cumulative distribution function by:

$$S(r_k) = \sum_{j=0}^{k} p_r(r_j), \qquad k = 0,1,2,3,\ldots$$

$$G(z_k) = \sum_{j=0}^{k} p_z(z_j), \qquad k = 0,1,2,3,\ldots,L$$

Where, L is the total number of gray level (256 for a standard image).

The idea is to map each r value in X to the z value that has the same probability in the desired pdf. I.e. $S(r_j) = G(z_i)$ or $z = G^{-1}(S(r))$.

Example:

The following input grayscale image is to be changed to match the reference histogram.

The input image has the following histogram.

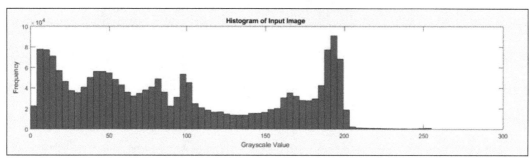

Histogram of input image.

It will be matched to this reference histogram to emphasize the lower gray levels.

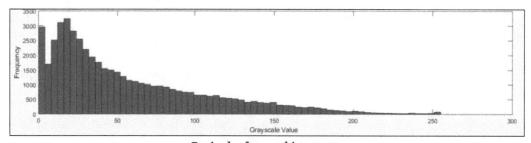

Desired reference histogram.

After matching, the output image has the following histogram.

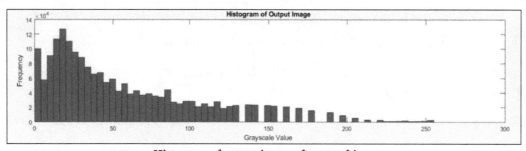

Histogram of output image after matching.

And looks like this:

Output image after histogram matching.

Algorithm

Given two images, the reference and the target images, we compute their histograms. Following, we calculate the cumulative distribution functions of the two images' histograms – $F_1()$, for the reference image and $F_2()$, for the target image. Then for each gray level $G_1 \in [0,255]$, we find the gray level G_2, for which $F_1(G_1) = F_2(G_2)$, and this is the result of histogram matching function: $M(G_1) = G_2$. Finally, we apply the function $M()$ on each pixel of the reference image.

Exact Histogram Matching

In typical real-world applications, with 8-bit pixel values (discrete values in range [0, 255]), histogram matching can only approximate the specified histogram. All pixels of a particular value in the original image must be transformed to just one value in the output image.

Exact histogram matching is the problem of finding a transformation for a discrete image so that its histogram exactly matches the specified histogram. Several techniques have been proposed for this. One simplistic approach converts the discrete-valued image into a continuous-valued image and adds small random values to each pixel so their values can be ranked without ties. However, this introduces noise to the output image.

Because of this there may be holes or open spots in the output matched histogram.

Multiple Histogram Matching

The histogram matching algorithm can be extended to find a monotonic mapping between two sets of histograms. Given two sets of histograms $P = \{p_i\}_{i=1}^k$ and $Q = \{q_i\}_{i=1}^k$, the optimal monotonic color mapping M is calculated to minimize the distance between the two sets simultaneously, namely $\text{argmin}_M \sum_k d(M(p_k), q_k)$ where $d(\cdot, \cdot)$ is a distance metric between two histograms. The optimal solution is calculated using dynamic programming.

Inpainting

Inpainting is a process of restorative conservation where damaged, deteriorating, or missing parts of an artwork are reconstructed, ultimately with the goal of presenting the artwork as it was originally created. This process can be applied to both physical and digital artistic mediums such as oil or acrylic paintings, chemical photographic prints, 3-dimensional sculptures, or digital images and video. In order to preserve the integrity of the original artwork, any treatment applied to physical or digital work should be reversible to the best of the conservators' ability so as to not permanently impact the original piece. Prior to any restoration work, conservators shall proceed under the code of ethics guidelines.

With its roots in physical artwork, such as painting and sculpture, traditional inpainting is performed by a trained art conservator who has carefully studied the artwork to determine the mediums and techniques used in the piece, potential risks of restoration, and ethical appropriateness of treatment. Before beginning any work, the conservator should present a treatment proposal to the owner of the object, whether an individual or institution, to discuss the goals of preserving and presenting the piece for future generations. Depending on the integrity of the object and careful research, the various techniques and mediums used for inpainting are decided.

Original and restored image.

Since the mid-1990s, the process of inpainting has evolved to include digital media. More commonly known as image or video interpolation, a form of estimation, digital inpainting includes the use of computer software that relies on sophisticated algorithms to replace lost or corrupted parts of the image data. There are currently many programs in use that are able to reconstruct missing or damaged areas of digital photographs and videos. Most widely known for use with digital images is Adobe Photoshop. Since the digital files are able to be duplicated, any restorative alterations should be made to the duplicate file, while maintaining the original files in an archive.

Applications

The applications of this technique depend on the desired goal and type of image being treated.

In the conservation and restoration of paintings, "the term inpainting refers to the compensation of paint losses—aiming at the recomposition of the missing parts of an image in order to improve its perception by making damages less visible". In other words, inpainting aims to make a visual improvement to the artwork as a whole by repairing missing or damaged parts using methods and materials equivalent to the original artist's work.

In photography and cinema, it is used for film restoration to reverse, repair, or mitigate deterioration (e.g. physical damage such as cracks in photographs or scratches and dust spots in film or chemical damage resulting in image loss). It can also be used for removing red-eye, the stamped date from photographs, and removing objects for creative effect.

This technique can be used to replace any lost blocks in the coding and transmission of images, for example, in a streaming video. It can also be used to remove logos in videos.

Deep learning neural network based inpainting can be used for decensoring images.

With all applications of inpainting, it is important to keep detailed records of the initial state of the images, treatments done and justification for treatment, and the original copies when applicable (e.g. original digital images).

Methods

"Helmut Ruhemann was a leading figure in the modernisation of the restoration profession. Prior to the 20th Century the methods of the picture restorer had been seen as dark secrets passed only between a select few". "One of his great contributions to the art of inpainting was his insistence on following the methods of the original painter exactly, and on understanding the painter's artistic intention" After his career of over 40 years as a conservator, Ruhemann published his treatise The Cleaning of Paintings: Problems & Potentialities in 1968. In describing his method, Ruhemann states that "The surface [of the fill] should be slightly lower than that of the surrounding paint to allow for the thickness of the inpainting...Inpainting medium should look and behave like the original medium, but must not darken with age." By studying the painting methods of various artists, the composition of paints used historically, and taking the time to carefully study the medium one is working with, conservators are able to, using an array of methodology, restore works very closely to their original visual appearance.

In Painting

Inpainting is rooted in the restoration of images. The underlying methodology of "inpainting" is as follows:

- The picture as a whole determines how to fill in the gap; the purpose of inpainting is to restore the unity of the work so it is crucial to know how the repaired piece will function within the rest of the image.

- The structure of the area surrounding the gap ought to be continued into the gap. Contour lines that end at the gap boundary are to be carried on into the gap.

- The different regions inside a gap, as defined by the contour lines, are filled with colors matching those of its boundary although the specific materials do not have to be identical. If alternate materials are to be used, it is important to test for potential reactivity.

- The small details are painted, i.e. "texture" is added to ensure the eye will not be drawn first to the inpainted region.

Computerized

Given the various abilities of the digital camera and the digitization of old photos, inpainting has become an automatic process that can be performed on digital images. More than mere scratch removal, the inpainting techniques can also be applied to object removal, text removal, and other automatic modifications of images and videos. Furthermore, they can also be observed in applications like image compression and super resolution.

Three main groups of 2D image inpainting algorithms can be found in literature. The first one to be noted is structural (or geometric) inpainting, the second one is texture inpainting, and the last one is a combination of these two techniques. All these inpainting methods have one thing in common: they use the information of the known or undestroyed image areas in order to fill the gap, similar to how physical images are restored.

Structural Inpainting

Structural or geometric inpainting is used for smooth images that have strong, defined borders.. There are many different approaches to geometric inpainting, but they all stem from the same idea that geometry can be recovered from similar areas or domains. Bertalmio proposed a method of structural inpainting that mimics how conservators address painting restoration. Bertalmio proposed that by progressively transferring similar information from the borders of an inpainting domain inwards, the gap can be filled.

Textural Inpainting

While structural/geometric inpainting works to repair smooth images, textural inpainting works best with images that are heavily textured. Texture has a repetitive pattern which means that a missing portion cannot be restored by continuing the level lines into the gap; level lines provide a complete, stable representation of an image. To repair texture in an image, one can combine frequency and spatial domain information to fill in a selected area with a desired texture. This method, while the most simple and very effective, works well when selecting a texture to be inpainted. For a texture that covers a wider area or a larger frame one would have to go through the image segmenting the areas to be inpainted and selecting the corresponding textures from throughout the image; there are programs that can help find the corresponding areas that work in a similar way as 'find and replace' works in a word processor.

Combined Structural and Textural Inpainting

Combined structural and textural inpainting approaches simultaneously try to perform texture- and structure-filling in regions of missing image information. Most parts of an image consist of texture and structure and the boundaries between image regions contain a large amount of structural information. This is the result when blending different textures together. That is why state of the art methods attempt to combine structural and textural inpainting.

A more traditional method is to use differential equations (such as the Laplace's equation) with Dirichlet boundary conditions for continuity so as to create a seemingly seamless fit. This works well if missing information lies within the homogeneous portion of an object area.

Other methods follow isophote directions (in an image, a contour of equal luminance), to do the inpainting. Recent investigations included the exploration of the wavelet transform properties to perform inpainting in the space-frequency domain, obtaining a better performance when compared to the frequency-based inpainting techniques.

Model based inpainting follows the Bayesian approach for which missing information is best fitted or estimated from the combination of the models of the underlying images, as well as the image data actually being observed. In deterministic language, this has led to various variational inpainting models.

Manual computer methods include using a clone tool to copy existing parts of the image to restore a damaged texture. Texture synthesis may also be used.

Exemplar-based image inpainting attempts to automate the clone tool process. It fills "holes" in the image by searching for similar patches in a nearby source region of the image, and copying the pixels from the most similar patch into the hole. By performing the fill at the patch level as opposed to the pixel level, the algorithm reduces blurring artifacts caused by prior techniques.

Tone Mapping

Tone mapping is a technique used in image processing and computer graphics to map one set of colors to another to approximate the appearance of high-dynamic-range images in a medium that has a more limited dynamic range. Print-outs, CRT or LCD monitors, and projectors all have a limited dynamic range that is inadequate to reproduce the full range of light intensities present in natural scenes. Tone mapping addresses the problem of strong contrast reduction from the scene radiance to the displayable range while preserving the image details and color appearance important to appreciate the original scene content.

Tone mapped high-dynamic-range (HDR) image of St. Kentigerns Roman
Catholic Church in Blackpool, Lancashire, England, UK.

The introduction of film-based photography created issues since capturing the enormous dynamic range of lighting from the real world on a chemically limited negative was very difficult. Early film developers attempted to remedy this issue by designing the film stocks and the print development systems that gave a desired S-shaped tone curve with slightly enhanced contrast (about 15%) in the middle range and gradually compressed highlights and shadows . Photographers have also used dodging and burning to overcome the limitations of the print process .

The advent of digital photography gave hope for better solutions to this problem. One of the earliest algorithms employed by Land and McCann in 1971 was Retinex, inspired by theories of lightness perception .This method is inspired by the eye's biological mechanisms of adaptation when lighting conditions are an issue. Gamut mapping algorithms were also extensively studied in the context of color printing. Computational models such as CIECAM02 or iCAM were used to predict color appearance. Despite this, if algorithms could not sufficiently map tones and colors, a skilled artist was still needed, as is the case with cinematographic movie post-processing.

Computer graphic techniques capable of rendering high-contrast scenes shifted the focus from color to luminance as the main limiting factor of display devices. Several tone mapping operators were developed to map high dynamic range (HDR) images to standard displays. More recently, this work has branched away from utilizing luminance to extend image contrast and towards other methods such as user-assisted image reproduction. Currently, image reproduction has shifted towards display-driven solutions since displays now possess advanced image processing algorithms that help adapt rendering of the image to viewing conditions, save power, up-scale color gamut and dynamic range.

Purpose and Methods

The goals of tone mapping can be differently stated depending on the particular application. In some cases producing just aesthetically pleasing images is the main goal, while other applications might emphasize reproducing as many image details as possible, or maximizing the image contrast. The goal in realistic rendering applications might be to obtain a perceptual match between a real scene and a displayed image even though the display device is not able to reproduce the full range of luminance values.

Various tone mapping operators have been developed in the recent years. They all can be divided in two main types:

- Global (or spatially uniform) operators: They are non-linear functions based on the luminance and other global variables of the image. Once the optimal function has been estimated according to the particular image, every pixel in the image is mapped in the same way, independent of the value of surrounding pixels in the image. Those techniques are simple and fast (since they can be implemented using look-up tables), but they can cause a loss of contrast. Examples of common global tone mapping methods are contrast reduction and color inversion.

- Local (or spatially varying) operators: The parameters of the non-linear function change in each pixel, according to features extracted from the surrounding parameters. In other words, the effect of the algorithm changes in each pixel according to the local features of the image. Those algorithms are more complicated than the global ones; they can show artifacts (e.g. halo effect and ringing); and the output can look unrealistic, but they can (if used correctly) provide the best performance, since human vision is mainly sensitive to local contrast.

A simple example of global tone mapping filter is $V_{out} = \dfrac{V_{in}}{V_{in}+1}$, where V_{in} is the luminance of the original pixel and V_{out} is the luminance of the filtered pixel. This function will map the luminance V_{in} in the domain $[0,\infty)$ to a displayable output range of $[0,1)$. While this filter provides a decent contrast for parts of the image with low luminance (particularly when $V_{in} < 1$), parts of the image with higher luminance will get increasingly lower contrast as the luminance of the filtered image goes to 1.

A perhaps more useful global tone mapping method is gamma compression, which has the filter $V_{out} = AV_{in}^{\gamma},$, where $A > 0$ and $0 < \gamma < 1$. This function will map the luminance Vin in the domain V_{in} in the domain $[0, A^{-1/\gamma}]$ to the output range $[0,1]$. γ regulates the contrast of the image; a lower value for lower contrast. While a lower constant γ gives a lower contrast and perhaps also a duller image, it increases the exposure of underexposed parts of the image while at the same time, if $A < 1$, it can decrease the exposure of overexposed parts of the image enough to prevent them from being overexposed.

An even more sophisticated group of tone mapping algorithms is based on contrast or gradient domain methods, which are 'local'. Such operators concentrate on preserving contrast between neighboring regions rather than absolute value, an approach motivated by the fact that the human perception is most sensitive to contrast in images rather than absolute intensities. Those tone mapping methods usually produce very sharp images, which preserve very well small contrast details; however, this is often done at the cost of flattening an overall image contrast, and may as a side effect produce halo-like glows around dark objects. Examples of such tone mapping methods include: gradient domain high dynamic range compression and A Perceptual Framework for Contrast Processing of High Dynamic Range Images (a tone mapping is one of the applications of this framework).

Another approach to tone mapping of HDR images is inspired by the anchoring theory of lightness perception. This theory explains many characteristics of the human visual system such as lightness constancy and its failures (as in the checker shadow illusion), which are important in the perception of images. The key concept of this tone mapping method (Lightness Perception in Tone Reproduction) is a decomposition of an HDR image into areas (frameworks) of consistent illumination and the local calculation of the lightness values. The net lightness of an image is calculated by merging of the frameworks proportionally to their strength. Particularly important is the anchoring—relating of the luminance to a known luminance, namely estimating which luminance value is perceived as white in the scene. This approach to tone mapping does not affect the local contrast and preserves the natural colors of an HDR image due to the linear handling of luminance.

One simple form of tone mapping takes a standard image (not HDR – the dynamic range already compressed) and applies unsharp masking with a large radius, which increases local contrast rather than sharpening.

One of the commonly used tone mapping algorithms is the iCAM06 which is based on both the color appearance model and hierarchical mapping. After bilateral filtering, the image is broken into a base layer and a detail layer. White point adaptation and chrominance adaptation are applied to the base layer, while detail enhancement is applied to the detail layer. Eventually the two layers are merged and converted to the IPT color space. In general, this method is good but has some shortcomings, specifically in how computationally heavy the filtering method is. A proposed solution[10] to this involves performance optimization of the filter. The base layer of the image is also converted to the RGB space for tone compression. This method also allows for more output adjustment and saturation enhancement, making it be less computationally intensive and better at reducing the overall halo effect.

Digital Photography

Tone mapped HDR image of Dundas Square; Tone mapping was done
as post-processing technique, using Photomatix photographic software.

Forms of tone mapping long precede digital photography. The manipulation of film and development process to render high contrast scenes, especially those shot in bright sunlight, on printing paper with a relatively low dynamic range, is effectively a form of tone mapping, although it is not usually called that. Local adjustment of tonality in film processing is primarily done via dodging and burning, and is particularly advocated by and associated with Ansel Adams.

The normal process of exposure compensation, brightening shadows and altering contrast applied globally to digital images as part of a professional or serious amateur workflow is also a form of tone mapping.

However, HDR tone mapping, usually using local operators, has become increasingly popular amongst digital photographers as a post-processing technique, where several exposures at different shutter speeds are combined to produce an HDR image and a tone mapping operator is then applied to the result. There are now many examples of locally tone mapped digital images, inaccurately known as "HDR photographs", on the internet, and these are of varying quality. This popularity is partly driven by the distinctive appearance of locally tone mapped images, which many people find attractive, and partly by a desire to capture high-contrast scenes that are hard or impossible to photograph in a single exposure, and may not render attractively even when they can be captured. Although digital sensors actually capture a higher dynamic range than film, they completely lose detail in extreme highlights, clipping them to pure white, producing an unattractive result when compared with negative film, which tends to retain color and some detail in highlights.

In some cases local tone mapping is used even though the dynamic range of the source image could be captured on the target media, either to produce the distinctive appearance of a locally tone mapped image, or to produce an image closer to the photographer's artistic vision of the scene by removing sharp contrasts, which often look unattractive. In some cases, tone mapped images are produced from a single exposure which is then manipulated with conventional processing tools to produce the inputs to the HDR image generation process. This avoids the artifacts that can appear when different exposures are combined, due to moving objects in the scene or camera shake. However, when tone mapping is applied to a single exposure in this way, the intermediate image has only normal dynamic range, and the amount of shadow or highlight detail that can be rendered is only that which was captured in the original exposure.

Display Devices

One of the original goals of tone mapping was to be able to reproduce a given scene or image onto a display device such that the brightness sensation of the image to a human viewer closely matches the real-world brightness sensation. However, a perfect match for this problem is never possible and thus the output image on a display is often built from a tradeoff between different image features. Choosing between features is often based on the necessary application, and given appropriate metrics for the application, one possible solution is to treat the issue as an optimization problem.

For this method, models for the Human Visual System (HVS) and the display are first generated, along with a simple tone mapping operator. The contrast distortions are weighted according to their individual visibilities approximated by the HVS. With these models, an objective function that defines the tone curve can be created and solved using a fast quadratic solver.

With the addition of filters, this method can also be extended to videos. The filters ensure that the rapid changing of the tone-curve between frames are not salient in the final output image.

Example of the Imaging Process

Tone mapped High dynamic range image example showing stained
glass windows in south alcove of Old Saint Paul's, Wellington, New Zealand.

The images on the right show the interior of a church, a scene which has a variation in radiance much larger than that which can be displayed on a monitor or recorded by a conventional camera. The six individual exposures from the camera show the radiance of the scene in some range transformed to the range of brightnesses that can be displayed on a monitor. The range of radiances recorded in each photo is limited, so not all details can be displayed at once: for example, details of the dark church interior cannot be displayed at the same time as those of the bright stained-glass window. An algorithm is applied to the six images to recreate the high dynamic range radiance map of the original scene (a high dynamic range image). Alternatively, some higher-end consumer and specialist scientific digital cameras are able to record a high dynamic range image directly, for example with RAW images.

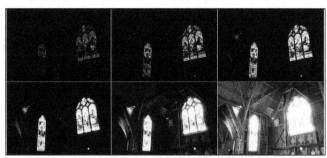

The six individual exposures used to create the previous image. In the low exposure images, the room is dark and unclear, but the details of the windows are visible. In the high exposure images, the windows are bright and unclear, but the details of the room are revealed.

In the ideal case, a camera might measure luminance directly and store this in the HDR image; however, most high dynamic range images produced by cameras today are not calibrated or even proportional to luminance, due to practical reasons such as cost and time required to measure accurate luminance values — it is often sufficient for artists to use multiple exposures to gain an "HDR image" which grossly approximates the true luminance signal.

The high dynamic range image is passed to a tone mapping operator, in this case a local operator, which transforms the image into a low dynamic range image suitable for viewing on a monitor. Relative to the church interior, the stained-glass window is displayed at a much lower brightness than a linear mapping between scene radiance and pixel intensity would produce. However, this inaccuracy is perceptually less important than the image detail, which can now be shown in both the window and the church interior simultaneously.

Visual Effect

Local tone mapping produces a number of characteristic effects in images. These include halos around dark objects, a "painting-like" or "cartoon-like" appearance due to a lack of large global contrasts, and highly saturated colors. Many people find the resulting images attractive and these effects to add an interesting new set of choices for post-processing in digital photography. Some people believe that the results stray too far from realism, or find them unattractive, but these are aesthetic judgements, and often concern the choices made by the photographer during the tone mapping process, rather than being a necessary consequence of using tone mapping.

Not all tone mapped images are visually distinctive. Reducing dynamic range with tone mapping is often useful in bright sunlit scenes, where the difference in intensity between direct illumination and shadow is great. In these cases the global contrast of the scene is reduced, but the local contrast maintained, while the image as a whole continues to look natural. Use of tone mapping in this context may not be apparent from the final image:

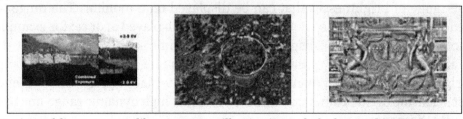

Regions of direct Cartoon-like appearance illumination and shadow on the Grand Canyon.

Tone mapping can also produce distinctive visual effects in the final image, such as the visible halo around the tower in the Cornell Law School image below. It can be used to produce these effects even when the dynamic range of the original image is not particularly high. Halos in images come about because the local tone mapping operator will brighten areas around dark objects, to maintain the local contrast in the original image, which fools the human visual system into perceiving the dark objects as being dark, even if their actual luminance is the same as that of areas of the image perceived as being bright. Usually this effect is subtle, but if the contrasts in the original image are extreme, or the photographer deliberately sets the luminance gradient to be very steep, the halos become visible.

Anisotropic Diffusion

In image processing and computer vision, anisotropic diffusion, also called Perona–Malik diffusion, is a technique aiming at reducing image noise without removing significant parts of the image content, typically edges, lines or other details that are important for the interpretation of the image. Anisotropic diffusion resembles the process that creates a scale space, where an image generates a parameterized family of successively more and more blurred images based on a diffusion process. Each of the resulting images in this family are given as a convolution between the image and a 2D isotropic Gaussian filter, where the width of the filter increases with the parameter. This diffusion process is a linear and space-invariant transformation of the original image. Anisotropic diffusion is a generalization of this diffusion process: it produces a family of parameterized images, but each resulting image is a combination between the original image and a filter that depends on the local content of the original image. As a consequence, anisotropic diffusion is a non-linear and space-variant transformation of the original image.

In its original formulation, presented by Perona and Malik in 1987, the space-variant filter is in fact isotropic but depends on the image content such that it approximates an impulse function close to edges and other structures that should be preserved in the image over the different levels of the resulting scale space. This formulation was referred to as anisotropic diffusion by Perona and Malik even though the locally adapted filter is isotropic, but it has also been referred to as inhomogeneous and nonlinear diffusion or Perona-Malik diffusion by other authors. A more general formulation allows the locally adapted filter to be truly anisotropic close to linear structures such as edges or lines: it has an orientation given by the structure such that it is elongated along the structure and narrow across. Such methods are referred to as shape-adapted smoothing or coherence enhancing diffusion. As a consequence, the resulting images preserve linear structures while at the same time smoothing is made along these structures. Both these cases can be described by a generalization of the usual diffusion equation where the diffusion coefficient, instead of being a constant scalar, is a function of image position and assumes a matrix (or tensor) value.

Although the resulting family of images can be described as a combination between the original image and space-variant filters, the locally adapted filter and its combination with the image do not have to be realized in practice. Anisotropic diffusion is normally implemented by means of an approximation of the generalized diffusion equation: each new image in the family is computed by applying this equation to the previous image. Consequently, anisotropic diffusion is an iterative process where a relatively simple set of computation are used to compute each successive image in the family and this process is continued until a sufficient degree of smoothing is obtained.

Formal Definition

Formally, let $\Omega \subset \mathbb{R}^2$ denote a subset of the plane and $I(\cdot,t):\Omega \to \mathbb{R}$ be a family of gray scale images, then anisotropic diffusion is defined as:

$$\frac{\partial I}{\partial t} = \mathrm{div}\left(c(x,y,t)\nabla I\right) = \nabla c \cdot \nabla I + c(x,y,t)\Delta I$$

Where, Δ denotes the Laplacian, ∇ denotes the gradient, $\mathrm{div}(\ldots)$ is the divergence operator and $c(x,y,t)$ is the diffusion coefficient. $c(x,y,t)$ controls the rate of diffusion and is usually chosen as a function of the image gradient so as to preserve edges in the image. Pietro Perona and Jitendra Malik pioneered the idea of anisotropic diffusion in 1990 and proposed two functions for the diffusion coefficient:

$$c\left(\|\nabla I\|\right) = e^{-(\|\nabla I\|/K)^2}$$

and

$$c\left(\|\nabla I\|\right) = \frac{1}{1+\left(\dfrac{\|\nabla I\|}{K}\right)^2}$$

The constant K controls the sensitivity to edges and is usually chosen experimentally or as a function of the noise in the image.

Let M denote the manifold of smooth images, then the diffusion equations presented above can be interpreted as the gradient descent equations for the minimization of the energy functional $E:M \to \mathbb{R}$ defined by:

$$E[I] = \frac{1}{2}\int_\Omega g\left(\|\nabla I(x)\|^2\right)dx$$

Where, $g:\mathbb{R} \to \mathbb{R}$ is a real-valued function which is intimately related to the diffusion coefficient. Then for any compactly supported infinitely differentiable test function h,

$$\left.\frac{d}{dt}\right|_{t=0} E[I+th] = \left.\frac{d}{dt}\right|_{t=0} \frac{1}{2}\int_\Omega g\left(\|\nabla(I+th)(x)\|^2\right)dx$$
$$= \int_\Omega g'\left(\|\nabla I(x)\|^2\right)\nabla I \cdot \nabla h\, dx$$
$$= -\int_\Omega \mathrm{div}(g'\left(\|\nabla I(x)\|^2\right)\nabla I)h\, dx$$

Where, the last line follows from multidimensional integration by parts. Letting ∇E_I denote the gradient of E with respect to the $L^2(\Omega,\mathbb{R})$ inner product evaluated at I, this gives:

$$\nabla E_I = -\mathrm{div}(g'\left(\|\nabla I(x)\|^2\right)\nabla I)$$

Therefore, the gradient descent equations on the functional E are given by:

$$\frac{\partial I}{\partial t} = -\nabla E_I = \operatorname{div}(g'(\|\nabla I(x)\|^2)\nabla I)$$

Thus by letting $c = g'$ the anisotropic diffusion equations are obtained.

Ill-posedness Problem

Diffusion coefficient, $c(x,y,t)$, which is proposed by Perona and Malik can be negative value when $\|\nabla I\|^2 > K^2$. From here, the system is restritced by one-dimension for simplicity. If flux function is defined as $\Phi(s) := g(|s|^2)s$, where $s = \nabla I(x,t)$ and $g(|s|^2) = \dfrac{1}{1+s^2/K^2}$, then the Perona-Malik equation can be rewritten based on the flux function by:

$\partial_t I = \nabla \cdot \Phi(s) = \partial_x(\Phi(\partial_x I)) = \Phi'(\partial_x I)\partial_{xx}I$. Here, $\partial_t, \partial_x, \partial_{xx}$ are denoted by first derivative of time, position, and second derivative of position, respectively.

Now, it is clear that $\Phi'(\partial_x I)$ plays a role in diffusion coefficient of linear heat equation. By calculating $\Phi'(\partial_x I)$,

$$\Phi'(\partial_x I) = \frac{\partial}{\partial s}\left(\frac{s}{1+s^2/K^2}\right) = \frac{1-s^2/K^2}{1+s^2/K^2}$$

If $1-s^2/K^2 < 0$, diffusion coefficient becomes negative and it leads to backward diffusion that enhances contrasts of image intensity rather than smoothes them in image processing.

In terms of theoretical perspective, backward diffusion is not only physically unnatural, but also gives numerically unstable solutions which are very sensitive to parameter (K). In addition, it is known that backward diffusion have numerous of solutions and this is called ill-posedness problem.

To avoid the problem, regularization is necessary and people have shown that spatial regularizations lead to converged and constant steady-state solution.

Regularization

Modified Perona-Malik model (that is also known as regularization of P-M equation) will be discussed here. In this approach, the unknown is convolved with a Gaussian inside the non-linearity to obtain the modified Perona-Malik equation:

$$\frac{\partial I}{\partial t} = \operatorname{div}\left(c(|DG_\sigma * I|)\nabla I\right)$$

Where, $G_\sigma = C\sigma^{-(1/2)}\exp\left(-|x|^2/4\sigma\right)$

The well-posedness of the equation can be achieved by regularization but it also introduces blurring effect, which is the main drawback of regularization. A prior knowledge of noise level is required as the choice of regularization parameter depends on it.

Applications

Anisotropic diffusion can be used to remove noise from digital images without blurring edges. With a constant diffusion coefficient, the anisotropic diffusion equations reduce to the heat equation which is equivalent to Gaussian blurring. This is ideal for removing noise but also indiscriminately blurs edges too. When the diffusion coefficient is chosen as an edge seeking function, such as in Perona-Malik, the resulting equations encourage diffusion (hence smoothing) within regions and prohibit it across strong edges. Hence the edges can be preserved while removing noise from the image.

Along the same lines as noise removal, anisotropic diffusion can be used in edge detection algorithms. By running the diffusion with an edge seeking diffusion coefficient for a certain number of iterations, the image can be evolved towards a piecewise constant image with the boundaries between the constant components being detected as edges.

IMAGE TRANSFORMATIONS

The function applied in the digital system that processes an image and converts it into output can be called as transformation function.

Consider this equation,

G(x,y) = T{ f(x,y) }

In this equation,

F(x,y) = input image on which transformation function has to be applied.

G(x,y) = the output image or processed image.

T is the transformation function.

This relation between input image and the processed output image can also be represented as.

s = T (r)

Where, r is actually the pixel value or gray level intensity of f(x,y) at any point. And s is the pixel value or gray level intensity of g(x,y) at any point.

Examples: Consider this transformation function.

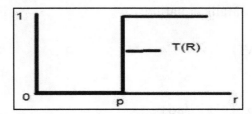

Let's take the point r to be 256, and the point p to be 127. Consider this image to be a one bpp image. That means we have only two levels of intensities that are 0 and 1. So in this case the transformation shown by the graph can be explained as.

All the pixel intensity values that are below 127 (point p) are 0, means black. And all the pixel intensity values that are greater than 127 are 1 that means white. But at the exact point of 127, there is a sudden change in transmission, so we cannot tell that at that exact point, the value would be 0 or 1.

Mathematically this transformation function can be denoted as:

$$g(x,y)= \begin{cases} 0 & f(x,y)<127 \\ 1 & f(x,y)<127 \end{cases}$$

Consider another transformation like this:

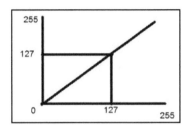

Now if you will look at this particular graph, you will see a straight transition line between input image and output image.

It shows that for each pixel or intensity value of input image, there is a same intensity value of output image. That means the output image is exact replica of the input image.

It can be mathematically represented as:

$$g(x,y) = f(x,y)$$

The input and output image would be in this case are shown below.

Hough Transform

The Hough transform is a feature extraction technique used in image analysis, computer vision, and digital image processing. The purpose of the technique is to find imperfect instances of objects within a certain class of shapes by a voting procedure. This voting procedure is carried out in a parameter space, from which object candidates are obtained as local maxima in a so-called accumulator space that is explicitly constructed by the algorithm for computing the Hough transform.

The classical Hough transform was concerned with the identification of lines in the image, but later the Hough transform has been extended to identifying positions of arbitrary shapes, most commonly circles or ellipses. The Hough transform as it is universally used today was invented by Richard Duda and Peter Hart in 1972, who called it a "generalized Hough transform" after the related 1962 patent of Paul Hough. The transform was popularized in the computer vision community by Dana H. Ballard through a 1981 journal article titled "Generalizing the Hough transform to detect arbitrary shapes".

Theory

In automated analysis of digital images, a subproblem often arises of detecting simple shapes, such as straight lines, circles or ellipses. In many cases an edge detector can be used as a pre-processing stage to obtain image points or image pixels that are on the desired curve in the image space. Due to imperfections in either the image data or the edge detector, however, there may be missing points or pixels on the desired curves as well as spatial deviations between the ideal line/circle/ellipse and the noisy edge points as they are obtained from the edge detector. For these reasons, it is often non-trivial to group the extracted edge features to an appropriate set of lines, circles or ellipses. The purpose of the Hough transform is to address this problem by making it possible to perform groupings of edge points into object candidates by performing an explicit voting procedure over a set of parameterized image objects.

The simplest case of Hough transform is detecting straight lines. In general, the straight line y = mx + b can be represented as a point (b, m) in the parameter space. However, vertical lines pose a problem. They would give rise to unbounded values of the slope parameter m. Thus, for computational reasons, Duda and Hart proposed the use of the Hesse normal form:

$$r = x \cos \theta + y \sin \theta$$

Where r is the distance from the origin to the closest point on the straight line, and θ is the angle between the x axis and the line connecting the origin with that closest point.

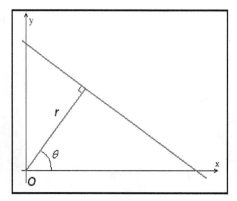

It is therefore possible to associate with each line of the image a pair (r, θ). The (r, θ) plane is sometimes referred to as Hough space for the set of straight lines in two dimensions. This representation makes the Hough transform conceptually very close to the two-dimensional Radon transform. In fact, the Hough transform is mathematically equivalent to the Radon transform, but the two transformations have different computational interpretations traditionally associated with them.

Given a single point in the plane, then the set of all straight lines going through that point corresponds to a sinusoidal curve in the (r, θ) plane, which is unique to that point. A set of two or more points that form a straight line will produce sinusoids which cross at the (r, θ) for that line. Thus, the problem of detecting collinear points can be converted to the problem of finding concurrent curves.

Implementation

The linear Hough transform algorithm uses a two-dimensional array, called an accumulator, to detect the existence of a line described by $r = x \cos \theta + y \sin \theta$. The dimension of the accumulator equals the number of unknown parameters, i.e., two, considering quantized values of r and θ in the pair (r, θ). For each pixel at (x, y) and its neighborhood, the Hough transform algorithm determines if there is enough evidence of a straight line at that pixel. If so, it will calculate the parameters (r, θ) of that line, and then look for the accumulator's bin that the parameters fall into, and increment the value of that bin. By finding the bins with the highest values, typically by looking for local maxima in the accumulator space, the most likely lines can be extracted, and their (approximate) geometric definitions read off. The simplest way of finding these peaks is by applying some form of threshold, but other techniques may yield better results in different circumstances – determining which lines are found as well as how many. Since the lines returned do not contain any length information, it is often necessary, in the next step, to find which parts of the image match up with which lines. Moreover, due to imperfection errors in the edge detection step, there will usually be errors in the accumulator space, which may make it non-trivial to find the appropriate peaks, and thus the appropriate lines.

The final result of the linear Hough transform is a two-dimensional array (matrix) similar to the accumulator—one dimension of this matrix is the quantized angle θ and the other dimension is the quantized distance r. Each element of the matrix has a value equal to the sum of the points or pixels that are positioned on the line represented by quantized parameters (r, θ). So the element with the highest value indicates the straight line that is most represented in the input image.

Examples:

1. Consider three data points, shown here as black dots.

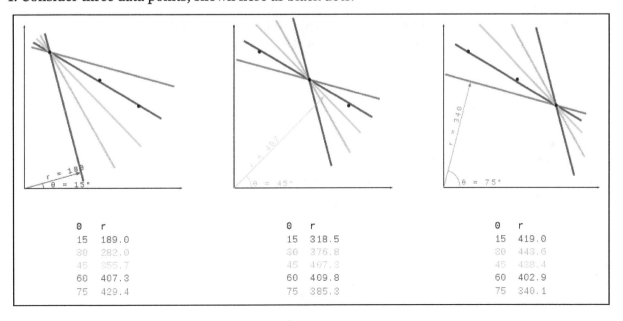

- For each data point, a number of lines are plotted going through it, all at different angles. These are shown here in different colors.

- To each line, a support line exists which is perpendicular to it and which intersects the origin. In each case, one of these is shown as an arrow.

- The length (i.e. perpendicular distance to the origin) and angle of each support line is calculated. Lengths and angles are tabulated below the diagrams.

From the calculations, it can be seen that in either case the support line at 60° has a similar length. Hence, it is understood that the corresponding lines (the blue ones in the above picture) are very similar. One can thus assume that all points lie close to the blue line.

2. The following is a different example showing the results of a Hough transform on a raster image containing two thick lines.

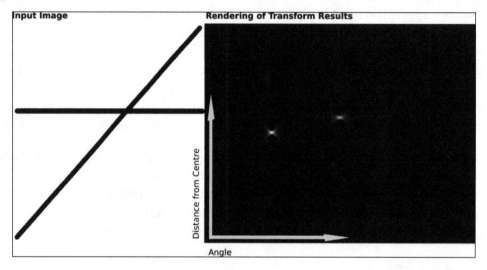

The results of this transform were stored in a matrix. Cell value represents the number of curves through any point. Higher cell values are rendered brighter. The two distinctly bright spots are the Hough parameters of the two lines. From these spots' positions, angle and distance from image center of the two lines in the input image can be determined.

Variations and Extensions

Using the Gradient Direction to Reduce the Number of Votes

An improvement suggested by O'Gorman and Clowes can be used to detect lines if one takes into account that the local gradient of the image intensity will necessarily be orthogonal to the edge. Since edge detection generally involves computing the intensity gradient magnitude, the gradient direction is often found as a side effect. If a given point of coordinates (x, y) happens to indeed be on a line, then the local direction of the gradient gives the θ parameter corresponding to said line, and the r parameter is then immediately obtained. The gradient direction can be estimated to within 20°, which shortens the sinusoid trace from the full 180° to roughly 45°. This reduces the computation time and has the interesting effect of reducing the number of useless votes, thus enhancing the visibility of the spikes corresponding to real lines in the image.

Kernel-based Hough Transform (KHT)

Fernandes and Oliveira suggested an improved voting scheme for the Hough transform that allows a software implementation to achieve real-time performance even on relatively large images (e.g., 1280×960). The Kernel-based Hough transform uses the same (r, θ) parameterization proposed by Duda and Hart but operates on clusters of approximately collinear pixels. For each cluster, votes are cast using an oriented elliptical-Gaussian kernel that models the uncertainty associated with the best-fitting line with respect to the corresponding cluster. The approach not only significantly improves the performance of the voting scheme, but also produces a much cleaner accumulator and makes the transform more robust to the detection of spurious lines.

3-D Kernel-based Hough Transform for Plane Detection (3DKHT)

Limberger and Oliveira suggested a deterministic technique for plane detection in unorganized point clouds whose cost is n log(n) in the number of samples, achieving real-time performance for relatively large datasets (up to 10^5 points on a 3.4 GHz CPU). It is based on a fast Hough-transform voting strategy for planar regions, inspired by the Kernel-based Hough transform (KHT). This 3D Kernel-based Hough transform (3DKHT) uses a fast and robust algorithm to segment clusters of approximately co-planar samples, and casts votes for individual clusters (instead of for individual samples) on a (θ, φ, ρ) spherical accumulator using a trivariate Gaussian kernel. The approach is several orders of magnitude faster than existing (non-deterministic) techniques for plane detection in point clouds, such as RHT and RANSAC, and scales better with the size of the datasets. It can be used with any application that requires fast detection of planar features on large datasets.

Hough Transform of Curves and its Generalization for Analytical and Non-analytical Shapes

Although the version of the transform described above applies only to finding straight lines, a similar transform can be used for finding any shape which can be represented by a set of parameters. A circle, for instance, can be transformed into a set of three parameters, representing its center and radius, so that the Hough space becomes three dimensional. Arbitrary ellipses and curves can also be found this way, as can any shape easily expressed as a set of parameters.

The generalization of the Hough transform for detecting analytical shapes in spaces having any dimensionality was proposed by Fernandes and Oliveira. In contrast to other Hough transform-based approaches for analytical shapes, Fernandes' technique does not depend on the shape one wants to detect nor on the input data type. The detection can be driven to a type of analytical shape by changing the assumed model of geometry where data have been encoded (e.g., euclidean space, projective space, conformal geometry, and so on), while the proposed formulation remains unchanged. Also, it guarantees that the intended shapes are represented with the smallest possible number of parameters, and it allows the concurrent detection of different kinds of shapes that best fit an input set of entries with different dimensionalities and different geometric definitions (e.g., the concurrent detection of planes and spheres that best fit a set of points, straight lines and circles).

For more complicated shapes in the plane (i.e., shapes that cannot be represented analytically in some 2D space), the Generalised Hough transform is used, which allows a feature to vote for a particular position, orientation and scaling of the shape using a predefined look-up table.

Detection of 3D Objects (Planes and Cylinders)

Hough transform can also be used for the detection of 3D objects in range data or 3D point clouds. The extension of classical Hough transform for plane detection is quite straightforward. A plane is represented by its explicit equation $z = a_x x + a_y y + d$ for which we can use a 3D Hough space corresponding to a_x, a_y and d. This extension suffers from the same problems as its 2D counterpart i.e., near horizontal planes can be reliably detected, while the performance deteriorates as planar direction becomes vertical (big values of a_x and a_y amplify the noise in the data). This formulation of the plane has been used for the detection of planes in the point clouds acquired from airborne laser scanning and works very well because in that domain all planes are nearly horizontal.

For generalized plane detection using Hough transform, the plane can be parametrized by its normal vector n (using spherical coordinates) and its distance from the origin ρ resulting in a three dimensional Hough space. This results in each point in the input data voting for a sinusoidal surface in the Hough space. The intersection of these sinusoidal surfaces indicates presence of a plane. A more general approach for more than 3 dimensions requires search heuristics to remain feasible.

Hough transform has also been used to find cylindrical objects in point clouds using a two-step approach. The first step finds the orientation of the cylinder and the second step finds the position and radius.

Using Weighted Features

One common variation detail. That is, finding the bins with the highest count in one stage can be used to constrain the range of values searched in the next.

Carefully Chosen Parameter Space

A high-dimensional parameter space for the Hough transform is not only slow, but if implemented without forethought can easily overrun the available memory. Even if the programming environment allows the allocation of an array larger than the available memory space through virtual memory, the number of page swaps required for this will be very demanding because the accumulator array is used in a randomly accessed fashion, rarely stopping in contiguous memory as it skips from index to index.

Consider the task of finding ellipses in an 800x600 image. Assuming that the radii of the ellipses are oriented along principal axes, the parameter space is four-dimensional. (x, y) defines the center of the ellipse, and a and b denote the two radii. Allowing the center to be anywhere in the image, adds the constraint 0<x<800 and 0<y<600. If the radii are given the same values as constraints, what is left is a sparsely filled accumulator array of more than 230 billion values.

A program thus conceived is unlikely to be allowed to allocate sufficient memory. This doesn't mean that the problem can't be solved, but only that new ways to constrain the size of the accumulator array are to be found, which makes it feasible. For instance:

- If it is reasonable to assume that the ellipses are each contained entirely within the image, the range of the radii can be reduced. The largest the radii can be is if the center of the ellipse is in the center of the image, allowing the edges of the ellipse to stretch to the edges. In this extreme case, the radii can only each be half the magnitude of the image size oriented in the same direction. Reducing the range of a and b in this fashion reduces the accumulator array to 57 billion values.

- Trade accuracy for space in the estimation of the center: If the center is predicted to be off by 3 on both the x and y axis this reduces the size of the accumulator array to about 6 billion values.

- Trade accuracy for space in the estimation of the radii: If the radii are estimated to each be off by 5 further reduction of the size of the accumulator array occurs, by about 256 million values.

- Crop the image to areas of interest. This is image dependent, and therefore unpredictable, but imagines a case where all of the edges of interest in an image are in the upper left quadrant of that image. The accumulator array can be reduced even further in this case by constraining all 4 parameters by a factor of 2, for a total reduction factor of 16.

By applying just the first three of these constraints to the example stated about, the size of the accumulator array is reduced by almost a factor of 1000, bringing it down to a size that is much more likely to fit within a modern computer's memory.

Circle Hough Transform

The circle Hough Transform (CHT) is a basic feature extraction technique used in digital image processing for detecting circles in imperfect images. The circle candidates are produced by "voting" in the Hough parameter space and then selecting local maxima in an accumulator matrix.

It is a specialization of Hough transform.

Theory

In a two-dimensional space, a circle can be described by:

$$(x-a)^2 + (y-b)^2 = r^2$$

Where, (a, b) is the center of the circle, and r is the radius. If a 2D point (x, y) is fixed, then the parameters can be found according to (1). The parameter space would be three dimensional, (a, b, r). And all the parameters that satisfy (x, y) would lie on the surface of an inverted right-angled cone whose apex is at (x, y, 0). In the 3D space, the circle parameters can be identified by the intersection of many conic surfaces that are defined by points on the 2D circle. This process can be divided into two stages. The first stage is fixing radius then find the optimal center of circles in a 2D parameter space. The second stage is to find the optimal radius in a one dimensional parameter space.

Find Parameters with Known Radius R

If the radius is fixed, then the parameter space would be reduced to 2D (the position of the circle center). For each point (x, y) on the original circle, it can define a circle centered at (x, y) with radius R according to (1). The intersection point of all such circles in the parameter space would be corresponding to the center point of the original circle.

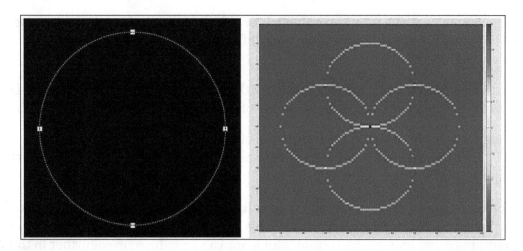

Consider 4 points on a circle in the original image (left). The circle Hough transform is shown in the right. Note that the radius is assumed to be known. For each (x, y) of the four points (white points) in the original image, it can define a circle in the Hough parameter space centered at (x, y) with radius r. An accumulator matrix is used for tracking the intersection point. In the parameter space, the voting number of points through which the circle passing would be increased by one. Then the local maxima point (the red point in the center in the right figure) can be found. The position (a, b) of the maxima would be the center of the original circle.

Multiple Circles with Known Radius R

Multiple circles with same radius can be found with the same technique.

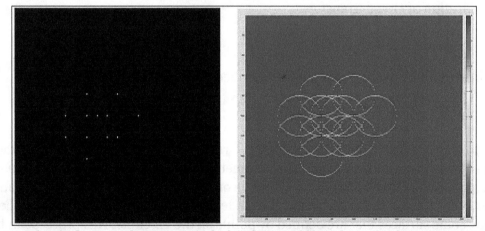

Note that, in the accumulator matrix (right fig), there would be at least 3 local maxima points.

Accumulator Matrix and Voting

In practice, an accumulator matrix is introduced to find the intersection point in the parameter space. First, we need to divide the parameter space into "buckets" using a grid and produce an accumulator matrix according to the grid. The element in the accumulator matrix denotes the number of "circles" in the parameter space that passing through the corresponding grid cell in the parameter space. The number is also called "voting number". Initially, every element in the matrix is zeros. Then for each "edge" point in the original space, we can formulate a circle in the parameter space and increase the voting number of the grid cell which the circle passing through. This process is called "voting".

After voting, we can find local maxima in the accumulator matrix. The positions of the local maxima are corresponding to the circle centers in the original space.

Find circle Parameter with Unknown Radius

Since the parameter space is 3D, the accumulator matrix would be 3D, too. We can iterate through possible radii; for each radius, we use the previous technique. Finally, find the local maxima in the 3D accumulator matrix. Accumulator array should be A [x, y, r] in the 3D space. Voting should be for each pixels, radius and theta A[x, y, r] += 1.

The algorithm:

- For each A [a, b, r] = 0;

- Process the filtering algorithm on image Gaussian Blurring, convert the image to grayscale (grayScaling), make Canny operator, The Canny operator gives the edges on image.

- Vote the all possible circles in accumulator.

- The local maximum voted circles of Accumulator A gives the circle Hough space.

- The maximum voted circle of Accumulator gives the circle.

The Voting:

For each pixel(x,y)

  For each radius r = 10 to r = 60 // the possible radius

  For each theta t = 0 to 360 // the possible theta 0 to 360

    a = x − r * cos(t * PI / 180); //polar coordinate for center

    b = y − r * sin(t * PI / 180); //polar coordinate for center

    A[a,b,r] +=1; //voting

  end

  end

end

Examples:

1. Find circles in a shoe-print

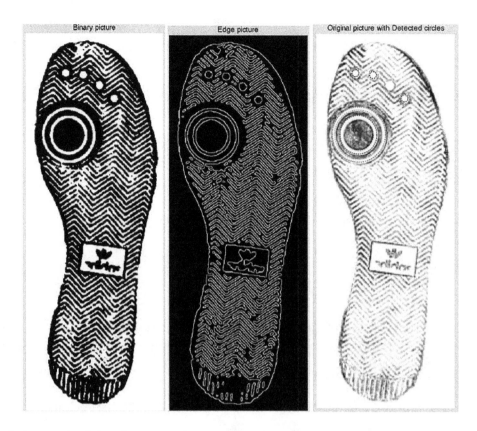

The original picture (right) is first turned into a binary image (left) using a threshold and Gaussian filter. Then edges (mid) are found from it using canny edge detection. After this, all the edge points are used by the Circle Hough Transform to find underlying circle structure.

Limitations

Since the parameter space of the CHT is three dimensional, it may require lots of storage and computation. Choosing a bigger grid size can ameliorate this problem.

However, choosing an appropriate grid size is difficult. Since too coarse a grid can lead to large values of the vote being obtained falsely because many quite different structures correspond to a single bucket. Too fine a grid can lead to structures not being found because votes resulting from tokens that are not exactly aligned end up in different buckets, and no bucket has a large vote.

Generalised Hough transform

The generalized Hough transform (GHT), introduced by Dana H. Ballard in 1981, is the modification of the Hough transform using the principle of template matching. The Hough transform was initially developed to detect analytically defined shapes (e.g., line, circle, ellipse etc.). In these cases, we have knowledge of the shape and aim to find out its location and orientation in the image. This modification enables the Hough transform to be used to detect an arbitrary object described with its model.

The problem of finding the object (described with a model) in an image can be solved by finding the model's position in the image. With the generalized Hough transform, the problem of finding the model's position is transformed to a problem of finding the transformation's parameter that maps the model into the image. Given the value of the transformation's parameter, the position of the model in the image can be determined.

The original implementation of the GHT used edge information to define a mapping from orientation of an edge point to a reference point of the shape. In the case of a binary image where pixels can be either black or white, every black pixel of the image can be a black pixel of the desired pattern thus creating a locus of reference points in the Hough space. Every pixel of the image votes for its corresponding reference points. The maximum points of the Hough space indicate possible reference points of the pattern in the image. This maximum can be found by scanning the Hough space or by solving a relaxed set of equations, each of them corresponding to a black pixel.

Theory of Generalized Hough Transform

To generalize the Hough algorithm to non-analytic curves, Ballard defines the following parameters for a generalized shape: $a = \{y, s, \theta\}$ where y is a reference origin for the shape, θ is its orientation and $s = (s_x, s_y)$ describes two orthogonal scale factors. An algorithm can compute the best set of parameters for a given shape from edge pixel data. These parameters do not have equal status. The reference origin location, y, is described in terms of a template table called the R table of possible edge pixel orientations. The computation of the additional parameters s and θ is then accomplished by straightforward transformations to this table. The key generalization to arbitrary shapes is the use of directional information. Given any shape and a fixed reference point on it, instead of a parametric curve, the information provided by the boundary pixels is stored in the form of the R-table in the transform stage. For every edge point on the test image, the properties of the point are looked up on the R-table and reference point is retrieved and the appropriate cell in a matrix called the Accumulator matrix is incremented. The cell with maximum 'votes' in the Accumulator matrix can be a possible point of existence of fixed reference of the object in the test image.

Building the R-table

Choose a reference point y for the shape (typically chosen inside the shape). For each boundary point x, compute $\phi(x)$, the gradient direction and $r = y - x$ as shown in the image. Store r as a function of ϕ. Notice that each index of ϕ may have many values of r. One can either store the co-ordinate differences between the fixed reference and the edge point $((x_c - x_{ij}),(y_c - y_{ij}))$ or as the radial distance and the angle between them (r_{ij} , α_{ij}). Having done this for each point, the R-table will fully represent the template object. Also, since the generation phase is invertible, we may use it to localise object occurrences at other places in the image.

i	ϕi	$R_{\phi i}$
1	0	(r11, α11) (r12, α12) (r1n, α1n)
2	$\Delta\phi$	(r21, α21) (r22, α22) (r2m, α2m)
3	2$\Delta\phi$	(r31, α31) (r32, α32) (r3k, α3k)

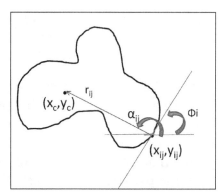

Geometry of shape detection for generalized Hough transform.

Object Localization

For each edge pixel x in the image, find the gradient φ and increment all the corresponding points x + r in the accumulator array A (initialized to a maximum size of the image) where r is a table entry indexed by φ, i.e., $r(\varphi)$. These entry points give us each possible position for the reference point. Although some bogus points may be calculated, given that the object exists in the image, a maximum will occur at the reference point. Maxima in A correspond to possible instances of the shape.

Generalization of Scale and Orientation

For a fixed orientation of shape, the accumulator array was two-dimensional in the reference point co-ordinates. To search for shapes of arbitrary orientation θ and scale s, these two parameters are added to the shape description. The accumulator array now consists of four dimensions corresponding to the parameters (y, s, θ). The R-table can also be used to increment this larger dimensional space since different orientations and scales correspond to easily computed transformations of the table. Denote a particular R-table for a shape S by $R(\phi)$. Simple transformations to this table will allow it to detect scaled or rotated instances of the same shape. For example, if the shape is scaled by s and this transformation is denoted by T_s. then $T_s[R(\phi)] = sR(\phi)$ i.e., all the vectors are scaled by s. Also, if the object is rotated by θ and this transformation is denoted by T_θ, then $T_\theta[R(\phi)] = Rot\{R[(\phi-\theta)mod2\pi],\theta\}$ i.e., all the indices are incremented by $-\theta$ modulo 2π, the appropriate vectors r are found, and then they are rotated by θ. Another property which will be useful in describing the composition of generalized Hough transforms is the change of reference point. If we want to choose a new reference point $\tilde{y}$ such that y- $\tilde{y}$ = z then the modification to the R-table is given by $R(\phi)+ z$, i.e. z is added to each vector in the table.

Alternate way using Pairs of Edges

A pair of edge pixels can be used to reduce the parameter space. Using the R-table and the properties as described above, each edge pixel defines a surface in the four-dimensional accumulator space of a = (y, s, θ). Two edge pixels at different orientations describe the same surface rotated by the same amount with respect to θ. If these two surfaces intersect, points where they intersect will correspond to possible parameters a for the shape. Thus it is theoretically possible to use the two points in image space to reduce the locus in parameter space to a single point. However, the difficulties of finding the intersection points of the two surfaces in parameter space will make this approach unfeasible for most cases.

Composite Shapes

If the shape S has a composite structure consisting of subparts S1, S2, .. SN and the reference points for the shapes S, S_1, S_2, ... SN are y, y_1, y_2, ... y_n, respectively, then for a scaling factor s and orientation θ, the generalized Hough transform $R_s(\phi)$ is given by $R_\phi = T_s \left\{ T_\theta \left[\bigcup_{k=1}^{N} R_{s_k}(\phi) \right] \right\}$. The concern with this transform is that the choice of reference can greatly affect the accuracy. To overcome this, Ballard has suggested smoothing the resultant accumulator with a composite smoothing template. The composite smoothing template H(y) is given as a composite convolution of individual smoothing templates of the sub-shapes.

$$H(y) = \sum_{i=1}^{N} h_i(y - y_i)$$

Then the improved Accumulator is given by $A_s = A*H$ and the maxima in A_s corresponds to possible instances of the shape.

Spatial Decomposition

Observing that the global Hough transform can be obtained by the summation of local Hough transforms of disjoint sub-region, Heather and Yang proposed a method which involves the recursive subdivision of the image into sub-images, each with their own parameter space, and organized in a quadtree structure. It results in improved efficiency in finding endpoints of line segments and improved robustness and reliability in extracting lines in noisy situations, at a slightly increased cost of memory.

Implementation

The implementation uses the following equations:

$$x = x_c + x' \text{ or } x_c = x - x'$$
$$y = y_c + y' \text{ or } y_c = y - y'$$
$$\cos(\pi - \alpha) = x'/r \text{ or } x' = r\cos(\pi - \alpha) = -r\cos(\alpha)$$
$$\sin(\pi - \alpha) = y'/r \text{ or } y' = r\sin(\pi - \alpha) = r\sin(\alpha)$$

Combining the previous equations we have:

$$x_c = x + r\cos(\alpha)$$
$$y_c = y + r\sin(\alpha)$$

Constructing the R-table

- Convert the sample shape image into an edge image using any edge detecting algorithm like Canny edge detector;

- Pick a reference point (e.g., (x_c, y_c));

- Draw a line from the reference point to the boundary;

- Compute ϕ;

- Store the reference point (x_c, y_c) as a function of ϕ in $R(\phi)$ table.

Detection:

- Convert the sample shape image into an edge image using any edge detecting algorithm like Canny edge detector.

- Initialize the Accumulator table: $A[x_{cmin} \dots x_{cmax}][y_{cmin} \dots y_{cmax}]$;

- For each edge point (x, y):

  ◦ Using the gradient angle ϕ, retrieve from the R-table all the (α, r) values indexed under ϕ.

  ◦ For each (α, r), compute the candidate reference points:

$$x_c = x + r\cos(\alpha)$$
$$y_c = y + r\sin(\alpha)$$

  ◦ Increase counters (voting):

$$++A\left(\left[\left[x_c\right]\right]\left[y_c\right]\right)$$

- Possible locations of the object contour are given by local maxima in $A[x_c][y_c]$. If $A[x_c][y_c] > T$, then the object contour is located at (x_c, y_c).

Suppose the object has undergone some rotation θ and uniform scaling s:

$$(x', y') \dashrightarrow (x'', y'')$$

$$x'' = (x'\cos(\theta) - y'\sin(\theta))s$$

$$y'' = (x'\sin(\theta) + y'\cos(\theta))s$$

Replacing x' by x'' and y' by y'':

$$x_c = x - x'' \text{ or } x_c = x - (x'\cos(\theta) - y'\sin(\theta))s$$

$$y_c = y - y'' \text{ or } y_c = y - (x'\sin(\theta) + y'\cos(\theta))s$$

- Initialize the Accumulator table: $A[x_{cmin} \dots x_{cmax}][y_{cmin} \dots y_{cmax}][q_{min} \dots q_{max}][s_{min} \dots s_{max}]$.

- For each edge point (x, y):

  ◦ Using its gradient angle ϕ, retrieve all the (α, r) values from the R-table

      ◦   For each (α, r), compute the candidate reference points:

$x' = r \cos(\alpha)$

$y' = r \sin(\alpha)$

for$(\theta = \theta_{min}; \theta \le \theta_{max}; \theta{+}{+})$

      for$(s = s_{min}; s \le s_{max}; s{+}{+})$

      $x_c = x - (x'\cos(\theta) - y'\sin(\theta))s$

      $y_c = y - (x'\sin(\theta) + y'\cos(\theta))s$

      $++(A[x_c][y_c][\theta][s])$

- Possible locations of the object contour are given by local maxima in $A[x_c][y_c][\theta][s]$.

If $A[x_c][y_c][\theta][s] > T$, then the object contour is located at (x_c, y_c), has undergone a rotation θ, and has been scaled by s.

Advantages

- It is robust to partial or slightly deformed shapes (i.e., robust to recognition under occlusion).

- It is robust to the presence of additional structures in the image.

- It is tolerant to noise.

- It can find multiple occurrences of a shape during the same processing pass.

Disadvantages

- It has substantial computational and storage requirements which become acute when object orientation and scale have to be considered.

Randomized Hough Transform

Hough transforms are techniques for object detection, a critical step in many implementations of computer vision, or data mining from images. Specifically, the Randomized Hough transform is a probabilistic variant to the classical Hough transform, and is commonly used to detect curves (straight line, circle, ellipse, etc.) The basic idea of Hough transform (HT) is to implement a voting procedure for all potential curves in the image, and at the termination of the algorithm, curves that do exist in the image will have relatively high voting scores. Randomized Hough transform (RHT) is different from HT in that it tries to avoid conducting the computationally expensive voting process for every nonzero pixel in the image by taking advantage of the geometric properties of analytical curves, and thus improve the time efficiency and reduce the storage requirement of the original algorithm.

Motivation

Although Hough transform (HT) has been widely used in curve detection, it has two major drawbacks: First, for each nonzero pixel in the image, the parameters for the existing curve and redundant ones are both accumulated during the voting procedure. Second, the accumulator array (or Hough space) is predefined in a heuristic way. The more accuracy needed, the higher parameter resolution should be defined. These two needs usually result in a large storage requirement and low speed for real applications. Therefore, RHT was brought up to tackle this problem.

Implementation

In comparison with HT, RHT takes advantage of the fact that some analytical curves can be fully determined by a certain number of points on the curve. For example, a straight line can be determined by two points, and an ellipse (or a circle) can be determined by three points. The case of ellipse detection can be used to illustrate the basic idea of RHT. The whole process generally consists of three steps:

- Fit ellipses with randomly selected points.

- Update the accumulator array and corresponding scores.

- Output the ellipses with scores higher than some predefined threshold.

Ellipse Fitting

One general equation for defining ellipses is $a(x-p)^2 + 2b(x-p)(y-q) + c(y-q)^2 = 1$: with restriction: $ac - b^2 > 0$

However, an ellipse can be fully determined if one knows three points on it and the tangents in these points.

RHT starts by randomly selecting three points on the ellipse. Let them be X_1, X_2 and X_3. The first step is to find the tangents of these three points. They can be found by fitting a straight line using least squares technique for a small window of neighboring pixels.

The next step is to find the intersection points of the tangent lines. This can be easily done by solving the line equations found in the previous step. Then let the intersection points be T_{12} and T_{23}, the midpoints of line segments X_1X_2 and X_2X_3 be M_{12} and M_{23}. Then the center of the ellipse will

lie in the intersection of $T_{12}M_{12}$ and $T_{23}M_{23}$. Again, the coordinates of the intersected point can be determined by solving line equations and the detailed process is skipped here for conciseness.

Let the coordinates of ellipse center found in previous step be (x_o, y_o). Then the center can be translated to the origin with $x' = x - x_o$ and $y' = y - y_o$ so that the ellipse equation can be simplified to:

$$ax'^2 + 2bx'y' + cy'^2 = 1$$

Now we can solve for the rest of ellipse parameters: a, b and c by substituting the coordinates of X_1, X_2 and X_3 into the equation above.

Accumulating

With the ellipse parameters determined from previous stage, the accumulator array can be updated correspondingly. Different from classical Hough transform, RHT does not keep "grid of buckets" as the accumulator array. Rather, it first calculates the similarities between the newly detected ellipse and the ones already stored in accumulator array. Different metrics can be used to calculate the similarity. As long as the similarity exceeds some predefined threshold, replace the one in the accumulator with the average of both ellipses and add 1 to its score. Otherwise, initialize this ellipse to an empty position in the accumulator and assign a score of 1.

Termination

Once the score of one candidate ellipse exceeds the threshold, it is determined as existing in the image (in other words, this ellipse is detected), and should be removed from the image and accumulator array so that the algorithm can detect other potential ellipses faster. The algorithm terminates when the number of iterations reaches a maximum limit or all the ellipses have been detected.

Pseudo code for RHT:

for(a fixed number of iterations) {

Find a potential ellipse.

if(the ellipse is similar to an ellipse in the accumulator)

Replace the one in the accumulator with the average of two ellipses and add 1 to the score;

else

Insert the ellipse into an empty position in the accumulator with a score of 1;

}

Select the ellipse with the best score and save it in a best ellipse table;

Eliminate the pixels of the best ellipse from the image;

Empty the accumulator;

}

Distance Transform

A distance transform, also known as distance map or distance field, is a derived representation of a digital image. The choice of the term depends on the point of view on the object in question: whether the initial image is transformed into another representation, or it is simply endowed with an additional map or field.

Distance fields can also be signed, in the case where it is important to distinguish whether the point is inside or outside of the shape.

The map labels each pixel of the image with the distance to the nearest obstacle pixel. A most common type of obstacle pixel is a boundary pixel in a binary image. See the image for an example of a Chebyshev distance transform on a binary image.

A distance transformation.

Usually the transform/map is qualified with the chosen metric. For example, one may speak of Manhattan distance transform, if the underlying metric is Manhattan distance. Common metrics are:

- Euclidean distance

- Taxicab geometry, also known as City block distance or Manhattan distance.

- Chebyshev distance

Applications are digital image processing (e.g., blurring effects, skeletonizing), motion planning in robotics, and even pathfinding.

Uniformly-sampled signed distance fields have been used for GPU-accelerated font smoothing, for example by Valve researchers.

Signed distance fields can also be used for (3D) solid modelling. Rendering on typical GPU hardware requires conversion to polygon meshes, e.g. by the marching cubes algorithm.

Discrete Fourier Transform

The Fourier Transform is an important image processing tool which is used to decompose an image into its sine and cosine components. The output of the transformation represents the image in the Fourier or frequency domain, while the input image is the spatial domain equivalent. In the Fourier domain image, each point represents a particular frequency contained in the spatial domain image.

The Fourier Transform is used in a wide range of applications, such as image analysis, image filtering, image reconstruction and image compression.

How it Works

As we are only concerned with digital images, we will restrict this discussion to the Discrete Fourier Transform (DFT).

The DFT is the sampled Fourier Transform and therefore does not contain all frequencies forming an image, but only a set of samples which is large enough to fully describe the spatial domain image. The number of frequencies corresponds to the number of pixels in the spatial domain image, i.e. the image in the spatial and Fourier domain is of the same size.

For a square image of size N×N, the two-dimensional DFT is given by:

$$F(k,l)=\sum_{i=0}^{N-1}\sum_{j=0}^{N-1}f(i,j)e^{-\iota 2\pi\left(\frac{ki}{N}+\frac{lj}{N}\right)}$$

where f(a, b) is the image in the spatial domain and the exponential term is the basis function corresponding to each point F(k, l) in the Fourier space. The equation can be interpreted as: the value of each point F(k, l) is obtained by multiplying the spatial image with the corresponding base function and summing the result.

The basic functions are sine and cosine waves with increasing frequencies, i.e. F(0,0) represents the DC-component of the image which corresponds to the average brightness and F(N-1,N-1) represents the highest frequency.

In a similar way, the Fourier image can be re-transformed to the spatial domain. The inverse Fourier transform is given by:

$$F(a,b)=\frac{1}{N^2}\sum_{k=0}^{N-1}\sum_{l=0}^{N-1}F(k,l)e^{\iota 2\pi\left(\frac{ka}{N}+\frac{lb}{N}\right)}$$

Note the $\frac{1}{N^2}$ normalization term in the inverse transformation. This normalization is sometimes applied to the forward transform instead of the inverse transform, but it should not be used for both.

To obtain the result for the above equations, a double sum has to be calculated for each image point. However, because the Fourier Transform is separable, it can be written as:

$$F(k,l)=\frac{1}{N}\sum_{b=0}^{N-1}P(k,b)e^{-\iota 2\pi\frac{lb}{N}}$$

Where,

$$F(k,b)=\frac{1}{N}\sum_{a=0}^{N-1}P(a,b)e^{-\iota 2\pi\frac{ka}{N}}$$

Using these two formulas, the spatial domain image is first transformed into an intermediate image using N one-dimensional Fourier Transforms. This intermediate image is then transformed into the final image, again using N one-dimensional Fourier Transforms. Expressing the two-dimensional Fourier Transform in terms of a series of 2N one-dimensional transforms decreases the number of required computations.

Even with these computational savings, the ordinary one-dimensional DFT has N^2 complexity. This can be reduced to $N \log_2 N$ if we employ the Fast Fourier Transform (FFT) to compute the one-dimensional DFTs. This is a significant improvement, in particular for large images. There are various forms of the FFT and most of them restrict the size of the input image that may be transformed, often to $N = 2^n$ where n is an integer.

The Fourier Transform produces a complex number valued output image which can be displayed with two images, either with the real and imaginary part or with magnitude and phase. In image processing, often only the magnitude of the Fourier Transform is displayed, as it contains most of the information of the geometric structure of the spatial domain image. However, if we want to re-transform the Fourier image into the correct spatial domain after some processing in the frequency domain, we must make sure to preserve both magnitude and phase of the Fourier image.

The Fourier domain image has a much greater range than the image in the spatial domain. Hence, to be sufficiently accurate, its values are usually calculated and stored in float values.

Guidelines for Use:

The Fourier Transform is used if we want to access the geometric characteristics of a spatial domain image. Because the image in the Fourier domain is decomposed into its sinusoidal components, it is easy to examine or process certain frequencies of the image, thus influencing the geometric structure in the spatial domain.

In most implementations the Fourier image is shifted in such a way that the DC-value (i.e. the image mean) F(0,0) is displayed in the center of the image. The further away from the center an image point is, the higher is its corresponding frequency.

We start off by applying the Fourier Transform of:

The magnitude calculated from the complex result is shown in:

We can see that the DC-value is by far the largest component of the image. However, the dynamic range of the Fourier coefficients (i.e. the intensity values in the Fourier image) is too large to be displayed on the screen, therefore all other values appear as black.

The result shows that the image contains components of all frequencies, but that their magnitude gets smaller for higher frequencies. Hence, low frequencies contain more image information than the higher ones. The transform image also tells us that there are two dominating directions in the Fourier image, one passing vertically and one horizontally through the center. These originate from the regular patterns in the background of the original image.

The phase of the Fourier transform of the same image is shown in:

The value of each point determines the phase of the corresponding frequency. As in the magnitude image, we can identify the vertical and horizontal lines corresponding to the patterns in the original image. The phase image does not yield much new information about the structure of the spatial domain image; therefore, in the following examples, we will restrict ourselves to displaying only the magnitude of the Fourier Transform.

Before we leave the phase image entirely, however, note that if we apply the inverse Fourier Transform to the above magnitude image while ignoring the phase (and then histogram equalizes the output) we obtain:

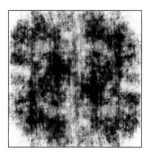

Although this image contains the same frequencies (and amount of frequencies) as the original input image, it is corrupted beyond recognition. This shows that the phase information is crucial to reconstruct the correct image in the spatial domain.

We will now experiment with some simple images to better understand the nature of the transform. The response of the Fourier Transform to periodic patterns in the spatial domain images can be seen very easily in the following artificial images.

The image,

Shows 2 pixel wide vertical stripes. The magnitude of the Fourier transform of this image is shown in:

If we look carefully, we can see that it contains 3 main values: the DC-value and, since the Fourier image is symmetrical to its center, two points corresponding to the frequency of the stripes in the original image. Note that the two points lie on a horizontal line through the image center, because the image intensity in the spatial domain changes the most if we go along it horizontally.

The distance of the points to the center can be explained as follows: the maximum frequencies which can be represented in the spatial domain are two pixel wide stripe pairs (one white, one black).

$$f_{max} = \frac{1}{2\,pixels}$$

Hence, the two pixel wide stripes in the above image represent:

$$f = \frac{1}{4\,pixels} = \frac{f_{max}}{2}$$

Thus, the points in the Fourier image are halfway between the center and the edge of the image, i.e. the represented frequency is half of the maximum.

Further investigation of the Fourier image shows that the magnitude of other frequencies in the image is less than 1/100 of the DC-value, i.e. they don't make any significant contribution to the image. The magnitudes of the two minor points are each two-thirds of the DC-value.

Similar effects as in the previous example can be seen when applying the Fourier Transform to:

Which consists of diagonal stripes. In,

Showing the magnitude of the Fourier Transform, we can see that, again, the main components of the transformed image are the DC-value and the two points corresponding to the frequency of the stripes. However, the logarithmic transform of the Fourier Transform,

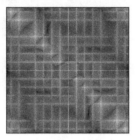

Shows that now the image contains many minor frequencies. The main reason is that a diagonal can only be approximated by the square pixels of the image, hence, additional frequencies are needed to compose the image. The logarithmic scaling makes it difficult to tell the influence of single frequencies in the original image. To find the most important frequencies we threshold the original Fourier magnitude image at level 13. The resulting Fourier image,

shows all frequencies whose magnitude is at least 5% of the main peak. Compared to the original Fourier image, several more points appear. They are all on the same diagonal as the three main components, i.e. they all originate from the periodic stripes. The represented frequencies are all multiples of the basic frequency of the stripes in the spatial domain image. This is because a rectangular signal, like the stripes, with the frequency $_{rect}$ is a composition of sine waves with the frequencies $f_{sin\varepsilon} = n \times f_{rect}$, known as the harmonics of f_{rect}. All other frequencies disappeared from the Fourier image, i.e. the magnitude of each of them is less than 5% of the DC-value.

A Fourier-Transformed image can be used for frequency filtering. A simple example is illustrated with the above image. If we multiply the (complex) Fourier image obtained above with an image containing a circle (of r = 32 pixels), we can set all frequencies larger than f_{rect} to zero as shown in the logarithmic transformed image.

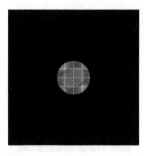

By applying the inverse Fourier Transform we obtain:

The resulting image is a lowpass filtered version of the original spatial domain image. Since all other frequencies have been suppressed, this result is the sum of the constant DC-value and a sine-wave with the frequency f_{rect}. Further examples can be seen in the worksheet on frequency filtering.

A property of the Fourier Transform which is used, for example, for the removal of additive noise, is its distributivity over addition. We can illustrate this by adding the complex Fourier images of the two previous example images. To display the result and emphasize the main peaks, we threshold the magnitude of the complex image, as can be seen in figure:

Applying the inverse Fourier Transform to the complex image yields,

According to the distributivity law, this image is the same as the direct sum of the two original spatial domain images.

Finally, we present an example (i.e. text orientation finding) where the Fourier Transform is used to gain information about the geometric structure of the spatial domain image. Text recognition using image processing techniques is simplified if we can assume that the text lines are in a predefined direction. Here we show how the Fourier Transform can be used to find the initial orientation of the text and then a rotation can be applied to correct the error. We illustrate this technique using,

A binary image of English text. The logarithm of the magnitude of its Fourier transform is:

and

Is the thresholded magnitude of the Fourier image. We can see that the main values lie on a vertical line, indicating that the text lines in the input image are horizontal.

If we proceed in the same way with,

Which was rotated about 45°, we obtain,

and

In the Fourier space. We can see that the line of the main peaks in the Fourier domain is rotated according to rotation of the input image. The second line in the logarithmic image (perpendicular to the main direction) originates from the black corners in the rotated image.

Although we managed to find a threshold which separates the main peaks from the background, we have a reasonable amount of noise in the Fourier image resulting from the irregular pattern of the letters. We could decrease these background values and therefore increase the difference to the main peaks if we were able to form solid blocks out of the text-lines. This could, for example, be done by using a morphological operator.

Common Variants

Another sinusoidal transform (i.e. transform with sinusoidal base functions) related to the DFT is the Discrete Cosine Transform (DCT). For an N×N image, the DCT is given by;

$$C(k,n)=\alpha(k,n)\sum_{i=0}^{N-1}\sum_{j=0}^{N-1}f(i,j)\cos\left(\frac{(2i+1)k\pi}{2N}\right)\cos\left(\frac{(2j+1)n\pi}{2N}\right)$$

with

$$\alpha(k,n)=\begin{cases}\dfrac{1}{N} & \text{for } k,n=0 \\[2ex] \dfrac{2}{N} & \text{for } k,n=1,2,...,N-1\end{cases}$$

The main advantages of the DCT are that it yields a real valued output image and that it is a fast transform. A major use of the DCT is in image compression - i.e. trying to reduce the amount of data needed to store an image. After performing a DCT it is possible to throw away the coefficients that encode high frequency components that the human eye is not very sensitive to. Thus the amount of data can be reduced, without seriously affecting the way an image looks to the human eye.

Discrete Cosine Transform

Discrete Cosine Transform is used in lossy image compression because it has very strong energy compaction, i.e., its large amount of information is stored in very low frequency component of a signal and rest other frequency having very small data which can be stored by using very less number of bits (usually, at most 2 or 3 bit).

To perform DCT Transformation on an image, first we have to fetch image file information (pixel value in term of integer having range 0 – 255) which we divides in block of 8 X 8 matrix and then we apply discrete cosine transform on that block of data.

After applying discrete cosine transform, we will see that its more than 90% data will be in lower frequency component. For simplicity, we took a matrix of size 8 X 8 having all value as 255 (considering image to be completely white) and we are going to perform 2-D discrete cosine transform on that to observe the output.

Image Foresting Transform

The Image Foresting Transform is a general tool for the design, implementation, and evaluation of image processing operators based on connectivity. The IFT defines a minimum-cost path forest in a graph, whose nodes are the image pixels and whose arcs are defined by an adjacency relation between pixels. The cost of a path in this graph is determined by an application-specific path-cost function, which usually depends on local image properties along the path—such as color, gradient, and pixel position. The roots of the forest are drawn from a given set of seed pixels. For suitable path-cost functions, the IFT assigns one minimum-cost path from the seed set to each pixel, in such a way that the union of those paths is an oriented forest, spanning the whole image. The IFT outputs three attributes for each pixel: its predecessor in the optimum path, the cost of that path, and the corresponding root (or some label associated with it). A great variety of powerful image operators, old and new, can be implemented by simple local processing of these attributes.

We describe a general algorithm for computing the IFT, which is essentially Dijkstra's shortest-path algorithm, slightly modified for multiple sources and general path-cost functions. Since our conditions on the path costs apply only to optimum paths, and not to all paths, we found it necessary to rewrite and extend the classical proof of correctness of Dijkstra's algorithm. In many practical applications, the path costs are integers with limited increments and the graph is sparse; therefore, the optimizations described by Dial and Ahuja et al. will apply and the running time will be linear on the number of pixels.

The IFT unifies and extends many image analysis techniques which, even though based on similar underlying concepts (ordered propagation, flooding, geodesic dilations, dynamic programming, region growing, A graph search, etc.), are usually presented as unrelated methods. Those techniques can all be reduced to a partition of the image into influence zones associated with a given seed set, where the zone of each seed consists of the pixels that are "more closely connected" to that seed than to any other, in some appropriate sense. These influence zones are simply the trees of the forest defined by the IFT. Examples are watershed transforms and fuzzy-connected segmentation. The IFT also provides a mathematically sound framework for many image-processing operations that are not obviously related to image partition, such as morphological reconstruction, distance transforms multiscale skeletons, shape saliences and multiscale fractal dimension, and boundary tracking.

By separating the general forest computation procedure from the application-specific path-cost function, the IFT greatly simplifies the implementation of image operators, and provides a fair testbed for their evaluation and tuning. For many classical operators, the IFT-based implementation is much closer to the theoretical definition than the published algorithms. Indeed, many algorithms which have been used without proof have their correctness established by being reformulated in terms of the IFT. By clarifying the relationship between different image transforms, the IFT approach often leads to novel image operators and considerably faster (but still provably correct) algorithms.

The IFT definition and algorithms are independent of the nature of the pixels and of the dimension of the image, and therefore they apply to color and multispectral images, as well as to higher-dimensional images such as video sequences and tomography data.

Grassfire Transform

In image processing, the grassfire transform is the computation of the distance from a pixel to the border of a region. It can be described as "setting fire" to the borders of an image region to yield descriptors such as the region's skeleton or medial axis. Harry Blum introduced the concept in 1967.

Motivation

A region's skeleton can be a useful descriptor, because it describes things such as the symmetry of the region as well as subparts, depressions and protrusions. It also provides a way of relating the interior of a region to the shape of the boundary. In the grassfire transform, the skeleton forms at the points in the region where the "fires" meet. In the literature this is described as the locus of meeting waveforms.

Another advantage of using the outcome of the grassfire transform as a descriptor is that it is invertible. Assuming information about when the medial axis or skeleton is created by meeting waveforms is kept, then the skeleton can be restored by radiating outward.

Example Algorithm

The algorithm below is a simple two pass method for computing the Manhattan distance from the border of a region. Of course there are several other algorithms for performing the grassfire transform.

for each row in image left to right

    for each column in image top to bottom

```
if(pixel is in region){

set pixel to 1 + minimum value of the north and west neighbours

}else{

set pixel to zero

}

}

}

for each row right to left

    for each column bottom to top

    if(pixel is in region){

    set pixel to min(value of the pixel,1 + minimum value of the south and east neighbours)

    }else{

    set pixel to zero

    }

    }

}
```

Below is the result of this transform. It is important to note that the most intense lines make up the skeleton.

Source image.

Result image.

Applications

The grassfire transform can be abstracted to suit a variety of computing problems. It has been shown that it can be extended beyond the context of images to arbitrary functions. This includes applications in energy minimization problems such as those handled by the Viterbi algorithm, max-product belief propagation, resource allocation, and in optimal control methods.

It can also be used to compute the distance between regions by setting the background to be as a region.

Phase Stretch Transform

Phase stretch transform (PST) is a computational approach to signal and image processing. One of its utilities is for feature detection and classification. PST is related to time stretch dispersive Fourier transform. It transforms the image by emulating propagation through a diffractive medium with engineered 3D dispersive property (refractive index). The operation relies on symmetry of the dispersion profile and can be understood in terms of dispersive eigenfunctions or stretch modes. PST performs similar functionality as phase-contrast microscopy, but on digital images. PST can be applied to digital images and temporal (time series) data.

Wavelet Transform

The word "wavelet" has been introduced by Morlet and Grossmann in the early 1980s. They used the French word ondelette, meaning "small wave" originated from the study of time-frequency signal analysis and wave propagation, sampling theory. Morlet first introduce the idea of wavelets as a family of functions constructed by using translation and dilation of single function, called mother wavelets, for analysis of nonstationary signals. Wavelets are a mathematical tool they can be used to extract information from many different kinds of data, including audio signals and images. The subject of wavelet analysis has recently drawn a great deal of attention from mathematical scientists in various disciplines. It is creating a common link between mathematicians, physicists, and electrical engineers with modern application as diverse as wave propagation, data compression, image processing, pattern recognition, computer graphics and other medical image technology. Sets of wavelets are generally needed to analyze data fully. The wavelet transform decompose the signal with finite energy in the spatial domain into a set of function as a standard in the modular spatial domain of orthogonal. Then we analyze the characteristics of the signal in the modular spatial domain. Compared with the traditional Fourier analysis, the wavelet transform can analyze the function in the modular spatial domain and timing domain which has better local capacity of the frequency and time. It is the development and sublimation of Fourier transform, which has a lot of advantages.

The main objective of wavelet transform is to define the powerful wavelet basis functions and find efficient methods for their computation. Fourier methods are not always good tools to recapture the signal or image, particularly if it is highly non- smooth. The wavelet transform is done similar like to Short Term Fourier Transform (STFT) analysis. The signal to be analysed is multiplied with a wavelet function just as it is multiplied with a window function in STFT, and then the transform is computed for each segment generated. However, unlike STFT, in Wavelet Transform, the width of the wavelet function changes with each spectral component. The Wavelet Transform, at high frequencies, gives good time resolution and poor frequency resolution, while at low frequencies; the Wavelet Transform gives good frequency resolution and poor time resolution. In these cases the wavelet analysis is often very effective because it provides a simple approach for dealing with the local aspects of a signal, therefore particular properties of the Haar or wavelet transforms allow to analyze the original image on spectral domain effectively. Wavelet transforms have advantages over traditional Fourier methods in analyzing physical situations where the signal contains discontinuities and sharp spikes. Wavelets were developed independently in the fields of mathematics, quantum physics, electrical engineering, and seismic geology.

The first literature that relates to the wavelet transform is Haar wavelet. It was proposed by the mathematician Alfred Haar in 1909. However, the concept of the wavelet did not exist at that time. Until 1981, the concept was proposed by the geophysicist Jean Morlet. Later, Morlet and Grossman invented the term wavelet in 1984. Before 1985, Haar wavelet was the only orthogonal wavelet known to the people. Fortunately, the Mathematician Yves Meyer constructed the second orthogonal wavelet called Meyer wavelet in 1985. As more and more scholars joined in this field, the 1st international conference was held in France in 1987.

A wavelet is a mathematical function used to divide a given function or continuous-time signal into different scale components. Usually one can assign a frequency range to each scale component. Each scale component can then be studied with a resolution that matches its scale. A wavelet transform is the representation of a function by wavelets. The wavelets are scaled and translated copies (known as "daughter wavelets") of a finite-length or fastdecaying oscillating waveform (known as the "mother wavelet").

$$\psi_{a,b}(t) = \frac{1}{\sqrt{|a|}} \psi\left(\frac{t-b}{a}\right), \ a,b \in R, a \neq 0,$$

Where, Ψ is a wavelet function, a, is a scaling parameter which measure the degree of compression or scale, and b, is a translation parameter which determines the time location of the wavelet. Wavelet transforms have advantages over traditional Fourier transforms for representing functions that have discontinuities and sharp peaks, and for accurately deconstructing and reconstructing finite, non-periodic and non-stationary signals.

References

- Digital-images, computing -news-wires-white-papers-and-books: encyclopedia.com, Retrieved 17 June, 2019

- Image-enhancement- 26314: techopedia.com, Retrieved 16 March, 2019

- Image-denoising-techniques-a-review, open-access- 46252: rroij.com, Retrieved 12 August, 2019

- Criminisi, A. Perez, P. Toyama, K. (2003). "Object Removal by Exemplar-Based Inpainting". 2003 IEEE Computer Society Conference on Computer Vision and Pattern Recognition, 2003. Proceedings. Proceedings of the 2003 IEEE Computer Society Conference on Computer Vision and Pattern Recognition. 2. pp. II-721–II-728. doi:10.1109/CVPR.2003.1211538. ISBN 0-7695-1900-8

- Image-transformations, dip: tutorialspoint.com, Retrieved 15 April, 2019

- Discrete-cosine-transform-algorithm-program: geeksforgeeks.org, Retrieved 25 January, 2019

- Wavelet-tranformations-its-major-applications-in-digital-image-processing-IJERTV2IS3538: ijert.org, Retrieved 29 May, 2019

- Gonzalez, Rafael (2018). Digital image processing. New York, NY: Pearson. ISBN 978-0-13-335672-4. OCLC 966609831

Color Vision

The capability of differentiating lights of various wavelengths and frequencies by the means of computer machines is termed as color vision. Color management, color space, color mapping, color constancy, visual perception, color appearance model, etc. are some of its concepts. These diverse concepts of color vision have been thoroughly discussed in this chapter.

The experimental laws of color-matching state that over a wide range of conditions of observation, colors can be matched by additive mixtures of three fixed primary colors. These primaries must be such that none of them can be matched by a mixture of the other two. Furthermore those matches are linear over a wide range of observing conditions which implies two facts. First, the match between two colors continues to hold if the corresponding stimuli are increased or reduced by the same amount, their respective relative spectral energy distributions being unchanged. Second, if colors C and D match and colors E and F match, then the additive mixture of colors C and E matches the corresponding additive mixture of colors D and F.

Colors can therefore be represented by three-dimensional vectors whereas color matches can be represented by linear equations between such vectors. If C represents a given color and R, G, B represent unit amounts of three fixed primaries then the equation,

$$C = RR + GG + BB,$$

Where, $R \geq 0, G \geq 0, B \geq 0$

Expresses the fact that the given color is matched by an additive mixture of quantities R, G, B, respectively, of the given primaries. R, G, B are called the tristimulus values of the given color in the particular set of primaries used. Another set of important quantities is the chromaticity coordinates r, g, b defined by,

$$r = \frac{R}{R+G+B}$$

$$g = \frac{G}{R+G+B}$$

$$b = \frac{B}{R+G+B}$$

The linearity property also allows us to define completely the color-matching properties of the observing eye in the given primary system by three functions of wavelength $r(\lambda)$, $g(\lambda)$, $b(\lambda)$ called color-matching functions. If the color C has a spectral energy distribution p(λ) then its tristimulus values are:

$$R = \int p(\lambda)\, r(\lambda)\, d\lambda$$
$$G = \int p(\lambda)\, g(\lambda)\, d\lambda$$
$$B = \int p(\lambda)\, b(\lambda)\, d\lambda$$

Where, the integrals are taken over the visible spectrum. In additive color-matching experiments, colors C_1 and C_2 of spectral energy distributions $p_1(\lambda)$ and $p_2(\lambda)$ match if and only if,

$$\int p_1(\lambda)\, r(\lambda)\, d\lambda = \int p_2(\lambda)\, r(\lambda)\, d\lambda$$
$$\int p_1(\lambda)\, g(\lambda)\, d\lambda = \int p_2(\lambda)\, g(\lambda)\, d\lambda$$
$$\int p_1(\lambda)\, b(\lambda)\, d\lambda = \int p_2(\lambda)\, b(\lambda)\, d\lambda$$

In the case of physical object colors, the properties of the illuminant and the object surface reflectance become critical. Land has demonstrated that under certain conditions color matches may be attained without satisfying previous three equations and those previous three equations do not always lead to color matches. His experiments, however, deal with varying illuminants between the two object colors being matched as well as varying surrounds. Judd discusses some of Land's phenomena and explains them using traditional arguments. Land's observations are based on a concept of Helmholtz; that is, in judging the color of objects in a real scene, we make an allowance for the color of the iUuminant. In other words, if the viewer knows certain objects in the picture to be white under "normal" conditions of illumination, then the eye and brain effect an inevitable and unconscious color transformation that makes this true. Another explanation of Land's results is based on simultaneous contrast and chromatic adaptation. The same illuminant is utilized throughout and the surrounds of the object colors are ignored due to the point theory the model assumes of the human visual system. Additionally, the color-matching experiments to be cited here are not affected by illumination (due to the nature of the experiments) and are also based on constant surrounds, thereby avoiding the effects observed by Land. It may then be said that (below equations) are equivalent to previous three equations but deal with object color matches as opposed to additive color matches,

$$\int p_1(\lambda)\, S(\lambda)\, r(\lambda)\, d\lambda = \int p_2(\lambda)\, S(\lambda)\, r(\lambda)\, d\lambda$$
$$\int p_1(\lambda)\, S(\lambda)\, g(\lambda)\, d\lambda = \int p_2(\lambda)\, S(\lambda)\, g(\lambda)\, d\lambda$$
$$\int p_1(\lambda)\, S(\lambda)\, b(\lambda)\, d\lambda = \int p_2(\lambda)\, S(\lambda)\, b(\lambda)\, d\lambda$$

Where, $p_1(\lambda)$ and $p_2(\lambda)$ are the spectral reflectance functions of the surface materials and $S(\lambda)$ is the spectral energy distribution of the illuminant. These equations are also in agreement with Land's retinex theory since a match is made when the reflectivities of the two surfaces match for a given illuminant.

We may also describe a change of primaries as a simple matrix multiplication operation whereby the new tristimulus values L, M, S of a given color and the new color-matching functions l(λ), m(λ), s(λ) are given by,

$$T_n = AT_o$$
$$t_n = At_o$$

Where, $T_n = [L,M,S]^t$, $T_o = [R,G,B]^t$, $t_n = [l(\lambda), m(\lambda), s(\lambda)]^t$, $t_o = [r(\lambda), g(\lambda), b(\lambda)]^t$, and A is a three-by-three matrix whose rows are the tristimulus values of the new primaries in the system of the old primaries.

A standard observer has been developed in 1931 by the CIE, whose color-matching functions are denoted by x(λ), y(λ), z(λ). The matches predicted with their aid using ($\int p_1(\lambda)\, r(\lambda)\, d\lambda = \int p_2(\lambda)\, r(\lambda)\, d\lambda$, $\int p_1(\lambda)\, g(\lambda)\, d\lambda = \int p_2(\lambda)\, g(\lambda)\, d\lambda$, $\int p_1(\lambda)\, b(\lambda)\, d\lambda = \int p_2(\lambda)\, b(\lambda)\, d\lambda$) represent average matches for humans with normal color vision as opposed to humans with any one of the several forms of color blind vision.

Psychophysics of the Human Visual System

The physiological basis of trichromatic color matches is the linear absorption of light at photopic levels of illumination (when the effect of rod receptors is negligible) by three types of cone receptors in the human fovea. However, specification of the spectral absorption characteristics of the three different cone types has been difficult since it has not been possible to extract cone pigments from the eyes of primates. A number of different approaches have been taken to yield this information which is essential to understanding color vision. All these approaches agree on two points. First, there are three types of cones with their absorption curves peaking at about 445, 540, and 570 nm. Second, these absorptions curves are quite abroad and fit to a first approximation the Dartnall nomogram.

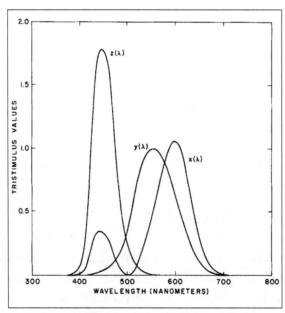

Color-matching functions x(λ), y(λ), and z(λ).

The terms L-cones (containing the long-wavelength peaking pigment), M-cones (containing the medium-wavelength peaking pigment) and S cones (containing the short-wavelength peaking pigment) will be used to denote the cone types containing the 570, 540, and 445 nm peaking pigments, respectively.

Physiological studies have shown that the activity or response of the cone receptors is proportional not to the intensity of the stimulus but rather to its logarithm. This idea is supported by Fechner's law, which states that the just-noticeable brightness difference is proportional to the logarithm of the stimulus intensity.

Further results obtained by neurophysiological experiments on lateral geniculate nucleus (LGN) cells of primates are now summarized. Four types of spectrally opponent cells exist in the LGN, a part of the brain to which the retina projects itself. They showed excitation to some wavelengths and inhibition to others when the eye was stimulated with flashes of monochromatic lights. The cells whose response showed maximum excitation around 500 nm and maximum inhibition around 630 nm were called green excitatory, red inhibitory (+G- R). Other cells showing opposite responses were called red excitatory, green inhibitory cells (+ R- G). The cells showing maximum excitation (inhibition) at 600 nm and maximum inhibition (excitation) at 440 nm were called yellow excitatory, blue inhibitory cells (+ Y - B) and blue excitatory, yellow inhibitory (+ B - Y), respectively.

In addition to these four varieties of spectrally opponent cells, two other classes of cells were found that did not give spectrally opponent responses but rather responded in the same direction to lights of all wavelengths. Those cells, which are not involved with color vision, are called white excitatory, black inhibitory cells (+ Wh - Bl) and black excitatory, white inhibitory cells (+ Bl - Wh).

Evidence also exists in favor of the assumption of separate chromatic and achromatic channels, each gaining its information from the same receptors but processing it in different ways. Spectrally non-opponent cells which correspond to the achromatic channel add together the (Log) outputs of the L- and M-cones (and possibly S-cones as well). Spectrally opponent cells which correspond to the chromatic channels subtract the (Log) outputs of the L- and M-cones for the red-green system, of the L- and S-cones for the yellow-blue system.

A Color Vision Model

Psychophysical Approach

There are three cone types involved in human photopic (day) vision, each of which contains a pigment with different spectral absorption characteristics. From color-matching experiments, the CIE derived a set of three color-matching functions which, according to Grassman laws of color mixture, have to be a linear combination of the pigment absorption curves. There is an infinite number of such combinations but we are restricted by the fact that the resulting curves should be positive in the visible spectrum and have a single maximum at a wavelength close to the ones indicated previously. Despite these restrictions there are still many of these "fundamentals" in the literature.

Faugeras has decided to adopt the fundamentals proposed by Stiles . However, a more recent model proposed by Pokorny and Smith seems to be much more readily acceptable today. This model is in accordance with the idea, proposed by other investigators as well, that the luminous efficiency function of the normal trichromat is mediated only by the red- and green-cone mechanisms and that the blue-cone mechanism makes no contribution to "luminance signals." In other words, a color blind person or dichromat, lacking in the tritanope or blue relative spectral sensitivity, $s(\lambda)$, perceives luminance information as well as does a trichromat. This statement, together with the fact that the CIE luminous efficiency function, $V(\lambda)$, has values at short wavelengths that are considered excessively low, have prompted us to adopt the Pokorny and Smith fundamentals. It should be mentioned that the CIE luminous efficiency function is, by definition, equal to the CIE curve $y(\lambda)$, and that it has been modified by Judd to take into account its low values at short wavelengths.

The fundamentals of Pokorny and Smith may be related to the CIE curves, $x'(\lambda), y'(\lambda), z'(\lambda)$, which are the Judd modified CIE 1931 standard functions , by a matrix transformation,

$$\begin{bmatrix} l(\lambda) \\ m(\lambda) \\ s(\lambda) \end{bmatrix} = T \begin{bmatrix} x'(\lambda) \\ y'(\lambda) \\ z'(\lambda) \end{bmatrix}, \quad \text{where } T = \begin{bmatrix} 0.15514 & 0.54312 & -0.03286 \\ -0.15514 & 0.45684 & 0.03286 \\ 0.0 & 0.0 & -0.00801 \end{bmatrix}$$

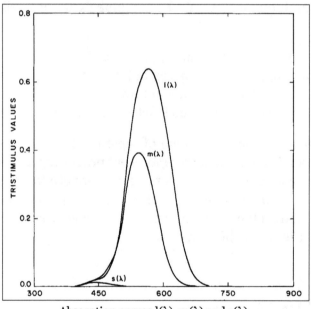

Absorption curves $l(\lambda)$, $m(\lambda)$ and $s(\lambda)$.

Since the blue-cone mechanism, $s(\lambda)$, makes no contribution to luminance, below equation also results.

$$V_{mod}(\lambda) = l(\lambda) + m(\lambda)$$

This constraint on $\left(\begin{bmatrix} l(\lambda) \\ m(\lambda) \\ s(\lambda) \end{bmatrix} = T \begin{bmatrix} x'(\lambda) \\ y'(\lambda) \\ z'(\lambda) \end{bmatrix}, \quad \text{where } T = \begin{bmatrix} 0.15514 & 0.54312 & -0.03286 \\ -0.15514 & 0.45684 & 0.03286 \\ 0.0 & 0.0 & -0.00801 \end{bmatrix} \right)$ helps to

improve the agreement between predicted and observed color-matching functions of tritanopes. Figure shows the resulting absorption curves $l(\lambda)$, $m(\lambda)$, $s(\lambda)$, which are positive in the visible spectrum and have single maxima at, respectively, 575, 540, and 445 nm.

A precise description, similar to that given by Faugeras , of the cone absorption stage of the model may now be presented. Let I(x, y, X) be an image, where x and y are the spatial coordinates and h is the wavelength of the light. Then the absorption of this light energy by the three pigments yields the three signals,

$$L(x,y) = \int I(x,y,\lambda)\, l(\lambda)\, d\lambda$$
$$M(x,y) = \int I(x,y,\lambda)\, m(\lambda)\, d\lambda$$
$$S(x,y) = \int I(x,y,\lambda)\, s(\lambda)\, d\lambda$$

Where each integral is taken over the visible spectrum.

The nonlinear response of the cones transforms those signals in the following way:

$$L^*(x,y) = Log[L(x,y)]$$
$$M^*(x,y) = Log[M(x,y)]$$
$$S^*(x,y) = Log[S(x,y)]$$

It has been mentioned that there exist separate chromatic and achromatic channels in the human visual path, each gaining its information from the same receptors but processing it in different ways. The achromatic response will be called A and the two chromatic responses will be called C_1 and C_2. Equations below express mathematically the ideas,

$$A = \alpha(\alpha L^* + \beta M^*) = \alpha(\alpha Log L + \beta Log M)$$
$$C_1 = u_1(L^* - M^*) = u_1 Log(L/M)$$
$$C_2 = u_2(L^* - M^*) = u_2 Log(L/S)$$

Where, A is a mathematical description of the response of (+ B1- Wh) and (+ Wh- B1) cells which add the Log outputs of the L-cones and M-cones (in agreement with the Pokorny and Smith fundamentals and spectral non-opponent cells). C_1 and C_2 are mathematical descriptions of the responses of (+ R - G), (+ G - R), and (+ B - Y), (+ Y - B) cells which subtract the Log outputs of the L- and M-cones and L- and S-cones, respectively (in agreement with the response of spectrally opponent cells).

This model is in agreement with Stockham's model for achromatic vision. For an achromatic image the outputs of the cone absorption stage are by definition equal,

$$L(x,\ y) = M(x,\ y) = S(x,\ y)$$

And thus,

$$C_1(x,\ y) = C_2(x,\ y) = 0$$

In that case only the achromatic channel A is active,

$$A = a(\alpha + \beta)L^*(x,y)$$

This is exactly Stockham's model. It may then be stated that A carries the brightness information.

Consider figure which describes the color space spanned by our model. It provides a three-dimensional vector space as a quantitative definition of some perceptually important parameters. If A, brightness, is now considered constant, the relationship of C_1 and C_2 to the perception of hue and saturation may be discussed. For a color at point Q, saturation is related to the distance O_q while hue is related to the angle θ. Saturation is thus proportional to the sum of the activities in the C_1 and C_2 channels while hue is proportional to the ratio of these activities.

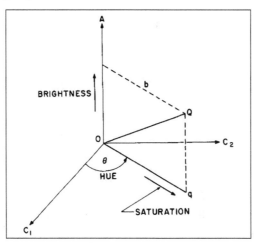

The AC_1C_2 space.

Colorimetric Analysis A line element will now be derived to quantitatively determine perceived color differences from the properties of the three fundamental color response systems. Line elements aim to specify pairs of color stimuli that present a particular perceived color difference, for example, a just-noticeable difference, by the position and distance apart in tristimulus space of the points representing these stimuli. In ordinary or Euclidean space, the distance ds between two neighboring points P_1 and P_2 whose rectangular coordinates (tristimulus values) are (U_1, U_2, U_3) and $(U_1 + dU_1, U_2 + dU_2, U_3 + dU_3)$ is given by:

$$(ds)^2 = (dU_1)^2 + (dU_2)^2 + (dU_3)^2$$

In AC_1C_2 space this line element may be expressed as:

$$(ds)^2 = (dA)^2 + (dC_1)^2 + (dC_2)^2$$

In other words, the AC_1C_2 space is assumed to be a uniform perceptual space in the sense that at a given point the locus of all points corresponding to a just-noticeable difference in perception (brightness or chromaticity) is a sphere of radius 1 centered at that point. This is approximated by adjusting the values of the parameters a, u_1, u_2, of ($A = \alpha(\alpha L^* + \beta M^*) = \alpha(\alpha \operatorname{Log} L + \beta \operatorname{Log} M)$, $C_1 = u_1(L^* - M^*) = u_1 \operatorname{Log}(L/M)$, $C_2 = u_2(L^* - M^*) = u_2 \operatorname{Log}(L/S)$).

The following Riemannian line element in LMS space is easily derived by substituting $(A = \alpha(\alpha L^* + \beta M^*) = \alpha(\alpha \operatorname{Log} L + \beta \operatorname{Log} M)$, $C_1 = u_1(L^* - M^*) = u_1 \operatorname{Log}(L/M)$, $C_2 = u_2(L^* - M^*) = u_2 \operatorname{Log}(L/S)$) into $((ds)^2 = (dA)^2 + (dC_1)^2 + (dC_2)^2)$,

$$(ds)^2 = \left(a^2\,\alpha^2 + u_1^2 + u_2^2\right)\left[\frac{dL}{L}\right]^2 + \left(a^2\,\beta^2 + u_1^2\right)\left[\frac{dM}{M}\right]^2 + u_2^2\left[\frac{dS}{S}\right]^2$$
$$+ 2\left(a^2\,\alpha\beta - u_1^2\right)\left[\frac{dL}{L}\right]\left[\frac{dM}{M}\right] - 2u_2^2\left[\frac{dL}{L}\right]\left[\frac{dS}{S}\right]$$

This line element is based on theoretical considerations regarding the functioning of the visual mechanism coupled with certain qualitative experimental data. It includes cross-product terms of the cone responses to account for the interdependence of the cone systems, a property that the Stiles line element does not possess. As noted in previous equation a number of undefined parameters exist which these inductive lines dement does not quantify. By minimizing the computed deviations from empirical data the best values for these parameters are determined.

According to Grassman's laws of additive color mixture it can be shown that the, function $V_{mod}(\lambda)$ should be a linear combination of the cones' spectral absorption curves, as is indeed the case (Pokorny and Smith). Our model should also account for the measurements yielding to the function $V_{mod}(\lambda)$. One method that may be used to measure this function is called the step by step method. Two juxtaposed monochromatic lights of slightly different wavelengths are viewed and the radiance of one is varied until the total difference between the patches is minimum. The wavelength difference can be made so small that the difference in color at this minimum setting is barely perceptible. This procedure is repeated step by step along the spectrum.

A relative luminous efficiency function can be derived from our model and previous equation by a corresponding procedure and is given by,

$$\hat{V}_{mod}(\lambda) = kl(\lambda)^{\alpha/(\alpha+\beta)}\,m(\lambda)^{\beta/(\alpha+\beta)}$$

Where, k has been adjusted to yield a maximum of 1. The parameters α and β have

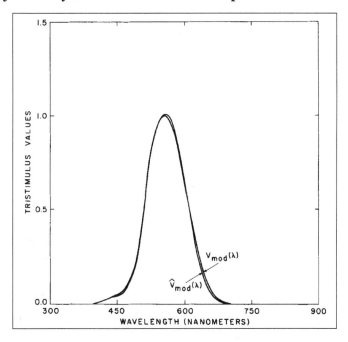

Been determined such that ($V_{mod}(\lambda) = l(\lambda) +$ (λ)) and ($\hat{V}_{mod}(\lambda) = kl(\lambda)^{\alpha/(\alpha+\beta)} m(\lambda)^{\beta/(\alpha+\beta)}$) are simultaneously satisfied, i.e.,

$$l(\lambda) + m(\lambda) = kl(\lambda)^{\alpha/(\alpha+\beta)} m(\lambda)^{\beta/(\alpha+\beta)}$$

The optimum values for α and β are 0.7186 and 0.2814, respectively, where $\alpha + \beta = 1$. They produce the best least squares estimate of previous equation. Figure plots ($\hat{V}_{mod}(\lambda) = kl(\lambda)^{\alpha/(\alpha+\beta)} m(\lambda)^{\beta/(\alpha+\beta)}$) and the true $V_{mod}(\lambda)$ given by ($V_{mod}(\lambda) = l(\lambda) + m(\lambda)$). It is quite evident that the two curves are in very good agreement for the entire visible spectrum.

The line element may also be used to predict the human observer's ability to discriminate between the wavelengths of two just-noticeable different monochromatic stimuli of equal brightness. Utilizing and making appropriate substitutions for dL, dM, dS, L, M, and S in terms of dl(λ), din(λ), ds(λ), l, m, and s, results.

$$(ds)^2 = (d\lambda)^2 \left\{ \left(a^2\alpha^2 + u_1^2 + u_2^2\right) \right.$$

$$\times \left[\frac{dl(\lambda)}{d\lambda} \frac{1}{l(\lambda)} - \left(\frac{dl(\lambda)}{d\lambda} \frac{\alpha}{l(\lambda)} + \frac{dm(\lambda)}{d\lambda} \frac{\beta}{m(\lambda)} \right) \right]^2$$

$$+ \left(a^2\beta^2 + u_1^2\right) \left[\frac{dm(\lambda)}{d\lambda} \frac{1}{m(\lambda)} - \left(\frac{dl(\lambda)}{d\lambda} \frac{\alpha}{l(\lambda)} + \frac{dm(\lambda)}{d\lambda} \frac{\beta}{m(\lambda)} \right) \right]^2$$

$$+ u_2^2 \left[\frac{ds(\lambda)}{d\lambda} \frac{1}{s(\lambda)} - \left(\frac{dl(\lambda)}{d\lambda} \frac{\alpha}{l(\lambda)} + \frac{dm(\lambda)}{d\lambda} \frac{\beta}{m(\lambda)} \right) \right]^2$$

$$+ 2\left(a^2\alpha\beta + u_1^2\right) \left[\frac{dl(\lambda)}{d\lambda} \frac{1}{l(\lambda)} - \left(\frac{dl(\lambda)}{d\lambda} \frac{\alpha}{l(\lambda)} + \frac{dm(\lambda)}{d\lambda} \frac{\beta}{m(\lambda)} \right) \right]$$

$$\times \left[\frac{dm(\lambda)}{d\lambda} \frac{1}{m(\lambda)} - \left(\frac{dl(\lambda)}{d\lambda} \frac{\alpha}{l(\lambda)} + \frac{dm(\lambda)}{d\lambda} \frac{\beta}{m(\lambda)} \right) \right]$$

$$- 2u_2^2 \left[\frac{dl(\lambda)}{d\lambda} \frac{1}{l(\lambda)} - \left(\frac{dl(\lambda)}{d\lambda} \frac{\alpha}{l(\lambda)} + \frac{dm(\lambda)}{d\lambda} \frac{\beta}{m(\lambda)} \right) \right]$$

$$\times \left. \left[\frac{ds(\lambda)}{d\lambda} \frac{1}{s(\lambda)} - \left(\frac{dl(\lambda)}{d\lambda} \frac{\alpha}{l(\lambda)} + \frac{dm(\lambda)}{d\lambda} \frac{\beta}{m(\lambda)} \right) \right] \right\}$$

For a sequence of pairs of stimuli spanning the spectrum of all the same small-step brightness (constant ds) determined from the line element, the variation of dλ with λ calculated from (previous equation) is compared with the mean experimental data reported by Wright and Pitt , as shown in figure. This comparison must be carefully considered since wavelength discrimination has been studied by many researchers , each producing results which vary considerably from the others' results. However, the data reported by Wright and Pitt seem to exhibit the features most commonly observed.

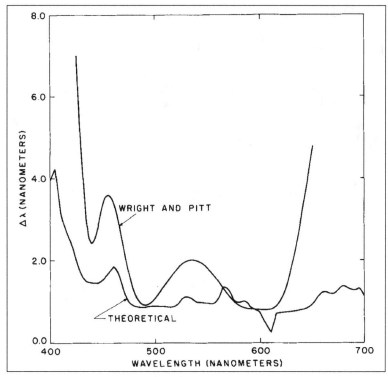

Wavelength discrimination.

The line element given in $((\mathrm{ds})^2 = (a^2\,\alpha^2 + u_1^2 + u_2^2)\left[\dfrac{dL}{L}\right]^2 + (a^2\,\beta^2 + u_1^2)\left[\dfrac{dM}{M}\right]^2 + u_2^2\left[\dfrac{dS}{S}\right]^2 + 2(a^2\,\alpha\beta - $ $u_1^2)\left[\dfrac{dL}{L}\right]\left[\dfrac{dM}{M}\right] - 2u_2^2\left[\dfrac{dL}{L}\right]\left[\dfrac{dS}{S}\right])$ may also be expressed in terms of CIE (x, y) chromaticity coordinates and luminance, Y, though,

$$\begin{bmatrix} l(\lambda) \\ m(\lambda) \\ s(\lambda) \end{bmatrix} = \begin{bmatrix} t_{11} & t_{12} & t_{13} \\ t_{21} & t_{22} & t_{23} \\ t_{31} & t_{32} & t_{33} \end{bmatrix} \begin{bmatrix} x(\lambda) \\ y(\lambda) \\ z(\lambda) \end{bmatrix}$$

Where,

$$T = \begin{bmatrix} 0.1195 & 0.5494 & -2.429 \times 10^{-2} \\ -0.1361 & 0.4348 & 3.025 \times 10^{-2} \\ 1.250 \times 10^{-5} & -1.049 \times 10^{-5} & 7.227 \times 10^{-3} \end{bmatrix}$$

Where, T is obtained by minimizing the least squares errors between the approximation obtained by (previous equation) and the true $l(\lambda)$, $m(\lambda)$, $s(\lambda)$ functions. Substituting this transformation into

$$((\mathrm{ds})^2 = (a^2\,\alpha^2 + u_1^2 + u_2^2)\left[\frac{dL}{L}\right]^2 + (a^2\,\beta^2 + u_1^2)\left[\frac{dM}{M}\right]^2 + u_2^2\left[\frac{dS}{S}\right]^2 + 2(a^2\,\alpha\beta - u_1^2)\left[\frac{dL}{L}\right]\left[\frac{dM}{M}\right] - 2u_2^2\left[\frac{dL}{L}\right]\left[\frac{dS}{S}\right])$$

determines the desired line element expressed by:

$$(ds)^2 = (dx)^2 \left\{ \left(a^2\alpha^2 + u_1^2 + u_2^2\right)\left(\frac{P_{11}}{L}\right)^2 + \left(a^2\beta^2 + u_1^2\right)\left(\frac{P_{21}}{L}\right)^2 + u_2^2\left(\frac{P_{31}}{S}\right)^2 \right.$$

$$\left. + 2\left(a^2\alpha\beta + u_1^2\right)\left(\frac{P_{11}}{L}\right)\left(\frac{P_{21}}{M}\right) - 2u_2^2\left(\frac{P_{11}}{L}\right)\left(\frac{P_{31}}{S}\right) \right\}$$

$$+ dx\,dy \left\{ \left(a^2\alpha^2 + u_1^2 + u_2^2\right)\left(\frac{P_{11}P_{12}}{L^2}\right) + \left(a^2\beta^2 + u_1^2\right)\left(\frac{P_{21}P_{22}}{M^2}\right) \right.$$

$$\left. + u_2^2\left(\frac{P_{31}P_{32}}{S^2}\right) + \left(a^2\alpha\beta + u_1^2\right)\left(\frac{P_{11}P_{22} + P_{12}P_{21}}{LM}\right) - u_2^2\left(\frac{P_{11}P_{32} + P_{12}P_{31}}{LS}\right) \right\}$$

$$+ (dy)^2 \left\{ \left(a^2\alpha^2 + u_1^2 + u_2^2\right)\left(\frac{P_{12}}{L}\right)^2 + \left(a^2\beta^2 + u_1^2\right)\left(\frac{P_{22}}{M}\right)^2 \right.$$

$$\left. + u_2^2\left(\frac{P_{32}}{S}\right)^2 + 2\left(a^2\alpha\beta + u_1^2\right)\left(\frac{P_{12}}{L}\right)\left(\frac{P_{22}}{M}\right) - 2u_2^2\left(\frac{P_{12}}{L}\right)\left(\frac{P_{32}}{S}\right) \right\}$$

Where,

$$P_{11} = \frac{Y}{y}\left(t_{11} - t_{13}\right)$$

$$P_{12} = \left[\frac{Y}{y^2}\left(t_{13} - t_{11}\right) - t_{13}\right]$$

$$P_{21} = \frac{Y}{y}\left(t_{21} - t_{23}\right)$$

$$P_{22} = \left[\frac{Y}{y^2}\left(t_{23} - t_{21}\right) - t_{23}\right]$$

$$P_{31} = \frac{Y}{y}\left(t_{31} - t_{33}\right)$$

$$P_{32} = \left[\frac{Y}{y^2}\left(t_{33} - t_{31}\right) - t_{33}\right]$$

Equation (previous) may be used to compute loci of constant ds around given points of chromaticity (x, y) for a constant level of luminance Y. Such loci are ellipses in the chromaticity diagram and circles in C_1C_2 space. If the positions of the given chromaticity points are appropriately chosen, a direct comparison of the computed ellipses with those measured by MacAdam can be made. It is assumed that chromaticity and brightness errors are independent, enabling us to optimize a and u_1u_2 independently. The optimization procedure for a is based on work by Brown and MacAdam and is detailed in . Optimization of parameters u_1u_2 is performed by mapping MacAdam's ellipses into C_1C_2 space and then computing the values for u_1u_2 which result in their least squares best fit with circles of radius 1/3. Figures give plots of MacAdam's ellipses and the corresponding ellipses predicted by the line element, respectively. There is a general similarity between the two sets of ellipses. The orientations of the ellipses correspond well, and their areas also show a reasonable correlation. The optimized values for a, u_1, u_2 are 22.6, 41.6 and 10.5, respectively.

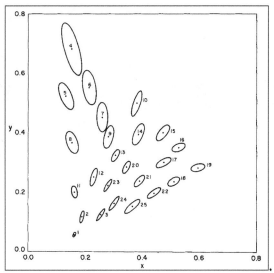

MacAdam ellipses in CIE space.

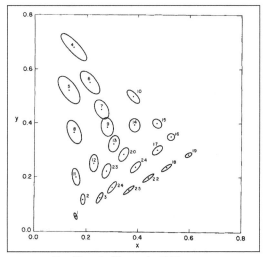

Predicted ellipses in CIE space.

Luo and Rigg have recently computed the chromaticity-discrimination ellipses for surface colors and provide an interesting discussion of their results. Due to the various errors in their original data, these ellipses were not used for the optimization.

Model Implementation

The previous description and analysis of the color model on which the system is to be based is only a theoretical one without any reference to practical considerations. The success or failure of the model is critically linked to the realizability of the CIE curves or cone sensitivity functions.

It has been decided to implement the CIE curves from which the LMS and AC1C 2 coordinates may be obtained. Due to the high cost of having the $x(\lambda)$, $y(\lambda)$, $z(\lambda)$ filters made for our particular vidicon camera a set of four standard filters have been purchased which approximate the desired responses. Two Kodak Wratten filters, f47 and f98, are used to approximate the $z(\lambda)$ and short wavelength part of the $x(\lambda)$ curves. They will be referred to as $b(\lambda)$ and $r_1(\lambda)$, respectively. Two additional Schott glass filters, VG9 and OG55, are used to approximate $y(\lambda)$ and the long wavelength part of the $x(\lambda)$ curves, to be referred to as $g(\lambda)$ and $r_2(\lambda)$, respectively. The camera response must also be taken into account. It should be noted that all of the aforementioned filters and the camera's spectral response are quite sensitive in the near infrared region. This is not an acceptable characteristic since none of the CIE curves have this property. An infrared absorbing filter from Schott, KG5, has therefore been used to eliminate this unwanted light. The resulting (r_1, r_2, g, b) curves after adjusting for the camera response and the infrared filtering are plotted in figure.

A linear transformation from R1R2GB space to XYZ space is now required and expressed by:

$$x(\lambda)=m_{11}r_1(\lambda)+m_{12}r_2(\lambda)+m_{13}g(\lambda)+m_{14}b(\lambda)$$
$$x(\lambda)=m_{21}r_1(\lambda)+m_{22}r_2(\lambda)+m_{23}g(\lambda)+m_{24}b(\lambda)$$
$$x(\lambda)=m_{31}r_1(\lambda)+m_{32}r_2(\lambda)+m_{33}g(\lambda)+m_{34}b(\lambda)$$

Where, m_{ij} are constants. Multiplying both sides by $p(\lambda)$, the spectral energy distribution of the source, and integrating over the wavelength limits yields,

$$\begin{bmatrix} X \\ Y \\ Z \end{bmatrix} = \begin{bmatrix} m_{11} & m_{12} & m_{13} & m_{14} \\ m_{21} & m_{22} & m_{23} & m_{24} \\ m_{31} & m_{32} & m_{33} & m_{34} \end{bmatrix} \begin{bmatrix} R_1 \\ R_2 \\ G \\ B \end{bmatrix}$$

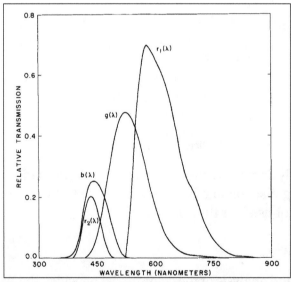

Spectral characteristics of $r_1 r_2$ gb appropriate adjustments.

Pratt suggests two strategies for determining the estimated tristimulus values XYZ for the sensor signals R_1R_2GB. One approach, method one, is to select four key colors and then compute the coefficients m_{ij} that result in exact colorimetric reproduction of the key colors. Then, hopefully, any other arbitrary color will not depart substantially from its true colorimetric values. The colors that are generally reproduced with the greatest error in chromaticity are the highly saturated colors. Therefore with saturated test colors C_i of known tristimulus values $R_1R_2G_iB_i$ and $X_iY_iZ_i$, four matrix equations are formed,

$$\begin{bmatrix} X_i \\ Y_i \\ Z_i \end{bmatrix} = \begin{bmatrix} m_{11} & m_{12} & m_{13} & m_{14} \\ m_{21} & m_{22} & m_{23} & m_{24} \\ m_{31} & m_{32} & m_{33} & m_{34} \end{bmatrix} \begin{bmatrix} R_{1i} \\ R_{2i} \\ G_i \\ B_i \end{bmatrix}, \quad i=1,2,3,4.$$

Equation (previous) may then be solved simultaneously for the coefficients m_{ij}.

Four calibration tiles of the three primary colors, red, green, blue, as well as grey have been used for this purpose. Through numerical methods, the reflectivities of the tiles without the effect of an illuminant as well as a tungsten lamp at a temperature of 3400 °K have been computed. It was decided to use this lamp as the source for the system since illuminant D_{65} could not be practically implemented and illuminant A lacks in power at short wavelengths and has a great deal of power at long wavelengths.

After numerically computing the XYZ tristimulus values of the four tiles as well as its R_1R_2GB coordinates with the tungsten lamp as the illuminant, previous equation are solved yielding the matrix M. It was noted that this method is very sensitive to noise since an incorrect value for one of the tristimulus values can produce quite erroneous results.

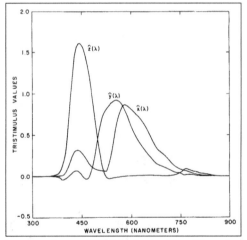

Approximation to CIE functions x(λ), y(λ), and z(λ).

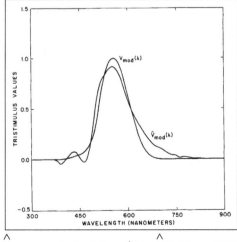

$\hat{V}_{mod}(\lambda)$ derived from $\hat{I}(\lambda)$, $m\,fn(\lambda)$, and $\hat{s}(\lambda)$.

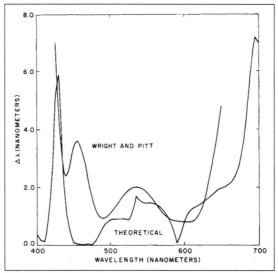

Wavelength discfimination.

Another approach, method two, to the estimation of tristimulus values is to select elements of the transformation matrix M to minimize the mean-square errors of $\hat{x}(\lambda)-x(\lambda)$, $\hat{y}(\lambda)-y(\lambda)$, and $\hat{z}(\lambda)-z(\lambda)$ for all wavelengths. $\hat{x}(\lambda)$, $\hat{y}(\lambda)$, and $\hat{z}(\lambda)$ are the approximated CIE functions estimated by $(x(\lambda)=m_{11}r_1(\lambda)+m_{12}r_2(\lambda)+m_{13}g(\lambda)+m_{14}b(\lambda)$, $x(\lambda)=m_{21}r_1(\lambda)+m_{22}r_2(\lambda)+m_{23}g(\lambda)+m_{24}b(\lambda)$, $x(\lambda)=$ [31] $=m_{31}r_1(\lambda)+m_{32}r_2(\lambda)+m_{33}g(\lambda)+m_{34}b(\lambda))$. The resulting matrix M (Eq. below) produces very good results when compared to the previous method and are plotted in figure,

$$M = \begin{bmatrix} 1.198\times10^{-2} & 1.106\times10^{-2} & 1.263\times10^{-3} & 3.593\times10^{-3} \\ 4.480\times10^{-3} & 3.771\times10^{-2} & 1.733\times10^{-2} & -2.955\times10^{-2} \\ 2.348\times10^{-4} & 1.892\times10^{-4} & -7.112\times10^{-4} & 6.380\times10^{-2} \end{bmatrix}$$

These approximation affect the color vision model as well as its predictions. Figure compares the true luminous efficiency function with that predicted using the approximations to x(λ), y(λ), and z(λ). The new values for α and β are 0.6782 and 0.3218, respectively. Figure compares the data reported by Wright and Pitt with that predicted by the approximation, in terms of wavelength discrimination for a constant small-step brightness. As noted by these plots the model has been significantly disrupted although it is still crudely consistent with experimental observations.

COLOR MANAGEMENT

In digital imaging systems, color management (or color management) is the controlled conversion between the color representations of various devices, such as image scanners, digital cameras, monitors, TV screens, film printers, computer printers, offset presses, and corresponding media.

The primary goal of color management is to obtain a good match across color devices; for example, the colors of one frame of a video should appear the same on a computer LCD monitor, on a plasma

TV screen, and as a printed poster. Color management helps to achieve the same appearance on all of these devices, provided the devices are capable of delivering the needed color intensities. With photography it is often critical that prints or online gallery appear how they were intended. Color management cannot guarantee identical color reproduction, as this is rarely possible, but it can at least give more control over any changes which may occur.

Parts of this technology are implemented in the operating system (OS), helper libraries, the application, and devices. A cross-platform view of color management is the use of an ICC-compatible color management system. The International Color Consortium (ICC) is an industry consortium that has defined:

- An open standard for a Color Matching Module (CMM) at the OS level,
- Color profiles for:
  - Devices, including devicelink-profiles that represent a complete color transformation from source device to target device,
  - Working spaces, the color spaces in which color data is meant to be manipulated.

There are other approaches to color management besides using ICC profiles. This is partly due to history and partly because of other needs than the ICC standard covers. The film and broadcasting industries make use of some of the same concepts, but they frequently rely on more limited boutique solutions. The film industry, for instance, often uses 3D LUTs (lookup table) to represent a complete color transformation for a specific RGB encoding. At the consumer level, color management currently applies more to still images than video, in which color management is still in its infancy.

Color Profiles

Embedding

Image formats themselves (such as TIFF, JPEG, PNG, EPS, PDF, and SVG) may contain embedded color profiles but are not required to do so by the image format. The International Color Consortium standard was created to bring various developers and manufacturers together. The ICC standard permits the exchange of output device characteristics and color spaces in the form of metadata. This allows the embedding of color profiles into images as well as storing them in a database or a profile directory.

Working Spaces

Working spaces, such as sRGB, Adobe RGB or ProPhoto are color spaces that facilitate good results while editing. For instance, pixels with equal values of R, G, B should appear neutral. Using a large (gamut) working space will lead to posterization, while using a small working space will lead to clipping. This trade-off is a consideration for the critical image editor.

Color Transformation

Color transformation, or color space conversion, is the transformation of the representation of a color from one color space to another. This calculation is required whenever data is exchanged inside a color-managed chain and carried out by a Color Matching Module. Transforming profiled color information to different output devices is achieved by referencing the profile data into a standard color space. It makes it easier to convert colors from one device to a selected standard color space and from that to the colors of another device. By ensuring that the reference color space covers the many possible colors that humans can see, this concept allows one to exchange colors between many different color output devices. Color transformations can be represented by two profiles (source profile and target profile) or by a devicelink profile. In this process there are approximations involved which make sure that the image keeps its important color qualities and also gives an opportunity to control on how the colors are being changed.

Profile Connection Space

In the terminology of the International Color Consortium, a translation between two color spaces can go through a profile connection space (PCS): Color Space 1 → PCS (CIELAB or CIEXYZ) → Color space 2; conversions into and out of the PCS are each specified by a profile.

Gamut Mapping

In nearly every translation process, we have to deal with the fact that the color gamut of different devices vary in range which makes an accurate reproduction impossible. They therefore need some rearrangement near the borders of the gamut. Some colors must be shifted to the inside of the gamut, as they otherwise cannot be represented on the output device and would simply be clipped. This so-called gamut mismatch occurs for example, when we translate from the RGB color space with a wider gamut into the CMYK color space with a narrower gamut range. In this example, the dark highly saturated purplish-blue color of a typical computer monitor's "blue" primary is impossible to print on paper with a typical CMYK printer. The nearest approximation within the printer's gamut will be much less saturated. Conversely, an inkjet printer's "cyan" primary, a saturated mid-brightness blue, is outside the gamut of a typical computer monitor. The color management system can utilize various methods to achieve desired results and give experienced users control of the gamut mapping behavior.

Rendering Intent

When the gamut of source color space exceeds that of the destination, saturated colors are liable to become clipped (inaccurately represented), or more formally burned. The color management module can deal with this problem in several ways. The ICC specification includes four different rendering intents, listed below. Before the actual rendering intent is carried out, one can temporarily simulate the rendering by soft proofing. It is a useful tool as it predicts the outcome of the colors and is available as an application in many color management systems:

1. Absolute colorimetric

Absolute colorimetry and relative colorimetry actually use the same table but differ in the adjustment for the white point media. If the output device has a much larger gamut than the source profile, i.e., all the colors in the source can be represented in the output, using the absolute colorimetry rendering intent would ideally (ignoring noise, precision, etc.) give an exact output of the specified CIELAB values. Perceptually, the colors may appear incorrect, but instrument measurements of the resulting output would match the source. Colors outside of the proof print system's possible color are mapped to the boundary of the color gamut.

Absolute colorimetry is useful to get an exact specified color (e.g., IBM blue), or to quantify the accuracy of mapping methods.

2. Relative colorimetric

The goal in relative colorimetry is to be truthful to the specified color, with only a correction for the media. Relative colorimetry is useful in proofing applications, since it can be used to get an idea of how a print on one device will appear on a different device. Media differences are the only thing that one really should adjust for, although some gamut mapping also needs to be applied. Usually this is done in a way where hue and lightness are maintained at the cost of reduced saturation.

Relative colorimetric is the default rendering intent on most systems.

3. Perceptual and Saturation

The perceptual and saturation intents are where the results really depend upon the profile maker. This is even how some of the competitors in this market differentiate themselves. These intents should be created by the profile maker so that pleasing images occur with the perceptual intent while eye-catching business graphics occur with the saturation intent. This is achieved through the use of different perceptual remaps of the data as well as different gamut mapping methods.

Perceptual rendering is recommended for color separation.

In practice, photographers almost always use relative or perceptual intent, as for natural images, absolute causes color cast, while saturation produces unnatural colors. Relative intent handles out-of-gamut by clipping (burning) these colors to the edge of the gamut, leaving in-gamut colors unchanged, while perceptual intent smoothly moves out-of-gamut colors into gamut, preserving gradations, but distorts in-gamut colors in the process. If an entire image is in-gamut, relative is perfect, but when there are out of gamut colors, which is preferable depends on a case-by-case basis.

Saturation intent is most useful in charts and diagrams, where there is a discrete palette of colors that the designer wants saturated to make them intense, but where specific hue is less important.

Implementation

Color Management Module

Color matching module (also -method or -system) is a software algorithm that adjusts the numerical values that get sent to or received from different devices so that the perceived color they produce remains consistent. The key issue here is how to deal with a color that cannot be reproduced on a certain device in order to show it through a different device as if it were visually the same color, just as when the reproducible color range between color transparencies and printed matters are different. There is no common method for this process, and the performance depends on the capability of each color matching method.

Some well-known CMMs are ColorSync, Adobe CMM, Little CMS, and ArgyllCMS.

Operating System Level

Apple's classic Mac OS and macOS operating systems have provided OS-level color management APIs since 1993, through ColorSync. macOS has added automatic color management (assuming sRGB for most things) automatically in the OS, and applications have to work around this to provide more accurate color management.

Since 1997 color management in Windows is available through an ICC color management system (ICM). Beginning with Windows Vista, Microsoft introduced a new color architecture known as Windows Color System. WCS supplements the Image Color Management (ICM) system in Windows 2000 and Windows XP, originally written by Heidelberg.

Operating systems that use the X Window System for graphics can use ICC profiles, and support for color management on Linux, still less mature than on other platforms, is coordinated through OpenICC at freedesktop.org and makes use of LittleCMS.

File Level

Certain image file types (TIFF and Photoshop) include the notion of color channels for specifying the color mode of the file. The most commonly used channels are RGB (mainly for display (monitors) but also for some desktop printing) and CMYK (for commercial printing). An additional alpha channel may specify a transparency mask value. Some image software (such as Photoshop) perform automatic color separation to maintain color information in CMYK mode using a specified ICC profile such as US Web Coated (SWOP) v2.

Application Level

As of 2005, most web browsers ignored color profiles. Notable exceptions were Safari, starting with version 2.0, and Firefox starting with version 3. Although disabled by default in Firefox 3.0, ICC v2 and ICC v4 color management could be enabled by using an add-on or setting a configuration option.

As of 2012, notable browser support for color management is:

- Firefox: From version 3.5 enabled by default for ICC v2 tagged images, version 8.0 has ICC v4 profiles support, but it needs to be activated manually.

- Internet Explorer: Version 9 is the first Microsoft browser to partly support ICC profiles, but it does not render images correctly according to the Windows ICC settings (it only converts non-sRGB images to the sRGB profile) and therefore provides no real color management at all.

- Google Chrome: Uses the system provided ICC v2 and v4 support on macOS, and from version 22 supports ICC v2 profiles by default on other platforms.

- Safari: Has support starting with version 2.0.

- Opera: Has support since 12.10 for ICC v4.

- Pale Moon supported ICC v2 from its first release, and v4 since Pale Moon 20.2 (2013).

ICC Profile

In color management, an ICC profile is a set of data that characterizes a color input or output device, or a color space, according to standards promulgated by the International Color Consortium (ICC). Profiles describe the color attributes of a particular device or viewing requirement by defining a mapping between the device source or target color space and a profile connection space (PCS). This PCS is either CIELAB (L*a*b*) or CIEXYZ. Mappings may be specified using tables, to which interpolation is applied, or through a series of parameters for transformations.

Every device that captures or displays color can be profiled. Some manufacturers provide profiles for their products, and there are several products that allow an end-user to generate his or her own color profiles, typically through the use of a tristimulus colorimeter or a spectrophotometer (sometimes called a spectrocolorimeter).

The ICC defines the format precisely but does not define algorithms or processing details. This means there is room for variation between different applications and systems that work with ICC profiles. Two main generations are used: the legacy ICCv2 and the December 2001 ICCv4. Since late 2010, the current version of the format specification (ICC.1) is 4.3.

ICC has also published a preliminary specification for iccMAX (ICC.2) or ICCv5, a next-generation color management architecture with significantly expanded functionality and a choice of colorimetric, spectral or material connection space.

To see how this works in practice, suppose we have a particular RGB and CMYK color space, and want to convert from this RGB to that CMYK. The first step is to obtain the two ICC profiles concerned. To perform the conversion, each RGB triplet is first converted to the Profile connection space (PCS) using the RGB profile. If necessary the PCS is converted between CIELAB and CIEXYZ, a well-defined transformation. Then the PCS is converted to the four values of C, M, Y, K required using the second profile.

So a profile is essentially a mapping from a color space to the PCS, and from the PCS to the color space. The profile might do this using tables of color values to be interpolated (separate tables will be needed for the conversion in each direction), or using a series of mathematical formulae.

A profile might define several mappings, according to rendering intent. These mappings allow a choice between closest possible color matching, and remapping the entire color range to allow for different gamuts.

The reference illuminant of the Profile connection space (PCS) is a 16-bit fractional approximation of D50; its white point is XYZ = (0.9642, 1.000, 0.8249). Different source/destination white points are adapted using the Bradford transformation.

Another kind of profile is the device link profile. Instead of mapping between a device color space and a PCS, it maps between two specific device spaces. While this is less flexible, it allows for a more accurate or purposeful conversion of color between devices. For example, a conversion between two CMYK devices could ensure that colors using only black ink convert to target colors using only black ink.

Color Calibration

The aim of color calibration is to measure and adjust the color response of a device (input or output) to a known state. In International Color Consortium (ICC) terms, this is the basis for an additional color characterization of the device and later profiling. In non-ICC workflows, calibration refers sometimes to establishing a known relationship to a standard color space in one go. The device that is to be calibrated is sometimes known as a calibration source; the color space that serves as a standard is sometimes known as a calibration target. Color calibration is a requirement for all devices taking an active part of a color-managed workflow, and is used by many industries, such as television production, gaming, photography, engineering, chemistry, medicine and more.

Information Flow and Output Distortion

Input data can come from device sources like digital cameras, image scanners or any other measuring devices. Those inputs can be either monochrome (in which case only the response curve needs to be calibrated, though in a few select cases one must also specify the color or spectral power distribution that that single channel corresponds to) or specified in multidimensional color - most commonly in the three channel RGB model. Input data is in most cases calibrated against a profile connection space (PCS).

One of the most important factors to consider when dealing with color calibration is having a valid source. If the color measuring source does not match the displays capabilities, the calibration will be ineffective and give false readings.

The main distorting factors on the input stage stem from the amplitude nonlinearity of the channel responses, and in the case of a multidimensional datastream the non-ideal wavelength responses of the individual color separation filters (most commonly a color filter array (CFA)) in combination with the spectral power distribution of the scene illumination.

After this the data is often circulated in the system translated into a working space RGB for viewing and editing.

In the output stage when exporting to a viewing device such as a CRT or LCD screen or a digital projector, the computer sends a signal to the computer's graphic card in the form RGB [Red, Green, Blue]. The dataset [255, 0, 0] signals only a device instruction, not a specific color. This instruction [R, G, B] = [255,0,0] then causes the connected display to show Red at the maximum achievable brightness , while the Green and Blue components of the display remain dark . The resultant color being displayed, however, depends on two main factors:

- The phosphors or another system actually producing a light that falls inside the red spectrum;

- The overall brightness of the color resulting in the desired color perception: an extremely bright light source will always be seen as white, irrespective of spectral composition.

Hence every output device will have its unique color signature, displaying a certain color according to manufacturing tolerances and material deterioration through use and age. If the output device is a printer, additional distorting factors are the qualities of a particular batch of paper and ink.

The conductive qualities and standards-compliance of connecting cables, circuitry and equipment can also alter the electrical signal at any stage in the signal flow. (A partially inserted VGA connector can result in a monochrome display, for example, as some pins are not connected.)

Color Perception

Color perception is subject to ambient light levels, and the ambient white point; for example, a red object looks black in blue light. It is therefore not possible to achieve calibration that will make a device look correct and consistent in all capture or viewing conditions. The computer display and calibration target will have to be considered in controlled, predefined lighting conditions.

Calibration Techniques and Procedures

Calibration Target of the "Mars Hand Lens Imager (MAHLI)"
on the Mars Curiosity rover.

The most common form of calibration aims at adjusting cameras, scanners, monitors and printers for photographic reproduction. The aim is that a printed copy of a photograph appear identical in saturation and dynamic range to the original or a source file on a computer display. This means that three independent calibrations need to be performed:

- The camera or scanner needs a device-specific calibration to represent the original's estimated colors in an unambiguous way.

- The computer display needs a device-specific calibration to reproduce the colors of the image color space.

- The printer needs a device-specific calibration to reproduce the colors of the image color space.

These goals can either be realized via direct value translation from source to target, or by using a common known reference color space as middle ground. In the most commonly used color profile system, ICC, this is known as the PCS or "Profile Connection Space".

Camera

The camera calibration needs a known calibration target to be photographed and the resulting output from the camera to be converted to color values. A correction profile can then be built using the difference between the camera result values and the known reference values. When two or more cameras need to be calibrated relatively to each other, to reproduce the same color values, the technique of color mapping can be used.

Scanner

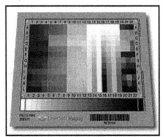

An IT8.7 Target by LaserSoft Imaging.

For creating a scanner profile it needs a target source, such as an IT8-target, an original with many small color fields, which was measured by the developer with a photometer. The scanner reads this original and compares the scanned color values with the target's reference values. Taking the differences of these values into account an ICC profile is created, which relates the device specific color space (RGB color space) to a device independent color space (L*a*b* color space). Thus, the scanner is able to output with color fidelity to what it reads.

Display

Color calibration of a monitor using ColorHug2,
an open source colorimeter, placed on the screen.

For calibrating the monitor a colorimeter is attached flat to the display's surface, shielded from all ambient light. The calibration software sends a series of color signals to the display and compares the values that were actually sent against the readings from the calibration device. This establishes the current offsets in color display. Depending on the calibration software and type of monitor used, the software either creates a correction matrix (i.e. an ICC profile) for color values before being sent to the display, or gives instructions for altering the display's brightness/contrast and RGB values through the OSD. This tunes the display to reproduce fairly accurately the in-gamut part of a desired color space. The calibration target for this kind of calibration is that of print stock paper illuminated by D65 light at 120 cd/m².

Printer

The ICC profile for a printer is created by comparing a test print result using a photometer with the original reference file. The testchart contains known CMYK colors, whose offsets to their actual

L*a*b* colors scanned by the photometer are resulting in an ICC profile. Another possibility to ICC profile a printer is to use a calibrated scanner as the measuring device for the printed CMYK testchart instead of a photometer. A calibration profile is necessary for each printer/paper/ink combination.

COLOR SPACE

A color space is a specific organization of colors. In combination with physical device profiling, it allows for reproducible representations of color, in both analog and digital representations. A color space may be arbitrary, with particular colors assigned to a set of physical color swatches and corresponding assigned color names or numbers (such as with the Pantone collection), or structured mathematically (as with the NCS System, Adobe RGB and sRGB).

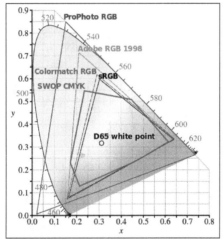

Comparison of some RGB and CMYK color gamuts
on a CIE 1931 xy chromaticity diagram.

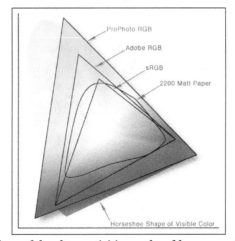

A comparison of the chromaticities enclosed by some color spaces.

A "color model" is an abstract mathematical model describing the way colors can be represented as tuples of numbers (e.g. triples in RGB or quadruples in CMYK); however, a color model with no associated mapping function to an absolute color space is a more or less arbitrary color system with no connection to any globally understood system of color interpretation. Adding a specific mapping function between a color model and a reference color space establishes within the reference color space a definite "footprint", known as a gamut, and for a given color model this defines a color space. For example, Adobe RGB and sRGB are two different absolute color spaces, both based on the RGB color model. When defining a color space, the usual reference standard is the CIELAB or CIEXYZ color spaces, which were specifically designed to encompass all colors the average human can see.

Since "color space" identifies a particular combination of the color model and the mapping function, the word is often used informally to identify a color model. However, even though identifying a color space automatically identifies the associated color model, this usage is incorrect in a strict sense. For example, although several specific color spaces are based on the RGB color model, there is no such thing as the singular RGB color space.

Examples:

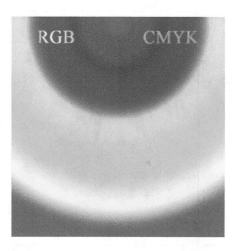

A comparison of CMYK and RGB color models. This image demonstrates the difference between how colors will look on a computer monitor (RGB) compared to how they will reproduce in a CMYK print process.

Colors can be created in printing with color spaces based on the CMYK color model, using the subtractive primary colors of pigment (cyan, magenta, yellow, and black). To create a three-dimensional representation of a given color space, we can assign the amount of magenta color to the representation's X axis, the amount of cyan to its Y axis, and the amount of yellow to its Z axis. The resulting 3-D space provides a unique position for every possible color that can be created by combining those three pigments.

Colors can be created on computer monitors with color spaces based on the RGB color model, using the additive primary colors (red, green, and blue). A three-dimensional representation would assign each of the three colors to the X, Y, and Z axes. Note that colors generated on given monitor will be limited by the reproduction medium, such as the phosphor (in a CRT monitor) or filters and backlight (LCD monitor).

Another way of creating colors on a monitor is with an HSL or HSV color space, based on hue, saturation, brightness (value/brightness). With such a space, the variables are assigned to cylindrical coordinates.

Many color spaces can be represented as three-dimensional values in this manner, but some have more, or fewer dimensions, and some, such as Pantone, cannot be represented in this way at all.

Conversion

Color space conversion is the translation of the representation of a color from one basis to another. This typically occurs in the context of converting an image that is represented in one color space to another color space, the goal being to make the translated image look as similar as possible to the original.

RGB Density

The RGB color model is implemented in different ways, depending on the capabilities of the system used. By far the most common general-used incarnation as of 2006 is the 24-bit implementation, with 8 bits, or 256 discrete levels of color per channel. Any color space based on such a 24-bit RGB model is thus limited to a range of 256×256×256 ≈ 16.7 million colors. Some implementations use 16 bits per component for 48 bits total, resulting in the same gamut with a larger number of distinct colors. This is especially important when working with wide-gamut color spaces (where most of the more common colors are located relatively close together), or when a large number of digital filtering algorithms are used consecutively. The same principle applies for any color space based on the same color model, but implemented in different bit depths.

Lists

CIE 1931 XYZ color space was one of the first attempts to produce a color space based on measurements of human color perception (earlier efforts were by James Clerk Maxwell, König & Dieterici, and Abney at Imperial College) and it is the basis for almost all other color spaces. The CIERGB color space is a linearly-related companion of CIE XYZ. Additional derivatives of CIE XYZ include the CIELUV, CIEUVW, and CIELAB.

Generic

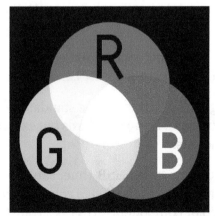

Additive color mixing: Three overlapping light bulbs
in a vacuum, adding together to create white.

RGB uses additive color mixing, because it describes what kind of light needs to be emitted to produce a given color. RGB stores individual values for red, green and blue. RGBA is RGB with an additional channel, alpha, to indicate transparency.

Common color spaces based on the RGB model include sRGB, Adobe RGB, ProPhoto RGB, scRGB, and CIE RGB.

CMYK uses subtractive color mixing used in the printing process, because it describes what kinds of inks need to be applied so the light reflected from the substrate and through the inks produces a given color. One starts with a white substrate (canvas, page, etc.), and uses ink to subtract color from white to create an image. CMYK stores ink values for cyan, magenta, yellow and black. There are many CMYK color spaces for different sets of inks, substrates, and press characteristics (which change the dot gain or transfer function for each ink and thus change the appearance).

Subtractive color mixing: Three splotches of paint on white paper, subtracting together to turn the paper black.

YIQ was formerly used in NTSC (North America, Japan and elsewhere) television broadcasts for historical reasons. This system stores a luma value roughly analogous to (and sometimes incorrectly identified as) luminance, along with two chroma values as approximate representations of the relative amounts of blue and red in the color. It is similar to the YUV scheme used in most video capture systems and in PAL (Australia, Europe, except France, which uses SECAM) television, except that the YIQ color space is rotated 33° with respect to the YUV color space and the color axes are swapped. The YDbDr scheme used by SECAM television is rotated in another way.

YPbPr is a scaled version of YUV. It is most commonly seen in its digital form, YCbCr, used widely in video and image compression schemes such as MPEG and JPEG.

xvYCC is a new international digital video color space standard published by the IEC (IEC 61966-2-4). It is based on the ITU BT.601 and BT.709 standards but extends the gamut beyond the R/G/B primaries specified in those standards.

HSV (hue, saturation, value), also known as HSB (hue, saturation, brightness) is often used by artists because it is often more natural to think about a color in terms of hue and saturation than in terms of additive or subtractive color components. HSV is a transformation of an RGB color space, and its components and colorimetry are relative to the RGB color space from which it was derived.

HSL (hue, saturation, lightness/luminance), also known as HLS or HSI (hue, saturation, intensity) is quite similar to HSV, with "lightness" replacing "brightness". The difference is that the brightness of a pure color is equal to the brightness of white, while the lightness of a pure color is equal to the lightness of a medium gray.

Commercial

- Munsell color system

- Pantone Matching System (PMS)

- Natural Color System (NCS)

Special-purpose

- The RG Chromaticity space is used in computer vision applications. It shows the color of light (red, yellow, green etc.), but not its intensity (dark, bright).

- The TSL color space (Tint, Saturation and Luminance) is used in face detection.

Obsolete

Early color spaces had two components. They largely ignored blue light because the added complexity of a 3-component process provided only a marginal increase in fidelity when compared to the jump from monochrome to 2-component color:

- RG for early Technicolor film

- RGK for early color printing

Absolute Color Space

In color science, there are two meanings of the term absolute color space:

- A color space in which the perceptual difference between colors is directly related to distances between colors as represented by points in the color space.

- A color space in which colors are unambiguous, that is, where the interpretations of colors in the space are colorimetrically defined without reference to external factors.

In this topic, we concentrate on the second definition.

CIEXYZ, sRGB, and ICtCp are examples of absolute color spaces, as opposed to a generic RGB color space.

A non-absolute color space can be made absolute by defining its relationship to absolute colorimetric quantities. For instance, if the red, green, and blue colors in a monitor are measured exactly, together with other properties of the monitor, then RGB values on that monitor can be considered as absolute. The L*a*b* is sometimes referred to as absolute, though it also needs a white point specification to make it so.

A popular way to make a color space like RGB into an absolute color is to define an ICC profile, which contains the attributes of the RGB. This is not the only way to express an absolute color, but it is the standard in many industries. RGB colors defined by widely accepted profiles include sRGB and Adobe RGB. The process of adding an ICC profile to a graphic or document is sometimes called tagging or embedding; tagging therefore marks the absolute meaning of colors in that graphic or document.

Conversion

A color in one absolute color space can be converted into another absolute color space, and back again, in general; however, some color spaces may have gamut limitations, and converting colors that lie outside that gamut will not produce correct results. There are also likely to be rounding errors, especially if the popular range of only 256 distinct values per component (8-bit color) is used.

One part of the definition of an absolute color space is the viewing conditions. The same color, viewed under different natural or artificial lighting conditions, will look different. Those involved professionally with color matching may use viewing rooms, lit by standardized lighting.

Occasionally, there are precise rules for converting between non-absolute color spaces. For example, HSL and HSV spaces are defined as mappings of RGB. Both are non-absolute, but the conversion between them should maintain the same color. However, in general, converting between two non-absolute color spaces (for example, RGB to CMYK) or between absolute and non-absolute color spaces (for example, RGB to L*a*b*) is almost a meaningless concept.

Arbitrary Spaces

A different method of defining absolute color spaces is familiar to many consumers as the swatch card, used to select paint, fabrics, and the like. This is a way of agreeing a color between two parties. A more standardized method of defining absolute colors is the Pantone Matching System, a proprietary system that includes swatch cards and recipes that commercial printers can use to make inks that are a particular color.

CIE 1931 Color Space

The International Commission on Illumination - commonly abbreviated as CIE (from its French name, "Commission internationale de l'éclairage") - is an organization founded in 1913 that creates international standards related to light and color. CIE 1931 color spaces were the first defined quantitative links between distributions of wavelengths in the electromagnetic visible spectrum, and physiologically perceived colors in human color vision. The mathematical relationships that define these color spaces are essential tools for color management, important when dealing with color inks, illuminated displays, and recording devices such as digital cameras.

The CIE 1931 RGB color space and CIE 1931 XYZ color space were created by the International Commission on Illumination (CIE) in 1931. They resulted from a series of experiments done in the late 1920s by William David Wright using ten observers and John Guild using seven observers. The experimental results were combined into the specification of the CIE RGB color space, from which the CIE XYZ color space was derived.

The CIE 1931 color spaces are still widely used, as is the 1976 CIELUV color space.

Tristimulus Values

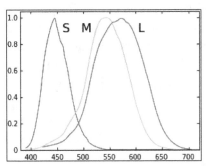

The normalized spectral sensitivity of human cone cells of
short-, middle- and long-wavelength types.

The human eye with normal vision has three kinds of cone cells that sense light, having peaks of spectral sensitivity in short ("S", 420 nm – 440 nm), middle ("M", 530 nm – 540 nm), and long ("L", 560 nm – 580 nm) wavelengths. These cone cells underlie human color perception in conditions of medium and high brightness; in very dim light color vision diminishes, and the low-brightness, monochromatic "night vision" receptors, denominated "rod cells", become effective. Thus, three parameters corresponding to levels of stimulus of the three kinds of cone cells, in principle describe any human color sensation. Weighting a total light power spectrum by the individual spectral sensitivities of the three kinds of cone cells renders three effective values of stimulus; these three values compose a tristimulus specification of the objective color of the light spectrum. The three parameters, denoted "S", "M", and "L", are indicated using a 3-dimensional space denominated the "LMS color space", which is one of many color spaces devised to quantify human color vision.

A color space maps a range of physically produced colors from mixed light, pigments, etc. to an objective description of color sensations registered in the human eye, typically in terms of tristimulus values, but not usually in the LMS color space defined by the spectral sensitivities of the cone cells. The tristimulus values associated with a color space can be conceptualized as amounts of three primary colors in a tri-chromatic, additive color model. In some color spaces, including the LMS and XYZ spaces, the primary colors used are not real colors in the sense that they cannot be generated in any light spectrum.

The CIE XYZ color space encompasses all color sensations that are visible to a person with average eyesight. That is why CIE XYZ (Tristimulus values) is a device-invariant representation of color. It serves as a standard reference against which many other color spaces are defined. A set of color-matching functions, like the spectral sensitivity curves of the LMS color space, but not restricted to non-negative sensitivities, associates physically produced light spectra with specific tristimulus values.

Consider two light sources composed of different mixtures of various wavelengths. Such light sources may appear to be the same color; this effect is denominated "metamerism". Such light sources have the same apparent color to an observer when they produce the same tristimulus values, regardless of the spectral power distributions of the sources.

Most wavelengths stimulate two or all three kinds of cone cell because the spectral sensitivity curves of the three kinds overlap. Certain tristimulus values are thus physically impossible, for example LMS tristimulus values those are non-zero for the M component and zero for both the L and S components. Furthermore, LMS tristimulus values for pure spectral colors would, in any normal trichromatic additive color space, e. g. the RGB color spaces, imply negative values for at least one of the three primaries because the chromaticity would be outside the color triangle defined by the primary colors. To avoid these negative RGB values, and to have one component that describes the perceived brightness, "imaginary" primary colors and corresponding color-matching functions were formulated. The CIE 1931 color space defines the resulting tristimulus values, in which they are denoted by "X", "Y", and "Z". In XYZ space, all combinations of non-negative coordinates are meaningful, but many, such as the primary locations [1, 0, 0], [0, 1, 0], and [0, 0, 1], correspond to imaginary colors outside the space of possible LMS coordinates; imaginary colors do not correspond to any spectral distribution of wavelengths and therefore have no physical reality.

Meaning of X, Y and Z

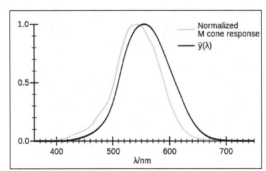

A comparison between a typical normalized M cone's spectral sensitivity and
the CIE 1931 luminosity function for a standard observer in photopic vision.

When judging the relative luminance (brightness) of different colors in well-lit situations, humans tend to perceive light within the green parts of the spectrum as brighter than red or blue light of equal power. The luminosity function that describes the perceived brightnesses of different wavelengths is thus roughly analogous to the spectral sensitivity of M cones.

The CIE model capitalizes on this fact by setting Y as luminance. Z is quasi-equal to blue, or the S cone response, and X is a mix of response curves chosen to be nonnegative. The XYZ tristimulus values are thus analogous to, but different from, the LMS cone responses of the human eye. Setting Y as luminance has the useful result that for any given Y value, the XZ plane will contain all possible chromaticities at that luminance.

The unit of the tristimulus values X, Y, and Z is often arbitrarily chosen so that $Y = 1$ or $Y = 100$ is the brightest white that a color display supports. In this case, the Y value is known as the relative luminance. The corresponding whitepoint values for X and Z can then be inferred using the standard illuminants.

CIE Standard Observer

Due to the distribution of cones in the eye, the tristimulus values depend on the observer's field of view. To eliminate this variable, the CIE defined a color-mapping function called the standard (colorimetric) observer, to represent an average human's chromatic response within a 2° arc inside the fovea. This angle was chosen owing to the belief that the color-sensitive cones resided within a 2° arc of the fovea. Thus the CIE 1931 Standard Observer function is also known as the CIE 1931 2° Standard Observer. A more modern but less-used alternative is the CIE 1964 10° Standard Observer, which is derived from the work of Stiles and Burch, and Speranskaya.

For the 10° experiments, the observers were instructed to ignore the central 2° spot. The 1964 Supplementary Standard Observer function is recommended when dealing with more than about a 4° field of view. Both standard observer functions are discretized at 5 nm wavelength intervals from 380 nm to 780 nm and distributed by the CIE. All corresponding values have been calculated from experimentally obtained data using interpolation. The standard observer is characterized by three color matching functions.

The derivation of the CIE standard observer from color matching experiments is given below, after the description of the CIE RGB space.

Color Matching Functions

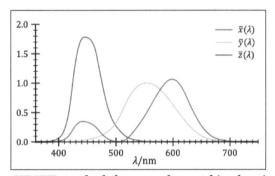

The CIE XYZ standard observer color matching functions.

The CIE's color matching functions $\bar{x}(\lambda)$, $\bar{y}(\lambda)$ and $\bar{z}(\lambda)$ are the numerical description of the chromatic response of the observer (described above). They can be thought of as the spectral sensitivity curves of three linear light detectors yielding the CIE tristimulus values X, Y and Z. Collectively, these three functions are known as the CIE standard observer.

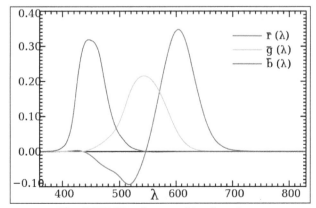

The CIE RGB color matching functions.

The CIE XYZ color matching functions can be approximated analytically, tristimulusXYZfromÅngstrøms λ = map(sum.map(stimulus))[

[[1056,5998,379,310],[362,4420,160,267],[-65,5011,204,262]],

[[821,5688,469,405],[286,5309,163,311]],

[[1217,4370,118,360],[681,4590,260,138]]]

where stimulus[α,μ,ς,σ]=α/1000*exp(-((λ-μ)/if λ<μ then ς else σ)^2/2)

The CIE XYZ color matching functions are nonnegative, and lead to nonnegative XYZ coordinates for all real colors (that is, for nonnegative light spectra). Other observers, such as for the CIE RGB space or other RGB color spaces, are defined by other sets of three color-matching functions, not generally nonnegative, and lead to tristimulus values in those other spaces, which may include negative coordinates for some real colors.

Computing XYZ from Spectral Data

Emissive Case

The tristimulus values for a color with a spectral radiance $L_{e,\Omega,\lambda}$ are given in terms of the standard observer by:

$$X = \int_\lambda L_{e,\Omega,\lambda}(\lambda)\,\bar{x}(\lambda)\,d\lambda$$

$$Y = \int_\lambda L_{e,\Omega,\lambda}(\lambda)\,\bar{y}(\lambda)\,d\lambda$$

$$Z = \int_\lambda L_{e,\Omega,\lambda}(\lambda)\,\bar{z}(\lambda)\,d\lambda$$

Where λ is the wavelength of the equivalent monochromatic light (measured in nanometers), and customary limits of the integral are $\lambda \in [380,780]$.

The values of X, Y, and Z are bounded if the radiance spectrum $L_{e,\Omega,\lambda}$ is bounded.

Reflective and Transmissive Cases

The reflective and transmissive cases are very similar to the emissive case, with a few differences. The spectral radiance $L_{e,\Omega,\lambda}$ is replaced by the spectral reflectance (or transmittance) S(λ) of the object being measured, multiplied by the spectral power distribution of the illuminant I(λ).

$$X = \frac{K}{N}\int_\lambda S(\lambda)\,I(\lambda)\,\bar{x}(\lambda)\,d\lambda,$$

$$Y = \frac{K}{N}\int_\lambda S(\lambda)\,I(\lambda)\,\bar{y}(\lambda)\,d\lambda,$$

$$Z = \frac{K}{N}\int_\lambda S(\lambda)\,I(\lambda)\,\bar{z}(\lambda)\,d\lambda,$$

Where,

$$N = \int_{\lambda} I(\lambda)\,\bar{y}(\lambda)\,d\lambda,$$

K is a scaling factor (usually 1 or 100), and λ is the wavelength of the equivalent monochromatic light (measured in nanometers), and the standard limits of the integral are $\lambda \in [380,780]$.

CIE xy Chromaticity Diagram and the CIE xyY Color Space

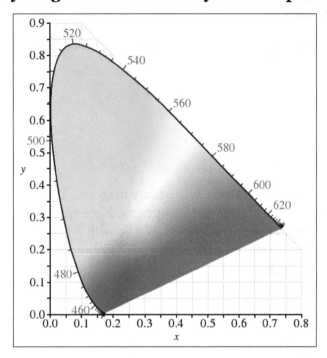

Figure shows, the CIE 1931 color space chromaticity diagram. The outer curved boundary is the spectral (or monochromatic) locus, with wavelengths shown in nanometers. Note that the colors your screen displays in this image are specified using sRGB, so the colors outside the sRGB gamut are not displayed properly. Depending on the color space and calibration of your display device, the sRGB colors may not be displayed properly either. This diagram displays the maximally saturated bright colors that can be produced by a computer monitor or television set.

Since the human eye has three types of color sensors that respond to different ranges of wavelengths, a full plot of all visible colors is a three-dimensional figure. However, the concept of color can be divided into two parts: brightness and chromaticity. For example, the color white is a bright color, while the color grey is considered to be a less bright version of that same white. In other words, the chromaticity of white and grey are the same while their brightness differs.

The CIE XYZ color space was deliberately designed so that the Y parameter is a measure of the luminance of a color. The chromaticity is then specified by the two derived parameters x and y, two of the three normalized values being functions of all three tristimulus values X, Y, and Z.

$$x = \frac{X}{X+Y+Z}$$

$$y = \frac{Y}{X+Y+Z}$$

$$z = \frac{Z}{X+Y+Z} = 1-x-y$$

The derived color space specified by x, y, and Y is known as the CIE xyY color space and is widely used to specify colors in practice.

The X and Z tristimulus values can be calculated back from the chromaticity values x and y and the Y tristimulus value:

$$X = \frac{Y}{y}x,$$

$$Z = \frac{Y}{y}(1-x-y)$$

The figure on the right shows the related chromaticity diagram. The outer curved boundary is the spectral locus, with wavelengths shown in nanometers. Note that the chromaticity diagram is a tool to specify how the human eye will experience light with a given spectrum. It cannot specify colors of objects (or printing inks), since the chromaticity observed while looking at an object depends on the light source as well.

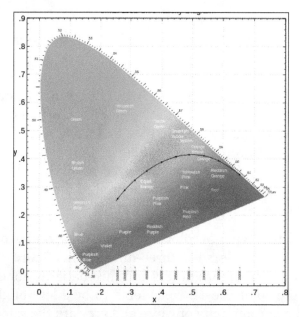

Figure shows the CIE 1931 color space chromaticity diagram rendered in terms of the colors of lower saturation and value than those displayed in the diagram above that can be produced by pigments, such as those used in printing. The color names are from the Munsell color system. The solid curve with dots on it, through the middle, is the Planckian locus, with the dots corresponding to a few select black-body temperatures that are indicated just above the x-axis.

Mathematically the colors of the chromaticity diagram occupy a region of the real projective plane.

The chromaticity diagram illustrates a number of interesting properties of the CIE XYZ color space:

- The diagram represents all of the chromaticities visible to the average person. These are shown in color and this region is called the gamut of human vision. The gamut of all visible chromaticities on the CIE plot is the tongue-shaped or horseshoe-shaped figure shown in color. The curved edge of the gamut is called the spectral locus and corresponds to monochromatic light (each point representing a pure hue of a single wavelength), with wavelengths listed in nanometers. The straight edge on the lower part of the gamut is called the line of purples. These colors, although they are on the border of the gamut, have no counterpart in monochromatic light. Less saturated colors appear in the interior of the figure with white at the center.

- It is seen that all visible chromaticities correspond to non-negative values of x, y, and z (and therefore to non-negative values of X, Y, and Z).

- If one chooses any two points of color on the chromaticity diagram, then all the colors that lie in a straight line between the two points can be formed by mixing these two colors. It follows that the gamut of colors must be convex in shape. All colors that can be formed by mixing three sources are found inside the triangle formed by the source points on the chromaticity diagram (and so on for multiple sources).

- An equal mixture of two equally bright colors will not generally lie on the midpoint of that line segment. In more general terms, a distance on the CIE xy chromaticity diagram does not correspond to the degree of difference between two colors. In the early 1940s, David MacAdam studied the nature of visual sensitivity to color differences, and summarized his results in the concept of a MacAdam ellipse. Based on the work of MacAdam, the CIE 1960, CIE 1964, and CIE 1976 color spaces were developed, with the goal of achieving perceptual uniformity (have an equal distance in the color space correspond to equal differences in color). Although they were a distinct improvement over the CIE 1931 system, they were not completely free of distortion.

- It can be seen that, given three real sources, these sources cannot cover the gamut of human vision. Geometrically stated, there are no three points within the gamut that form a triangle that includes the entire gamut; or more simply, the gamut of human vision is not a triangle.

- Light with a flat power spectrum in terms of wavelength (equal power in every 1 nm interval) corresponds to the point (x, y) = (1/3, 1/3).

Mixing Colors Specified with the CIE xy Chromaticity Diagram

When two or more colors are additively mixed, the x and y chromaticity coordinates of the resulting color (x_{mix}, y_{mix}) may be calculated from the chromaticities of the mixture components $(x_1, y_1;$

$x_2,y_2; ...; x_n,y_n$) and their corresponding luminances (L_1, L_2, ..., L_n) with the following formulas:

$$x_{mix} = \frac{\dfrac{x_1}{y_1}L_1 + \dfrac{x_2}{y_2}L_2 + ... + \dfrac{x_n}{y_n}L_n}{\dfrac{L_1}{y_1} + \dfrac{L_2}{y_2} + ... + \dfrac{L_n}{y_n}},$$

$$y_{mix} = \frac{L_1 + L_2 + ... + L_n}{\dfrac{L_1}{y_1} + \dfrac{L_2}{y_2} + ... + \dfrac{L_n}{y_n}}$$

These formulas can be derived from the previously presented definitions of x and y chromaticity coordinates by taking advantage of the fact that the tristimulus values X, Y, and Z of the individual mixture components are directly additive. In place of the luminance values (L1, L2, etc.) one can alternatively use any other photometric quantity that is directly proportional to the tristimulus value Y (naturally meaning that Y itself can also be used as well).

When two colors are mixed, the resulting color x_{mix},y_{mix} will lie on the straight line segment that connects these colors on the CIE xy chromaticity diagram. To calculate the mixing ratio of the component colors x_1,y_1 and x_2,y_2 that results in a certain x_{mix},y_{mix} on this line segment, one can use the formula:

$$\frac{L_1}{L_2} = \frac{y_1(x_2 - x_{mix})}{y_2(x_{mix} - x_1)} = \frac{y_1(y_2 - y_{mix})}{y_2(y_{mix} - y_1)}$$

Where, L_1 is the luminance of color x_1,y_1 and L_2 the luminance of color x_2,y_2. Note that because y_{mix} is unambiguously determined by x_{mix} and vice versa, knowing just one or the other of them is enough for calculating the mixing ratio. Also note that, in accordance with the remarks concerning the formulas for x_{mix} and y_{mix}, the mixing ratio L_1/L_2 may well be expressed in terms of other photometric quantities than luminance.

Definition of the CIE XYZ Color Space

CIE RGB Color Space

The CIE RGB color space is one of many RGB color spaces, distinguished by a particular set of monochromatic (single-wavelength) primary colors.

In the 1920s, two independent experiments on human color perception were conducted by W. David Wright with ten observers, and John Guild with seven observers. Their results laid the foundation for the trichromatic CIE XYZ color space specification.

The experiments were conducted by using a circular split screen (a bipartite field) 2 degrees in diameter, which is the angular size of the human fovea. On one side a test color was projected while on the other an observer-adjustable color was projected. The adjustable color was a mixture of three primary colors, each with fixed chromaticity, but with adjustable brightness.

The observer would alter the brightness of each of the three primary beams until a match to the test color was observed. Not all test colors could be matched using this technique. When this was the case, a variable amount of one of the primaries could be added to the test color, and a match with the remaining two primaries was carried out with the variable color spot. For these cases, the amount of the primary added to the test color was considered to be a negative value. In this way, the entire range of human color perception could be covered. When the test colors were monochromatic, a plot could be made of the amount of each primary used as a function of the wavelength of the test color. These three functions are called the color matching functions for that particular experiment.

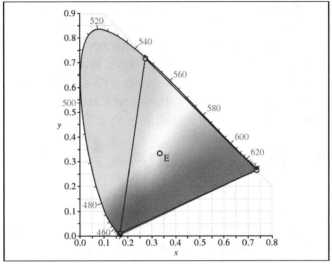

Gamut of the CIE RGB primaries and location of primaries
on the CIE 1931 xy chromaticity diagram.

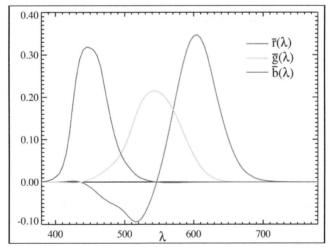

The CIE 1931 RGB color matching functions. The color matching functions are the amounts of primaries
needed to match the monochromatic test color at the wavelength shown on the horizontal scale.

Although Wright and Guild's experiments were carried out using various primaries at various intensities, and although they used a number of different observers, all of their results were summarized by the standardized CIE RGB color matching functions $\bar{r}(\lambda)$, $\bar{g}(\lambda)$ and $\bar{b}(\lambda)$, obtained using three monochromatic primaries at standardized wavelengths of 700 nm (red), 546.1 nm (green) and 435.8 nm (blue). The color matching functions are the amounts of primaries needed to match the monochromatic test primary. These functions are shown in the plot on the right (CIE 1931).

Note that $\bar{r}(\lambda)$ and $\bar{g}(\lambda)$ are zero at 435.8 nm, $\bar{r}(\lambda)$ and $\bar{b}(\lambda)$ are zero at 546.1 nm and $\bar{g}(\lambda)$ and $\bar{b}(\lambda)$ are zero at 700 nm, since in these cases the test color is one of the primaries. The primaries with wavelengths 546.1 nm and 435.8 nm were chosen because they are easily reproducible monochromatic lines of a mercury vapor discharge. The 700 nm wavelength, which in 1931 was difficult to reproduce as a monochromatic beam, was chosen because the eye's perception of color is rather unchanging at this wavelength, and therefore small errors in wavelength of this primary would have little effect on the results.

The color matching functions and primaries were settled upon by a CIE special commission after considerable deliberation. The cut-offs at the short- and long-wavelength side of the diagram are chosen somewhat arbitrarily; the human eye can actually see light with wavelengths up to about 810 nm, but with a sensitivity that is many thousand times lower than for green light. These color matching functions define what is known as the "1931 CIE standard observer". Note that rather than specify the brightness of each primary, the curves are normalized to have constant area beneath them. This area is fixed to a particular value by specifying that:

$$\int_0^\infty \bar{r}(\lambda)\,d\lambda = \int_0^\infty \bar{g}(\lambda)\,d\lambda = \int_0^\infty \bar{b}(\lambda)\,d\lambda$$

The resulting normalized color matching functions are then scaled in the r:g:b ratio of 1:4.5907:0.0601 for source luminance and 72.0962:1.3791:1 for source radiance to reproduce the true color matching functions. By proposing that the primaries be standardized, the CIE established an international system of objective color notation.

Given these scaled color matching functions, the RGB tristimulus values for a color with a spectral power distribution $S(\lambda)$ would then be given by:

$$R = \int_0^\infty S(\lambda)\,\bar{r}(\lambda)\,d\lambda,$$

$$G = \int_0^\infty S(\lambda)\,\bar{g}(\lambda)\,d\lambda,$$

$$B = \int_0^\infty S(\lambda)\,\bar{b}(\lambda)\,d\lambda.$$

These are all inner products and can be thought of as a projection of an infinite-dimensional spectrum to a three-dimensional color.

Grassmann's Law

One might ask: "Why is it possible that Wright and Guild's results can be summarized using different primaries and different intensities from those actually used?" One might also ask: "What about the case when the test colors being matched are not monochromatic?" The answer to both of these questions lies in the (near) linearity of human color perception. This linearity is expressed in Grassmann's law.

The CIE RGB space can be used to define chromaticity in the usual way: The chromaticity coordinates are r, g and b where:

$$r = \frac{R}{R+G+B}$$

$$g = \frac{G}{R+G+B}$$

$$b = \frac{B}{R+G+B}$$

Construction of the CIE XYZ Color Space from the Wright–Guild Data

Having developed an RGB model of human vision using the CIE RGB matching functions, the members of the special commission wished to develop another color space that would relate to the CIE RGB color space. It was assumed that Grassmann's law held, and the new space would be related to the CIE RGB space by a linear transformation. The new space would be defined in terms of three new color matching functions $\bar{x}(\lambda)$, $\bar{y}(\lambda)$ and $\bar{z}(\lambda)$. The new color space would be chosen to have the following desirable properties:

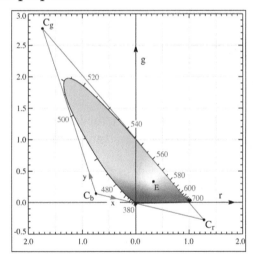

Diagram in CIE rg chromaticity space showing the construction of the triangle specifying the CIE XYZ color space. The triangle C_b-C_g-C_r is just the xy = (0, 0), (0, 1), (1, 0) triangle in CIE xy chromaticity space. The line connecting C_b and C_r is the alychne. Notice that the spectral locus passes through rg = (0, 0) at 435.8 nm, through rg = (0, 1) at 546.1 nm and through rg = (1, 0) at 700 nm. Also, the equal energy point (E) is at rg = xy = (1/3, 1/3).

- The new color matching functions were to be everywhere greater than or equal to zero. In 1931, computations were done by hand or slide rule, and the specification of positive values was a useful computational simplification.

- The $\bar{y}(\lambda)$ color matching function would be exactly equal to the photopic luminous efficiency function $V(\lambda)$ for the "CIE standard photopic observer". The luminance function describes the variation of perceived brightness with wavelength. The fact that the luminance function could be constructed by a linear combination of the RGB color matching functions was not guaranteed by any means but might be expected to be nearly true due to the near-linear nature of human sight. Again, the main reason for this requirement was computational simplification.

- For the constant energy white point, it was required that $x = y = z = 1/3$.

- By virtue of the definition of chromaticity and the requirement of positive values of x and y, it can be seen that the gamut of all colors will lie inside the triangle [1, 0], [0, 0], [0, 1]. It was required that the gamut fill this space practically completely.

- It was found that the $\bar{z}(\lambda)$ color matching function could be set to zero above 650 nm while remaining within the bounds of experimental error. For computational simplicity, it was specified that this would be so.

In geometrical terms, choosing the new color space amounts to choosing a new triangle in rg chromaticity space. In the figure above-right, the rg chromaticity coordinates are shown on the two axes in black, along with the gamut of the 1931 standard observer. Shown in red are the CIE xy chromaticity axes which were determined by the above requirements. The requirement that the XYZ coordinates be non-negative means that the triangle formed by C_r, C_g, C_b must encompass the entire gamut of the standard observer. The line connecting C_r and C_b is fixed by the requirement that the $\bar{y}(\lambda)$ function be equal to the luminance function. This line is the line of zero luminance, and is called the alychne. The requirement that the $\bar{z}(\lambda)$ function be zero above 650 nm means that the line connecting C_g and C_r must be tangent to the gamut in the region of K_r. This defines the location of point C_r. The requirement that the equal energy point be defined by $x = y = 1/3$ puts a restriction on the line joining C_b and C_g, and finally, the requirement that the gamut fill the space puts a second restriction on this line to be very close to the gamut in the green region, which specifies the location of C_g and C_b. The above described transformation is a linear transformation from the CIE RGB space to XYZ space. The standardized transformation settled upon by the CIE special commission was as follows:

The numbers in the conversion matrix below are exact, with the number of digits specified in CIE standards.

$$
\begin{bmatrix} X \\ Y \\ Z \end{bmatrix} = \frac{1}{b_{21}} \begin{bmatrix} b_{11} & b_{12} & b_{13} \\ b_{21} & b_{22} & b_{23} \\ b_{31} & b_{32} & b_{33} \end{bmatrix} \begin{bmatrix} R \\ G \\ B \end{bmatrix} = \frac{1}{0.17697} \begin{bmatrix} 0.49000 & 0.31000 & 0.20000 \\ 0.17697 & 0.81240 & 0.01063 \\ 0.00000 & 0.01000 & 0.99000 \end{bmatrix} \begin{bmatrix} R \\ G \\ B \end{bmatrix}
$$

While the above matrix is exactly specified in standards, going the other direction uses an inverse matrix that is not exactly specified, but is approximately:

$$
\begin{bmatrix} R \\ G \\ B \end{bmatrix} = \begin{bmatrix} 0.41847 & -0.15866 & -0.082835 \\ -0.091169 & 0.25243 & 0.015708 \\ 0.00092090 & -0.0025498 & 0.17860 \end{bmatrix} \cdot \begin{bmatrix} X \\ Y \\ Z \end{bmatrix}
$$

The integrals of the XYZ color matching functions must all be equal by requirement 3 above, and this is set by the integral of the photopic luminous efficiency function by requirement 2 above. The tabulated sensitivity curves have a certain amount of arbitrariness in them. The shapes of the individual X, Y and Z sensitivity curves can be measured with a reasonable accuracy. However, the overall luminosity curve (which in fact is a weighted sum of these three curves) is subjective, since it involves asking a test person whether two light sources have the same brightness, even if they are in completely different colors. Along the same lines, the relative magnitudes of the X, Y, and Z curves are arbitrary. Furthermore, one could define a valid color space with an X sensitivity curve that has twice the amplitude. This new color space would have a different shape. The sensitivity curves in the CIE 1931 and 1964 XYZ color spaces are scaled to have equal areas under the curves.

COLOR MAPPING

Color mapping is a function that maps (transforms) the colors of one (source) image to the colors of another (target) image. A color mapping may be referred to as the algorithm that results in the mapping function or the algorithm that transforms the image colors. Color mapping is also sometimes called color transfer or, when grayscale images are involved, brightness transfer function (BTF).

Source image. Reference image. Source image color mapped using histogram matching.

Algorithms

There are two types of color mapping algorithms: those that employ the statistics of the colors of two images, and those that rely on a given pixel correspondence between the images.

An example of an algorithm that employs the statistical properties of the images is histogram matching. This is a classic algorithm for color mapping, suffering from the problem of sensitivity to image content differences. Newer statistic-based algorithms deal with this problem. An example of such algorithm is adjusting the mean and the standard deviation of Lab channels of the two images.

A common algorithm for computing the color mapping when the pixel correspondence is given is building the joint-histogram of the two images and finding the mapping by using dynamic programming based on the joint-histogram values.

When the pixel correspondence is not given and the image contents are different (due to different point of view), the statistics of the image corresponding regions can be used as an input to statistics-based algorithms, such as histogram matching. The corresponding regions can be found by detecting the corresponding features.

Applications

Color mapping can serve two different purposes: one is calibrating the colors of two cameras for further processing using two or more sample images, the second is adjusting the colors of two images for perceptual visual compatibility.

Color calibration is an important pre-processing task in computer vision applications. Many applications simultaneously process two or more images and, therefore, need their colors to be calibrated. Examples of such applications are: Image differencing, registration, object recognition, multi-camera tracking, co-segmentation and stereo reconstruction.

Outline of Object Recognition

Object recognition – technology in the field of computer vision for finding and identifying objects in an image or video sequence. Humans recognize a multitude of objects in images with little effort, despite the fact that the image of the objects may vary somewhat in different viewpoints, in many different sizes and scales or even when they are translated or rotated. Objects can even be recognized when they are partially obstructed from view. This task is still a challenge for computer vision systems. Many approaches to the task have been implemented over multiple decades.

Image Registration

Image registration is the process of transforming different sets of data into one coordinate system. Data may be multiple photographs, data from different sensors, times, depths, or viewpoints. It is used in computer vision, medical imaging, military automatic target recognition, and compiling and analyzing images and data from satellites. Registration is necessary in order to be able to compare or integrate the data obtained from these different measurements.

Algorithm Classification

Intensity-based vs. Feature-based

Image registration or image alignment algorithms can be classified into intensity-based and feature-based. One of the images is referred to as the moving or source and the others are referred to as the target, fixed or sensed images. Image registration involves spatially transforming the source/moving images to align with the target image. The reference frame in the target image is stationary, while the other datasets are transformed to match to the target. Intensity-based methods compare intensity patterns in images via correlation metrics, while feature-based methods find correspondence between image features such as points, lines, and contours. Intensity-based methods register entire images or sub-images. If sub-images are registered, centers of corresponding sub images are treated as corresponding feature points. Feature-based methods establish a correspondence between a number of especially distinct points in images. Knowing the correspondence between a number of points in images, a geometrical transformation is then determined to map the target image to the reference images, thereby establishing point-by-point correspondence between the reference and target images. Methods combining intensity-based and feature-based information have also been developed.

Transformation Models

Image registration algorithms can also be classified according to the transformation models they use to relate the target image space to the reference image space. The first broad category of transformation models includes linear transformations, which include rotation, scaling, translation, and other affine transforms. Linear transformations are global in nature, thus, they cannot model local geometric differences between images.

The second categories of transformations allow 'elastic' or 'nonrigid' transformations. These transformations are capable of locally warping the target image to align with the reference image. Nonrigid transformations include radial basis functions (thin-plate or surface splines, multiquadrics, and compactly-supported transformations), physical continuum models (viscous fluids), and large deformation models (diffeomorphisms).

Transformations are commonly described by a parametrization, where the model dictates the number of parameters. For instance, the translation of a full image can be described by a single parameter, a translation vector. These models are called parametric models. Non-parametric models on the other hand, do not follow any parameterization, allowing each image element to be displaced arbitrarily.

There are a number of programs that implement both estimation and application of a warp-field. It is a part of the SPM and AIR programs.

Transformations of Coordinates via the Law of Function Composition Rather than Addition

Alternatively, many advanced methods for spatial normalization are building on structure preserving transformations homeomorphisms and diffeomorphisms since they carry smooth submanifolds smoothly during transformation. Diffeomorphisms are generated in the modern field of Computational Anatomy based on flows since diffeomorphisms are not additive although they form a group, but a group under the law of function composition. For this reason, flows which generalize the ideas of additive groups allow for generating large deformations that preserve topology, providing 1-1 and onto transformations. Computational methods for generating such transformation are often called LDDMM which provide flows of diffeomorphisms as the main computational tool for connecting coordinate systems corresponding to the geodesic flows of Computational Anatomy.

There are a number of programs which generate diffeomorphic transformations of coordinates via diffeomorphic mapping including MRI Studio and MRI Cloud.org

Spatial vs. Frequency Domain Methods

Spatial methods operate in the image domain, matching intensity patterns or features in images. Some of the feature matching algorithms are outgrowths of traditional techniques for performing manual image registration, in which an operator chooses corresponding control points (CP) in images. When the number of control points exceeds the minimum required to define the appropriate transformation model, iterative algorithms like RANSAC can be used to robustly estimate the parameters of a particular transformation type (e.g. affine) for registration of the images.

Frequency-domain methods find the transformation parameters for registration of the images while working in the transform domain. Such methods work for simple transformations, such as translation, rotation, and scaling. Applying the phase correlation method to a pair of images produces a third image which contains a single peak. The location of this peak corresponds to the relative translation between the images. Unlike many spatial-domain algorithms, the phase correlation method is resilient to noise, occlusions, and other defects typical of medical or satellite images. Additionally, the phase correlation uses the fast Fourier transform to compute the cross-correlation between the two images, generally resulting in large performance gains. The method can be extended to determine rotation and scaling differences between two images by first converting the images to log-polar coordinates. Due to properties of the Fourier transform, the rotation and scaling parameters can be determined in a manner invariant to translation.

Single- vs. Multi-Modality Methods

Another classification can be made between single-modality and multi-modality methods. Single-modality methods tend to register images in the same modality acquired by the same scanner/sensor type, while multi-modality registration methods tended to register images acquired by different scanner/sensor types.

Multi-modality registration methods are often used in medical imaging as images of a subject are frequently obtained from different scanners. Examples include registration of brain CT/MRI images or whole body PET/CT images for tumor localization, registration of contrast-enhanced CT images against non-contrast-enhanced CT images for segmentation of specific parts of the anatomy, and registration of ultrasound and CT images for prostate localization in radiotherapy.

Automatic vs. Interactive Methods

Registration methods may be classified based on the level of automation they provide. Manual, interactive, semi-automatic, and automatic methods have been developed. Manual methods provide tools to align the images manually. Interactive methods reduce user bias by performing certain key operations automatically while still relying on the user to guide the registration. Semi-automatic methods perform more of the registration steps automatically but depend on the user to verify the correctness of a registration. Automatic methods do not allow any user interaction and perform all registration steps automatically.

Similarity Measures for Image Registration

Image similarities are broadly used in medical imaging. An image similarity measure quantifies the degree of similarity between intensity patterns in two images. The choice of an image similarity measure depends on the modality of the images to be registered. Common examples of image similarity measures include cross-correlation, mutual information, sum of squared intensity differences, and ratio image uniformity. Mutual information and normalized mutual information are the most popular image similarity measures for registration of multimodality images. Cross-correlation, sum of squared intensity differences and ratio image uniformity are commonly used for registration of images in the same modality.

Many new features have been derived for cost functions based on matching methods via large deformations have emerged in the field Computational Anatomy including Measure matching which are pointsets or landmarks without correspondence, Curve matching and Surface matching via mathematical currents and varifolds.

Uncertainty

There is a level of uncertainty associated with registering images that have any spatio-temporal differences. A confident registration with a measure of uncertainty is critical for many change detection applications such as medical diagnostics.

In remote sensing applications where a digital image pixel may represent several kilometers of spatial distance (such as NASA's LANDSAT imagery), an uncertain image registration can mean that a solution could be several kilometers from ground truth. Several notable papers have attempted to quantify uncertainty in image registration in order to compare results. However, many approaches to quantifying uncertainty or estimating deformations are computationally intensive or are only applicable to limited sets of spatial transformations.

Applications

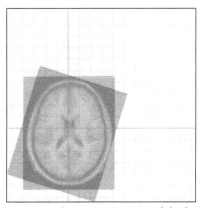

Registration of two MRI images of the brain.

Image registration has applications in remote sensing (cartography updating), and computer vision. Due to the vast range of applications to which image registration can be applied, it is impossible to develop a general method that is optimized for all uses.

Medical image registration (for data of the same patient taken at different points in time such as change detection or tumor monitoring) often additionally involves elastic (also known as nonrigid) registration to cope with deformation of the subject (due to breathing, anatomical changes, and so forth). Nonrigid registration of medical images can also be used to register a patient's data to an anatomical atlas, such as the Talairach atlas for neuroimaging.

In astrophotography image alignment and stacking are often used to increase the signal to noise ratio for faint objects. Without stacking it may be used to produce a timelapse of events such as a planets rotation of a transit across the Sun. Using control points (automatically or manually entered), the computer performs transformations on one image to make major features align with a second or multiple images. This technique may also be used for images of different sizes, to allow images taken through different telescopes or lenses to be combined.

In cryo-TEM instability causes specimen drift and many fast acquisitions with accurate image registration is required to preserve high resolution and obtain high signal to noise images. For low SNR data, the best image registration is achieved by cross-correlating all permutations of images in an image stack.

Image registration is an essential part of panoramic image creation. There are many different techniques that can be implemented in real time and run on embedded devices like cameras and camera-phones.

COLOR CONSTANCY

Color constancy is an example of subjective constancy and a feature of the human color perception system which ensures that the perceived color of objects remains relatively constant under varying illumination conditions. A green apple for instance looks green to us at midday, when the main illumination is white sunlight, and also at sunset, when the main illumination is red. This helps us identify objects.

Color constancy: The colors of a hot air balloon are
recognized as being the same in sun and shade.

Object Illuminance

The phenomenon of color constancy occurs when the source of illumination is not directly known. It is for this reason that color constancy takes a greater effect on days with sun and clear sky as opposed to days that are overcast. Even when the sun is visible, color constancy may affect color perception. This is due to an ignorance of all possible sources of illumination. Although an object may reflect multiple sources of light into the eye, color constancy causes objective identities to remain constant.

D. H. Foster states, "in the natural environment, the source itself may not be well defined in that the illumination at a particular point in a scene is usually a complex mixture of direct and indirect [light] distributed over a range of incident angles, in turn modified by local occlusion and mutual reflection, all of which may vary with time and position." The wide spectrum of possible illuminances in the natural environment and the limited ability of the human eye to perceive color mean that color constancy plays a functional role in daily perception. Color constancy allows for humans to interact with the world in a consistent or veridical manner and it allows for one to more effectively make judgements on the time of day.

Constancy makes square A appear darker than square B, when in
fact they are both exactly the same shade of grey.

Achieving luminance constancy by retinex filtering for image analysis.

Physiological Basis

In these two pictures, the second card from the left seems to be a stronger shade of pink in the upper
one than in the lower one. In fact they are the same color (since they have the same RGB values),
but perception is affected by the color cast of the surrounding photo.

The physiological basis for color constancy is thought to involve specialized neurons in the primary visual cortex that compute local ratios of cone activity, which is the same calculation that Land's retinex algorithm uses to achieve color constancy. These specialized cells are called double-opponent cells because they compute both color opponency and spatial opponency. Double-opponent cells were first described by Nigel Daw in the goldfish retina. There was considerable debate about the existence of these cells in the primate visual system; their existence was eventually proven using reverse-correlation receptive field mapping and special stimuli that selectively activate single cone classes at a time, so-called "cone-isolating" stimuli.

Color constancy works only if the incident illumination contains a range of wavelengths. The different cone cells of the eye register different but overlapping ranges of wavelengths of the light reflected by every object in the scene. From this information, the visual system attempts to determine the approximate composition of the illuminating light. This illumination is then discounted in order to obtain the object's "true color" or reflectance: the wavelengths of light the object reflects. This reflectance then largely determines the perceived color.

Neural Mechanism

There are two possible mechanisms for color constancy. The first mechanism is unconscious inference. The second view holds this phenomenon to be caused by sensory adaptation. Research suggests color constancy to be related changes in retinal cells as well as cortical areas related to vision. This phenomenon is most likely attributed to changes in various levels of the visual system.

Cone Adaptation

Cones, specialized cells within the retina, will adjust relative to light levels within the local environment. This occurs at the level of individual neurons. However, this adaptation is incomplete. Chromatic adaptation is also regulated by processes within the brain. Research in monkeys suggest that changes in chromatic sensitivity is correlated to activity in parvocellular lateral geniculate neurons. Color constancy may be both attributed to localized changes in individual retinal cells or to higher level neural processes within the brain.

Metamerism

Metamerism, the perceiving of colors within two separate scenes, can help to inform research regarding color constancy. Research suggests that when competing chromatic stimuli are presented, spatial comparisons must be completed early in the visual system. For example, when subjects are presented stimuli in a dichoptic fashion, an array of colors and a void color, such as grey, and are told to focus on a specific color of the array, the void color appears different than when perceived in a binocular fashion. This means that color judgements, as they relate to spatial comparisons, must be completed at or prior to the V1 monocular neurons. If spatial comparisons occur later in the visual system such as in cortical area V4, the brain would be able to perceive both the color and void color as though they were seen in a binocular fashion.

Retinex Theory

The "Land effect" refers to the capacity to see full color (if muted) images solely by looking at a photo with red and gray wavelengths. The effect was discovered by Edwin H. Land, who was attempting to reconstruct James Clerk Maxwell's early experiments in full-colored images. Land realized that, even when there were no green or blue wavelengths present in an image, the visual system would still perceive them as green or blue by discounting the red illumination. Land described this effect in a 1959 article in Scientific American. In 1977, Land wrote another Scientific American article that formulated his "retinex theory" to explain the Land effect. The word "retinex" is a portmanteau formed from "retina" and "cortex", suggesting that both the eye and the brain are involved in the processing. Land, with John McCann, also developed a computer program designed to imitate the retinex processes taking place in human physiology.

The effect can be experimentally demonstrated as follows. A display called a "Mondrian" (after Piet Mondrian whose paintings are similar) consisting of numerous colored patches is shown to a person. The display is illuminated by three white lights, one projected through a red filter, one projected through a green filter, and one projected through a blue filter. The person is asked to adjust the intensity of the lights so that a particular patch in the display appears white. The experimenter then measures the intensities of red, green, and blue light reflected from this white-appearing patch. Then the experimenter asks the person to identify the color of a neighboring patch, which, for example, appears green. Then the experimenter adjusts the lights so that the intensities of red, blue, and green light reflected from the green patch are the same as were originally measured from the white patch. The person shows color constancy in that the green patch continues to appear green, the white patch continues to appear white, and all the remaining patches continue to have their original colors.

Color constancy is a desirable feature of computer vision, and many algorithms have been developed for this purpose. These include several retinex algorithms. These algorithms receive as input the red/green/blue values of each pixel of the image and attempt to estimate the reflectances of each point. One such algorithm operates as follows: the maximal red value r_{max} of all pixels is determined, and also the maximal green value g_{max} and the maximal blue value b_{max}. Assuming that the scene contains objects which reflect all red light, and (other) objects which reflect all green light and still others which reflect all blue light, one can then deduce that the illuminating light source is described by $(r_{max}, g_{max}, b_{max})$. For each pixel with values (r, g, b) its reflectance is estimated as $(r/r_{max}, g/g_{max}, b/b_{max})$. The original retinex algorithm proposed by Land and McCann uses a localized version of this principle.

Although retinex models are still widely used in computer vision, actual human color perception has been shown to be more complex.

VISUAL PERCEPTION

Although the digital image processing field is built on a foundation of mathematical and probabilistic formulations, human intuition and analysis play a central role in the choice of one technique versus another, and this choice often is made based on subjective, visual judgments.

Brightness Adaptation and Discrimination

Because digital images are displayed as a discrete set of intensities, the eye's ability to discriminate between different intensity levels is an important consideration in presenting imageprocessing results. The range of light intensity levels to which the human visual system can adapt is enormous—on the order of 1010—from the scotopic threshold to the glare limit. Experimental evidence indicates that subjective brightness (intensity as perceived by the human visual system) is a logarithmic function of the light intensity incident on the eye. Figure shows a plot of light intensity versus subjective brightness, illustrates this characteristic. The long solid curve represents the range of intensities to which the visual system can adapt. In photopic vision alone, the range is about 106. The transition from scotopic to photopic vision is gradual over the approximate range from 0.001 to 0.1 millilambert (−3 to −1 mL in the log scale), as the double branches of the adaptation curve in this range show.

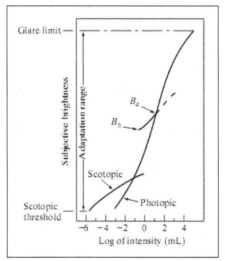

Range of Subjective brightness sensations showing a particular adaptation level.

The essential point in interpreting the impressive dynamic range depicted in figure is that the visual system cannot operate over such a range simultaneously. Rather, it accomplishes this large variation by changes in its overall sensitivity, a phenomenon known as brightness adaptation. The total range of distinct intensity levels it can discriminate simultaneously is rather small when compared with the total adaptation range. For any given set of conditions, the current sensitivity level of the visual system is called the brightness adaptation level, which may correspond, for example, to brightness Ba in Fig. 4.3. The short intersecting curve represents the range of subjective brightness that the eye can perceive when adapted to this level. This range is rather restricted, having a level Bb at and below which all stimuli are perceived as indistinguishable blacks. The upper (dashed) portion of the curve is not actually restricted but, if extended too far, loses its meaning because much higher intensities would simply raise the adaptation level higher than Ba.

COLOR MODEL

A color model is an abstract mathematical model describing the way colors can be represented as tuples of numbers, typically as three or four values or color components. When this model is associated with a precise description of how the components are to be interpreted (viewing conditions, etc.), the resulting set of colors is called "color space."

Tristimulus Color Space

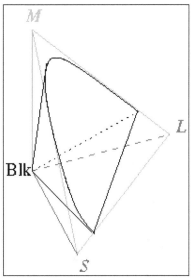

3D representation of the human color space.

One can picture this space as a region in three-dimensional Euclidean space if one identifies the x, y, and z axes with the stimuli for the long-wavelength (L), medium-wavelength (M), and short-wavelength (S) light receptors. The origin, (S,M,L) = (0,0,0), corresponds to black. White has no definite position in this diagram; rather it is defined according to the color temperature or white balance as desired or as available from ambient lighting. The human color space is a horse-shoe-shaped cone such as shown here, extending from the origin to, in principle, infinity. In practice, the human color receptors will be saturated or even be damaged at extremely high light intensities, but such behavior is not part of the CIE color space and neither is the changing color perception at low light levels. The most saturated colors are located at the outer rim of the region, with brighter colors farther removed from the origin. As far as the responses of the receptors in the eye are concerned, there is no such thing as "brown" or "gray" light. The latter color names refer to orange and white light respectively, with an intensity that is lower than the light from surrounding areas. One can observe this by watching the screen of an overhead projector during a meeting: one sees black lettering on a white background, even though the "black" has in fact not become darker than the white screen on which it is projected before the projector was turned on. The "black" areas have not actually become darker but appear "black" relative to the higher intensity "white" projected onto the screen around it.

The human tristimulus space has the property that additive mixing of colors corresponds to the adding of vectors in this space. This makes it easy to, for example, describe the possible colors (gamut) that can be constructed from the red, green, and blue primaries in a computer display.

CIE XYZ Color Space

One of the first mathematically defined color spaces is the CIE XYZ color space (also known as CIE 1931 color space), created by the International Commission on Illumination in 1931. These data were measured for human observers and a 2-degree field of view. In 1964, supplemental data for a 10-degree field of view were published.

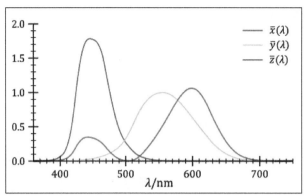

1931 Standard Colorimetric Observer functions between 380 nm and 780 nm (at 5 nm intervals).

Note that the tabulated sensitivity curves have a certain amount of arbitrariness in them. The shapes of the individual X, Y and Z sensitivity curves can be measured with a reasonable accuracy. However, the overall luminosity function (which in fact is a weighted sum of these three curves) is subjective, since it involves asking a test person whether two light sources have the same brightness, even if they are in completely different colors. Along the same lines, the relative magnitudes of the X, Y, and Z curves are arbitrarily chosen to produce equal areas under the curves. One could as well define a valid color space with an X sensitivity curve that has twice the amplitude. This new color space would have a different shape. The sensitivity curves in the CIE 1931 and 1964 xyz color space are scaled to have equal areas under the curves.

Sometimes XYZ colors are represented by the luminance, Y, and chromaticity coordinates x and y, defined by:

$$x = \frac{X}{X+Y+Z} \text{ and}$$
$$y = \frac{Y}{X+Y+Z}$$

Mathematically, x and y are projective coordinates and the colors of the chromaticity diagram occupy a region of the real projective plane. Because the CIE sensitivity curves have equal areas under the curves, light with a flat energy spectrum corresponds to the point $(x, y) = (0.333, 0.333)$.

The values for X, Y, and Z are obtained by integrating the product of the spectrum of a light beam and the published color-matching functions.

Additive and Subtractive Color Models

RGB Color Model

Media that transmit light (such as television) use additive color mixing with primary colors of red, green, and blue, each of which stimulates one of the three types of the eye's color receptors with as little stimulation as possible of the other two. This is called "RGB" color space. Mixtures of light of these primary colors cover a large part of the human color space and thus produce a large part of human color experiences. This is why color television sets or color computer monitors need only produce mixtures of red, green and blue light.

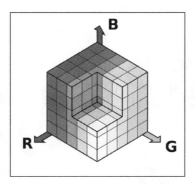

Other primary colors could in principle be used, but with red, green and blue the largest portion of the human color space can be captured. Unfortunately there is no exact consensus as to what loci in the chromaticity diagram the red, green, and blue colors should have, so the same RGB values can give rise to slightly different colors on different screens.

CMYK Color Model

It is possible to achieve a large range of colors seen by humans by combining cyan, magenta, and yellow transparent dyes/inks on a white substrate. These are the subtractive primary colors. Often a fourth ink, black, is added to improve reproduction of some dark colors. This is called the "CMY" or "CMYK" color space.

The cyan ink absorbs red light but transmits green and blue, the magenta ink absorbs green light but transmits red and blue, and the yellow ink absorbs blue light but transmits red and green. The white substrate reflects the transmitted light back to the viewer. Because in practice the CMY inks suitable for printing also reflect a little bit of color, making a deep and neutral black impossible, the K (black ink) component, usually printed last, is needed to compensate for their deficiencies. Use of a separate black ink is also economically driven when a lot of black content is expected, e.g. in text media, to reduce simultaneous use of the three colored inks. The dyes used in traditional color photographic prints and slides are much more perfectly transparent, so a K component is normally not needed or used in those media.

Cylindrical-coordinate Color Models

A number of color models exist in which colors are fit into conic, cylindrical or spherical shapes, with neutrals running from black to white along a central axis, and hues corresponding to angles around the perimeter. Arrangements of this type date back to the 18th century, and continue to be developed in the most modern and scientific models.

Background

Different color theorists have each designed unique color solids. Many are in the shape of a sphere, whereas others are warped three-dimensional ellipsoid figures—these variations being designed to express some aspect of the relationship of the colors more clearly. The color spheres conceived by Phillip Otto Runge and Johannes Itten are typical examples and prototypes for many other color solid schematics. The models of Runge and Itten are basically identical, and form the basis for the description below.

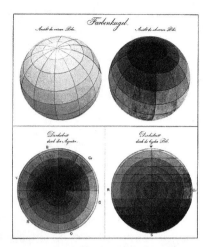
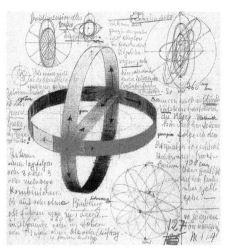

(Left) Philipp Otto Runge's Farbenkugel (color sphere), 1810, showing the outer surface of the sphere (top two images), and horizontal and vertical cross sections (bottom two images). (Right) Color sphere of Johannes Itten, 1919-20.

Pure, saturated hues of equal brightness are located around the equator at the periphery of the color sphere. As in the color wheel, contrasting (or complementary) hues are located opposite each other. Moving toward the center of the color sphere on the equatorial plane, colors become less and less saturated, until all colors meet at the central axis as a neutral gray. Moving vertically in the color sphere, colors become lighter (toward the top) and darker (toward the bottom). At the upper pole, all hues meet in white; at the bottom pole, all hues meet in black.

The vertical axis of the color sphere, then, is gray all along its length, varying from black at the bottom to white at the top. All pure (saturated) hues are located on the surface of the sphere, varying from light to dark down the color sphere. All impure (unsaturated hues, created by mixing contrasting colors) comprise the sphere's interior, likewise varying in brightness from top to bottom.

HSL and HSV

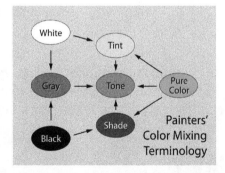
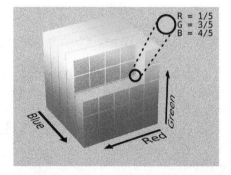

Painters long mixed colors by combining relatively bright pigments with black and white. Mixtures with white are called tints, mixtures with black are called shades, and mixtures with both are called tones.

The RGB gamut can be arranged in a cube. The RGB model is not very intuitive to artists used to using traditional models based on tints, shades and tones. The HSL and HSV color models were designed to fix this.

HSL and HSV are both cylindrical geometries, with hue, their angular dimension, starting at the red primary at 0°, passing through the green primary at 120° and the blue primary at 240°, and then wrapping back to red at 360°. In each geometry, the central vertical axis comprises the neutral, achromatic, or gray colors, ranging from black at lightness 0 or value 0, the bottom, to white at lightness 1 or value 1, the top.

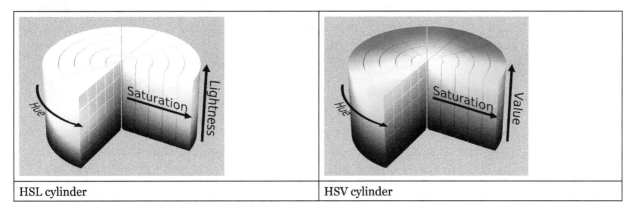

| HSL cylinder | HSV cylinder |

Most televisions, computer displays, and projectors produce colors by combining red, green, and blue light in varying intensities—the so-called RGB additive primary colors. However, the relationship between the constituent amounts of red, green, and blue light and the resulting color is unintuitive, especially for inexperienced users, and for users familiar with subtractive color mixing of paints or traditional artists' models based on tints and shades.

In an attempt to accommodate more traditional and intuitive color mixing models, computer graphics pioneers at PARC and NYIT developed the HSV model in the mid-1970s, formally described by Alvy Ray Smith in the August 1978 issue of Computer Graphics. In the same issue, Joblove and Greenberg described the HSL model—whose dimensions they labeled hue, relative chroma, and intensity—and compared it to HSV. Their model was based more upon how colors are organized and conceptualized in human vision in terms of other color-making attributes, such as hue, lightness, and chroma; as well as upon traditional color mixing methods—e.g., in painting—that involve mixing brightly colored pigments with black or white to achieve lighter, darker, or less colorful colors.

The following year, 1979, at SIGGRAPH, Tektronix introduced graphics terminals using HSL for color designation, and the Computer Graphics Standards Committee recommended it in their annual status report. These models were useful not only because they were more intuitive than raw RGB values, but also because the conversions to and from RGB were extremely fast to compute: they could run in real time on the hardware of the 1970s. Consequently, these models and similar ones have become ubiquitous throughout image editing and graphics software since then.

Natural Color System

The Swedish Natural Color System (NCS), widely used in Europe, takes a similar approach to the Ostwald bicone at right. Because it attempts to fit color into a familiarly shaped solid based on "phenomenological" instead of photometric or psychological characteristics, it suffers from some of the same disadvantages as HSL and HSV: in particular, its lightness dimension differs from perceived lightness, because it forces colorful yellow, red, green, and blue into a plane.

Preucil Hue Circle

In densitometry, a model quite similar to the hue defined above is used for describing colors of

CMYK process inks. In 1953, Frank Preucil developed two geometric arrangements of hue, the "Preucil hue circle" and the "Preucil hue hexagon", analogous to our H and H_2, respectively, but defined relative to idealized cyan, yellow, and magenta ink colors. The "Preucil hue error" of an ink indicates the difference in the "hue circle" between its color and the hue of the corresponding idealized ink color. The grayness of an ink is m/M, where m and M are the minimum and maximum among the amounts of idealized cyan, magenta, and yellow in a density measurement.

CIELCH$_{uv}$ and CIELCH$_{ab}$

The International Commission on Illumination (CIE) developed the XYZ model for describing the colors of light spectra in 1931, but its goal was to match human visual metamerism, rather than to be perceptually uniform, geometrically. In the 1960s and 1970s, attempts were made to transform XYZ colors into a more relevant geometry, influenced by the Munsell system. These efforts culminated in the 1976 CIELUV and CIELAB models. The dimensions of these models—(L*, u*, v*) and (L*, a*, b*), respectively—are cartesian, based on the opponent process theory of color, but both are also often described using polar coordinates—$(L^*, C^*_{uv}, h^*_{uv})$ and $(L^*, C^*_{ab}, h^*_{ab})$, respectively—where L* is lightness, C* is chroma, and h* is hue angle. Officially, both CIELAB and CIELUV were created for their color difference metrics ΔE^*_{ab} and ΔE^*_{uv}, particularly for use defining color tolerances, but both have become widely used as color order systems and color appearance models, including in computer graphics and computer vision. For example, gamut mapping in ICC color management is usually performed in CIELAB space, and Adobe Photoshop includes a CIELAB mode for editing images. CIELAB and CIELUV geometries are much more perceptually relevant than many others such as RGB, HSL, HSV, YUV/YIQ/YCbCr or XYZ, but are not perceptually perfect, and in particular have trouble adapting to unusual lighting conditions.[B]

The HCL color space seems to be synonymous with CIELCH.

CIECAM02

The CIE's most recent model, CIECAM02 (CAM stands for "color appearance model"), is more theoretically sophisticated and computationally complex than earlier models. Its aims are to fix several of the problems with models such as CIELAB and CIELUV, and to explain not only responses in carefully controlled experimental environments, but also to model the color appearance of real-world scenes. Its dimensions J (lightness), C (chroma), and h (hue) define a polar-coordinate geometry.

Color Systems

There are various types of color systems that classify color and analyse their effects. The American Munsell color system devised by Albert H. Munsell is a famous classification that organises various colors into a color solid based on hue, saturation and value. Other important color systems include the Swedish Natural Color System (NCS), the Optical Society of America's Uniform Color Space (OSA-UCS), and the Hungarian Coloroid system developed by Antal Nemcsics from the Budapest University of Technology and Economics. Of those, the NCS is based on the opponent-process color model, while the Munsell, the OSA-UCS and the Coloroid attempt to model color uniformity. The American Pantone and the German RAL commercial color-matching systems differ from the previous ones in that their color spaces are not based on an underlying color model.

Other uses of "Color Model"

Models of Mechanism of Color Vision

We also use "color model" to indicate a model or mechanism of color vision for explaining how color signals are processed from visual cones to ganglion cells. For simplicity, we call these models color mechanism models. The classical color mechanism models are Young–Helmholtz's trichromatic model and Hering's opponent-process model. Though these two theories were initially thought to be at odds, it later came to be understood that the mechanisms responsible for color opponency receive signals from the three types of cones and process them at a more complex level.

Vertebrate Evolution of Color Vision

Vertebrate animals were primitively tetrachromatic. They possessed four types of cones—long, mid, short wavelength cones, and ultraviolet sensitive cones. Today, fish, amphibians, reptiles and birds are all tetrachromatic. Placental mammals lost both the mid and short wavelength cones. Thus, most mammals do not have complex color vision—they are dichromatic but they are sensitive to ultraviolet light, though they cannot see its colors. Human trichromatic color vision is a recent evolutionary novelty that first evolved in the common ancestor of the Old World Primates. Our trichromatic color vision evolved by duplication of the long wavelength sensitive opsin, found on the X chromosome. One of these copies evolved to be sensitive to green light and constitutes our mid wavelength opsin. At the same time, our short wavelength opsin evolved from the ultraviolet opsin of our vertebrate and mammalian ancestors.

Human red-green color blindness occurs because the two copies of the red and green opsin genes remain in close proximity on the X chromosome. Because of frequent recombination during meiosis, these gene pairs can get easily rearranged, creating versions of the genes that do not have distinct spectral sensitivities.

Color Appearance Model

A color appearance model (CAM) is a mathematical model that seeks to describe the perceptual aspects of human color vision, i.e. viewing conditions under which the appearance of a color does not tally with the corresponding physical measurement of the stimulus source. (In contrast, a color model defines a coordinate space to describe colors, such as the RGB and CMYK color models.)

Color Appearance

Color originates in the mind of the observer; "objectively", there is only the spectral power distribution of the light that meets the eye. In this sense, any color perception is subjective. However, successful attempts have been made to map the spectral power distribution of light to human sensory response in a quantifiable way. In 1931, using psychophysical measurements, the International Commission on Illumination (CIE) created the XYZ color space which successfully models human color vision on this basic sensory level.

However, the XYZ color model presupposes specific viewing conditions (such as the retinal locus of stimulation, the luminance level of the light that meets the eye, the background behind the observed object, and the luminance level of the surrounding light). Only if all these conditions stay constant will two identical stimuli with thereby identical XYZ tristimulus values create an identical color appearance for a human observer. If some conditions change in one case, two identical stimuli with thereby identical XYZ tristimulus values will create different color appearances (and vice versa: two different stimuli with thereby different XYZ tristimulus values might create an identical color appearance).

Therefore, if viewing conditions vary, the XYZ color model is not sufficient, and a color appearance model is required to model human color perception.

Color Appearance Parameters

The basic challenge for any color appearance model is that human color perception does not work in terms of XYZ tristimulus values, but in terms of appearance parameters (hue, lightness, brightness, chroma, colorfulness and saturation). So any color appearance model needs to provide transformations (which factor in viewing conditions) from the XYZ tristimulus values to these appearance parameters (at least hue, lightness and chroma).

Color Appearance Phenomena

Chromatic Adaptation

Chromatic adaptation describes the ability of human color perception to abstract from the white point (or color temperature) of the illuminating light source when observing a reflective object. For the human eye, a piece of white paper looks white no matter whether the illumination is blueish or yellowish. This is the most basic and most important of all color appearance phenomena, and therefore a chromatic adaptation transform (CAT) that tries to emulate this behavior is a central component of any color appearance model.

This allows for an easy distinction between simple tristimulus-based color models and color appearance models. A simple tristimulus-based color model ignores the white point of the illuminant when it describes the surface color of an illuminated object; if the white point of the illuminant changes, so does the color of the surface as reported by the simple tristimulus-based color model. In contrast, a color appearance model takes the white point of the illuminant into account (which is why a color appearance model requires this value for its calculations); if the white point of the illuminant changes, the color of the surface as reported by the color appearance model remains the same.

Chromatic adaptation is a prime example for the case that two different stimuli with thereby different XYZ tristimulus values create an identical color appearance. If the color temperature of the illuminating light source changes, so do the spectral power distribution and thereby the XYZ tristimulus values of the light reflected from the white paper; the color appearance, however, stays the same (white).

Hue Appearance

Several effects change the perception of hue by a human observer:

- Bezold–Brücke hue shift: The hue of monochromatic light changes with luminance.

- Abney effect: The hue of monochromatic light changes with the addition of white light (which would be expected color-neutral).

Contrast Appearance

Bartleson–Breneman effect.

Several effects change the perception of contrast by a human observer:

- Stevens effect: Contrast increases with luminance.

- Bartleson–Breneman effect: Image contrast (of emissive images such as images on an LCD display) increases with the luminance of surround lighting.

Colorfulness Appearance

There is an effect which changes the perception of colorfulness by a human observer:

- Hunt effect: Colorfulness increases with luminance.

Brightness Appearance

There is an effect which changes the perception of brightness by a human observer:

- Helmholtz–Kohlrausch effect: Brightness increases with saturation.

Spatial Phenomena

Spatial phenomena only affect colors at a specific location of an image, because the human brain interprets this location in a specific contextual way (e.g. as a shadow instead of gray color). These phenomena are also known as optical illusions. Because of their contextuality, they are especially hard to model; color appearance models that try to do this are referred to as image color appearance models (iCAM).

Color Appearance Models

Since the color appearance parameters and color appearance phenomena are numerous and the task is complex, there is no single color appearance model that is universally applied; instead, various models are used.

The chromatic adaptation transforms for some of these models are listed in LMS color space.

CIELAB

In 1976, the CIE set out to replace the many existing, incompatible color difference models by a new, universal model for color difference. They tried to achieve this goal by creating a perceptually uniform color space, i.e. a color space where identical spatial distance between two colors equals identical amount of perceived color difference. Though they succeeded only partially, they thereby created the CIELAB ("L*a*b*") color space which had all the necessary features to become the first color appearance model. While CIELAB is a very rudimentary color appearance model, it is one of the most widely used because it has become one of the building blocks of color management with ICC profiles. Therefore, it is basically omnipresent in digital imaging.

One of the limitations of CIELAB is that it does not offer a full-fledged chromatic adaptation in that it performs the von Kries transform method directly in the XYZ color space (often referred to as "wrong von Kries transform"), instead of changing into the LMS color space first for more precise results. ICC profiles circumvent this shortcoming by using the Bradford transformation matrix to the LMS color space (which had first appeared in the LLAB color appearance model) in conjunction with CIELAB.

Nayatani et al. model: The Nayatani et al. color appearance model focuses on illumination engineering and the color rendering properties of light sources.

Hunt Model

The Hunt color appearance model focuses on color image reproduction (its creator worked in the Kodak Research Laboratories). Development already started in the 1980s and by 1995 the model had become very complex (including features no other color appearance model offers, such as incorporating rod cell responses) and allowed to predict a wide range of visual phenomena. It had a very significant impact on CIECAM02, but because of its complexity the Hunt model itself is difficult to use.

RLAB

RLAB tries to improve upon the significant limitations of CIELAB with a focus on image reproduction. It performs well for this task and is simple to use, but not comprehensive enough for other applications.

LLAB

LLAB is similar to RLAB, also tries to stay simple, but additionally tries to be more comprehensive than RLAB. In the end, it traded some simplicity for comprehensiveness, but was still not fully comprehensive. Since CIECAM97s was published soon thereafter, LLAB never gained widespread usage.

CIECAM97s

After starting the evolution of color appearance models with CIELAB, in 1997, the CIE wanted to follow up itself with a comprehensive color appearance model. The result was CIECAM97s, which was comprehensive, but also complex and partly difficult to use. It gained widespread acceptance as a standard color appearance model until CIECAM02 was published.

IPT

Ebner and Fairchild addressed the issue of non-constant lines of hue in their color space dubbed IPT. The IPT color space converts D65-adapted XYZ data (XD65, YD65, ZD65) to long-medium-short cone response data (LMS) using an adapted form of the Hunt–Pointer–Estevez matrix ($M_{HPE(D65)}$).

The IPT color appearance model excels at providing a formulation for hue where a constant hue value equals a constant perceived hue independent of the values of lightness and chroma (which is the general ideal for any color appearance model, but hard to achieve). It is therefore well-suited for gamut mapping implementations.

ICtCp

ITU-R BT.2100 includes a color space called ICtCp, which improves the original IPT by exploring higher dynamic range and larger color gamuts.

CIECAM02

After the success of CIECAM97s, the CIE developed CIECAM02 as its successor and published it in 2002. It performs better and is simpler at the same time. Apart from the rudimentary CIELAB model, CIECAM02 comes closest to an internationally agreed upon "standard" for a (comprehensive) color appearance model.

iCAM06

iCAM06 is an image color appearance model. As such, it does not treat each pixel of an image independently, but in the context of the complete image. This allows it to incorporate spatial color appearance parameters like contrast, which makes it well-suited for HDR images. It is also a first step to deal with spatial appearance phenomena.

References

- Bumbaca-smith-computer-vision: eecg.toronto.edu, Retrieved 13 June, 2019

- Hsien-Che Lee (2005). Introduction to color imaging science. Cambridge University Press. ISBN 0-521-84388-X

- Logvinenko, A. D. (2015). The geometric structure of color. Journal of Vision, 15(1), 15.1.16. http://doi.org/10.1167/15.1.16

- Foster, David H. (2011). "Color Constancy". Vision Research. 51 (7): 674–700. doi:10.1016/j.visres.2010.09.006. PMID 20849875

- Steven K. Shevell (2003) The Science of Color. 2nd ed. Elsevier Science & Technology. ISBN 0-444-51251-9

- Explain-about-elements-of-visual-perception: legendtechz.blogspot.com, Retrieved 05 July, 2019

- Fairchild, Mark D. (2013). Color Appearance Models. Wiley-IS&T Series in Imaging Science and Technology (3 ed.). Hoboken: John Wiley & Sons. ISBN 978-1-119-96703-3

- Rodney, Andrew (2005). Color Management for Photographers. Focal Press. pp. 32–33. ISBN 0-240-80649-2

Geometry in Computer Vision

Geometry has numerous uses in terms of computer vision. Projective geometry, epipolar geometry, etc. are some of its types. Some of its aspects are bundle adjustment, fundamental matrix of computer vision, essential matrix, camera matrix, camera resectioning, structure from motion and image rectification. The topics elaborated in this chapter will help in gaining a better perspective about the use of geometry in computer vision.

PROJECTIVE GEOMETRY

The straightforward way to model geometry in 3D space is with the 3 dimensional Euclidean vector space R^3. For geometry on the plane (drawings and images) the equivalent choice is R^2. A Euclidean vector space implies the existence of the Euclidean vector norm. A vector norm is what is needed to define lengths and angles.

When dealing with 2D images being the projections of the 3D world, Euclidean geometry does not suffice anymore as a mathematical model. To obtain a feeling for the necessity of projective geometry, we take a quick look at the basic imaging device: the pinhole camera, before we introduce the math of projective geometry.

Imagine standing in a darkened room with only a small hole in one of the walls and a semi-transparent screen a short distance from the hole. The 3D outside world is projected onto the screen. Such a room (or device as you can build miniature versions) is called a camera obscura.

A picture of trees. The image as would have been projected in the camera obscura in case the camera obscura was placed on the middle of the road.

From the image of the road with trees in figure we can observe that in the projected space:

- Points on a line in the real world are projected as points on a line on the retina,

- Lines which are parallel in 3d space are projected on lines that meet at the horizon,

- Lengths are not preserved (a tree far away is projected much smaller then a nearby tree),

- Angles are not preserved.

Note that not all parallel lines in 3D will meet in a point in the projection. Two lines parallel to the horizon will not meet in a point. I.e. not in a point nearby, but mathematically we say that the lines meet in a point at infinity. Euclidean geometry is not capable of dealing with points (and lines) at infinity. In projective geometry the points at infinity are treated as all other points in space.

The most important invariance in projective space (indeed its defining property) is that colinearity is preserved. Points on a line will stay points on a line (although maybe a different line).

Projective Geometry in 2D

By definition a projective transform preserves colinearity of points. It can be shown that any 2D projective transform is a linear operator in homogeneous 3D space (i.e. using vectors in 3D space). And therefore any 2D projective transform P can be represented with a 3×3 matrix working on the homogeneous 3D vectors. Also any 3×3 matrix represents a projective 2D transform.

We will write homogeneous vectors with a tilde: $\tilde{\mathbf{x}}$. So for a 2D point:

$$\mathbf{x} = \begin{pmatrix} x_1 \\ x_2 \end{pmatrix}$$

the corresponding homogeneous vectors are all of the form:

$$\tilde{\mathbf{x}} = \begin{pmatrix} sx_1 \\ sx_2 \\ s \end{pmatrix}$$

for any s≠0. So two homogeneous vectors $\tilde{\mathbf{x}}$ and $\tilde{\mathbf{y}}$ such that $\tilde{\mathbf{x}} \neq \tilde{\mathbf{y}}$ can still correspond with the same 2D point (in case $\tilde{\mathbf{y}}$ is a multiple of $\tilde{\mathbf{x}}$). Such homogeneous vectors that are not mathematically the same, but do have the same interpretation are said to be similar and denoted as:

$$\tilde{\mathbf{y}} \sim \tilde{\mathbf{x}}$$

Projective Geometry in 3D

For projective geometry in 3D space we need to use homogeneous vectors in 4D. Projective transforms in 3D space are then represented as 4×4 matrices.

In 2D space lines can be represented with a homogeneous vector like points in 2D space. In 3D space a point is represented with a 4D homogeneous vector and we can also represent planes with a 4D homogeneous vector.

EPIPOLAR GEOMETRY

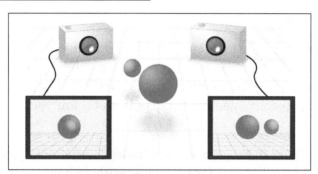

Typical use case for epipolar geometry
Two cameras take a picture of the same scene from different points of view. The epipolar geometry then describes the relation between the two resulting views.

Epipolar geometry is the geometry of stereo vision. When two cameras view a 3D scene from two distinct positions, there are a number of geometric relations between the 3D points and their projections onto the 2D images that lead to constraints between the image points. These relations are derived based on the assumption that the cameras can be approximated by the pinhole camera model.

The figure below depicts two pinhole cameras looking at point X. In real cameras, the image plane is actually behind the focal center, and produces an image that is symmetric about the focal center of the lens. Here, however, the problem is simplified by placing a *virtual image plane* in front of the focal center i.e. optical center of each camera lens to produce an image not transformed by the symmetry. O_L and O_R represent the centers of symmetry of the two cameras lenses. X represents the point of interest in both cameras. Points x_L and x_R are the projections of point X onto the image planes.

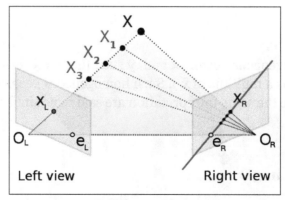

Epipolar geometry.

Each camera captures a 2D image of the 3D world. This conversion from 3D to 2D is referred to as a perspective projection and is described by the pinhole camera model. It is common to model this projection operation by rays that emanate from the camera, passing through its focal center. Note that each emanating ray corresponds to a single point in the image.

Epipole or Epipolar Point

Since the optical centers of the cameras lenses are distinct, each center projects onto a distinct point into the other camera's image plane. These two image points, denoted by e_L and e_R, are called *epipoles* or *epipolar points*. Both epipoles e_L and e_R in their respective image planes and both optical centers O_L and O_R lie on a single 3D line.

Epipolar Line

The line O_L–X is seen by the left camera as a point because it is directly in line with that camera's lens optical center. However, the right camera sees this line as a line in its image plane. That line $(e_R$–$x_R)$ in the right camera is called an *epipolar line*. Symmetrically, the line O_R–X seen by the right camera as a point is seen as epipolar line e_L–x_L by the left camera.

An epipolar line is a function of the position of point X in the 3D space, i.e. as X varies, a set of epipolar lines is generated in both images. Since the 3D line O_L–X passes through the optical center of the lens O_L, the corresponding epipolar line in the right image must pass through the epipole e_R (and correspondingly for epipolar lines in the left image). All epipolar lines in one image contain the epipolar point of that image. In fact, any line which contains the epipolar point is an epipolar line since it can be derived from some 3D point X.

Epipolar Plane

As an alternative visualization, consider the points X, O_L & O_R that form a plane called the *epipolar plane*. The epipolar plane intersects each camera's image plane where it forms lines—the epipolar lines. All epipolar planes and epipolar lines intersect the epipole regardless of where X is located.

Epipolar Constraint and Triangulation

If the relative position of the two cameras is known, this leads to two important observations:

- Assume the projection point x_L is known, and the epipolar line e_R–x_R is known and the point X projects into the right image, on a point x_R which must lie on this particular epipolar line. This means that for each point observed in one image the same point must be observed in the other image on a known epipolar line. This provides an *epipolar constraint*: the projection of X on the right camera plane x_R must be contained in the e_R–x_R epipolar line. Note also that all points X e.g. X_1, X_2, X_3 on the O_L–X_L line will verify that constraint. It means that it is possible to test if two points correspond to the same 3D point. Epipolar constraints can also be described by the essential matrix or the fundamental matrix between the two cameras.

- If the points x_L and x_R are known, their projection lines are also known. If the two image points correspond to the same 3D point X the projection lines must intersect precisely at X. This means that X can be calculated from the coordinates of the two image points, a process called *triangulation*.

Simplified Cases

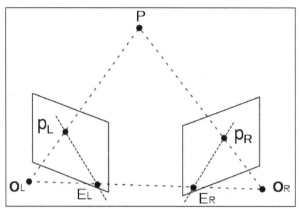

Example of epipolar geometry.

If the two camera plane coincide then the two epipoles are undetermined as intersection of one optical center of one camera with the other camera plane is not a point but a line. Two cameras, with their respective centers of projection points O_L and O_R, observe a point P. The projection of P onto each of the image planes is denoted p_L and p_R. Points E_L and E_R are the epipoles.

The epipolar geometry is simplified if the two camera image planes coincide. In this case, the epipolar lines also coincide (E_L–P_L = E_R–P_R). Furthermore, the epipolar lines are parallel to the line O_L–O_R between the centers of projection, and can in practice be aligned with the horizontal axes of the two images. This means that for each point in one image, its corresponding point in the other image can be found by looking only along a horizontal line. If the cameras cannot be positioned in this way, the image coordinates from the cameras may be transformed to emulate having a common image plane. This process is called image rectification.

Epipolar Geometry of Pushbroom Sensor

In contrast to the conventional frame camera which uses a two-dimensional CCD, pushbroom camera adopts an array of one-dimensional CCDs to produce long continuous image strip which is called "image carpet". Epipolar geometry of this sensor is quite different from that of pinhole projection cameras. First, the epipolar line of pushbroom sensor is not straight, but hyperbola-like curve. Second, epipolar 'curve' pair does not exist. However, in some special conditions, the epipolar geometry of the satellite images could be considered as a linear model.

POSE

In computer vision and robotics, a typical task is to identify specific objects in an image and to determine each object's position and orientation relative to some coordinate system. This information can then be used, for example, to allow a robot to manipulate an object or to avoid moving into the object. The combination of *position* and *orientation* is referred to as the pose of an object, even though this concept is sometimes used only to describe the orientation. *Exterior orientation* and *translation* are also used as synonyms of pose.

The image data from which the pose of an object is determined can be either a single image, a stereo image pair, or an image sequence where, typically, the camera is moving with a known velocity. The objects which are considered can be rather general, including a living being or body parts, e.g., a head or hands. The methods which are used for determining the pose of an object, however, are usually specific for a class of objects and cannot generally be expected to work well for other types of objects.

The pose can be described by means of a rotation and translation transformation which brings the object from a reference pose to the observed. This rotation transformation can be represented in different ways, e.g., as a rotation matrix or a quaternion.

3D Pose Estimation

3D pose estimation is the problem of determining the transformation of an object in a 2D image which gives the 3D object. One of the requirements of 3D pose estimation arises from the limitations of feature-based pose estimation. There exist environments where it is difficult to extract corners or edges from an image. To circumvent these issues, the object is dealt with as a whole in noted techniques through the use of free-form contours.

From an Uncalibrated 2D Camera

It is possible to estimate the 3D rotation and translation of a 3D object from a single 2D photo, if an approximate 3D model of the object is known and the corresponding points in the 2D image are known. A common technique for solving this has recently been "POSIT", where the 3D pose is estimated directly from the 3D model points and the 2D image points, and corrects the errors iteratively until a good estimate is found from a single image. Most implementations of POSIT only work on non-coplanar points (in other words, it won't work with flat objects or planes).

Another approach is to register a 3D CAD model over the photograph of a known object by optimizing a suitable distance measure with respect to the pose parameters. The distance measure is computed between the object in the photograph and the 3D CAD model projection at a given pose. Perspective projectionor orthogonal projection is possible depending on the pose representation used. This approach is appropriate for applications where a 3D CAD model of a known object (or object category) is available.

From a Calibrated 2D Camera

Given a 2D image of an object, and the camera that is calibrated with respect to a world coordinate system, it is also possible to find the pose which gives the 3D object in its object coordinate system. This works as follows.

Extracting 3D from 2D

Starting with a 2D image, image points are extracted which correspond to corners in an image. The projection rays from the image points are reconstructed from the 2D points so that the 3D points, which must be incident with the reconstructed rays, can be determined.

Pseudocode

The algorithm for determining pose estimation is based on the iterative closest point algorithm. The main idea is to determine the correspondences between 2D image features and points on the 3D model curve.

(a) Reconstruct projection rays from the image points

(b) Estimate the nearest point of each projection ray to a point on the 3D contour

(c) Estimate the pose of the contour with the use of this correspondence set

(d) goto (b)

The above algorithm does not account for images containing an object that is partially occluded. The following algorithm assumes that all contours are rigidly coupled, meaning the pose of one contour defines the pose of another contour.

(a) Reconstruct projection rays from the image points

(b) For each projection ray R:

  (c) For each 3D contour:

    (c1) Estimate the nearest point P1 of ray R to a point on the contour

    (c2) if (n == 1) choose P1 as actual P for the point-line correspondence

    (c3) else compare P1 with P:

      if dist(P1, R) is smaller than dist(P, R) then

        choose P1 as new P

(d) Use (P, R) as correspondence set.

(e) Estimate pose with this correspondence set

(f) Transform contours, goto (b)

Estimating Pose through Comparison

Systems exist which use a database of an object at different rotations and translations to compare an input image against to estimate pose. These systems accuracy is limited to situations which are represented in their database of images, however the goal is to recognize a pose, rather than determine it.

Software

- Posest, a GPL C/C++ library for 6dof pose estimation from 3D-2D correspondences.

- Diffgeom2pose, fast Matlab solver for 6dof pose estimation from only *two* 3D-2D correspondences of points with directions (vectors), or points at curves (point-tangents). The points can be SIFT attributed with feature directions.

- MINUS, C++ package for (relative) pose estimation of three views. Includes cases of three corresponding points with lines at these points (as in feature positions and orientations, or curve points with tangents), and also for three corresponding points and one line correspondence.

BUNDLE ADJUSTMENT

Given a set of images depicting a number of 3D points from different viewpoints, bundle adjustment can be defined as the problem of simultaneously refining the 3D coordinates describing the scene geometry, the parameters of the relative motion, and the optical characteristics of the camera employed to acquire the images, according to an optimality criterion involving the corresponding image projections of all points.

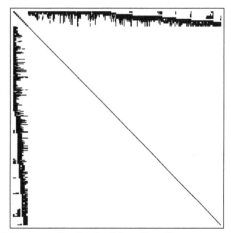

A sparse matrix obtained when solving a modestly sized bundle adjustment problem. This is the sparsity pattern of a 992×992 normal-equation (i.e. approximate Hessian) matrix. Black regions correspond to nonzero blocks.

Uses

Bundle adjustment is almost always used as the last step of every feature-based 3D reconstruction algorithm. It amounts to an optimization problem on the 3D structure and viewing parameters (i.e., camera pose and possibly intrinsic calibration and radial distortion), to obtain a reconstruction which is optimal under certain assumptions regarding the noise pertaining to the observed image features: If the image error is zero-mean Gaussian, then bundle adjustment is the Maximum Likelihood Estimator. Its name refers to the bundles of light rays originating from each 3D feature and converging on each camera's optical center, which are adjusted optimally with respect to both the structure and viewing parameters (similarity in meaning to categorical bundle seems a pure coincidence). Bundle adjustment was originally conceived in the field of photogrammetry during the 1950s and has increasingly been used by computer vision researchers during recent years.

Bundle adjustment boils down to minimizing the reprojection error between the image locations of observed and predicted image points, which is expressed as the sum of squares of a large number of nonlinear, real-valued functions. Thus, the minimization is achieved using nonlinear least-squares algorithms. Of these, Levenberg–Marquardt has proven to be one of the most successful due to its ease of implementation and its use of an effective damping strategy that lends it the ability to converge quickly from a wide range of initial guesses. By iteratively linearizing the function to be minimized in the neighborhood of the current estimate, the Levenberg–Marquardt algorithm involves the solution of linear systems termed the normal equations. When solving the minimization problems arising in the framework of bundle adjustment, the normal equations have a sparse block structure owing to the lack of interaction among parameters for different 3D points and cameras. This can be exploited to gain tremendous computational benefits by employing a sparse variant of the Levenberg–Marquardt algorithm which explicitly takes advantage of the normal equations zeros pattern, avoiding storing and operating on zero-elements.

Bundle adjustment amounts to jointly refining a set of initial camera and structure parameter estimates for finding the set of parameters that most accurately predict the locations of the observed points in the set of available images. More formally, assume that n 3D points are seen in m views and let x_{ij} be the projection of the i th point on image j. Let v_{ij} denote the binary variables that equal 1 if point i is visible in image j and 0 otherwise. Assume also that each camera j is parameterized by a vector a_j and each 3D point i by a vector b_i. Bundle adjustment minimizes the total reprojection error with respect to all 3D point and camera parameters, specifically:

$$\min_{a_j, b_i} \sum_{i=1}^{n} \sum_{j=1}^{m} v_{ij} d(Q(a_j, b_i), x_{ij})^2,$$

where $Q(a_j, b_i)$ is the predicted projection of point i on image j and d(x, y) denotes the Euclidean distance between the image points represented by vectors x and y . Clearly, bundle adjustment is by definition tolerant to missing image projections and minimizes a physically meaningful criterion.

FUNDAMENTAL MATRIX

In computer vision, the fundamental matrix F is a 3×3 matrix which relates corresponding points in stereo images. In epipolar geometry, with homogeneous image coordinates, x and x′, of corresponding points in a stereo image pair, Fx describes a line (an epipolar line) on which the corresponding point x′ on the other image must lie. That means, for all pairs of corresponding points holds:

$$x'^{\top} F x = 0$$

Being of rank two and determined only up to scale, the fundamental matrix can be estimated given at least seven point correspondences. Its seven parameters represent the only geometric information about cameras that can be obtained through point correspondences alone.

The term "fundamental matrix" was coined by QT Luong in his influential PhD thesis. It is sometimes also referred to as the "bifocal tensor". As a tensor it is a two-point tensor in that it is a bilinear form relating points in distinct coordinate systems.

The above relation which defines the fundamental matrix was published in 1992 by both Olivier Faugeras and Richard Hartley. Although H. Christopher Longuet-Higgins' essential matrix satisfies a similar relationship, the essential matrix is a metric object pertaining to calibrated cameras, while the fundamental matrix describes the correspondence in more general and fundamental terms of projective geometry. This is captured mathematically by the relationship between a fundamental matrix F and its corresponding essential matrix E, which is:

$$E = (K')^\top F K$$

K and K' being the intrinsic calibration matrices of the two images involved.

The fundamental matrix is a relationship between any two images of the same scene that constrains where the projection of points from the scene can occur in both images. Given the projection of a scene point into one of the images the corresponding point in the other image is constrained to a line, helping the search, and allowing for the detection of wrong correspondences. The relation between corresponding image points which the fundamental matrix represents is referred to as epipolar constraint, matching constraint, discrete matching constraint, or incidence relation.

Projective Reconstruction Theorem

The fundamental matrix can be determined by a set of point correspondences. Additionally, these corresponding image points may be triangulated to world points with the help of camera matrices derived directly from this fundamental matrix. The scene composed of these world points is within a projective transformation of the true scene.

Proof

Say that the image point correspondence $x \leftrightarrow x'$ derives from the world point x under the camera matrices (P, P') as:

$$x = PX$$
$$x' = P'X$$

Say we transform space by a general homography matrix $H_{4\times4}$ such that $X_0 = HX$.

The cameras then transform as:

$$P_0 = PH^{-1}$$
$$P'_0 = P'H^{-1}$$
$$P_0 X_0 = PH^{-1}HX = PX = x$$

The Fundamental Matrix for Satellite Images

The fundamental matrix expresses the epipolar geometry in stereo images. Although, the Epipolar geometry in images taken with perspective cameras appears as straight lines, however, in satellite images, the image is formed during the sensor movement along its orbit, therefore, there are multiple projection centers for one image scene and the epipolar line is formed as the epipolar curve.

However, in special conditions such as small image tiles, the satellite images could be rectified using the fundamental matrix.

ESSENTIAL MATRIX

In computer vision, the essential matrix is a 3×3 matrix, E, with some additional properties described below, which relates corresponding points in stereo images assuming that the cameras satisfy the pinhole camera model.

Function

More specifically, if y and y' are homogeneous normalized image coordinates, respectively, then:

$$(y')^{\top} E y = 0$$

if y and y' correspond to the same 3D point in the scene.

The above relation which defines the essential matrix was published in 1981 by H. Christopher Longuet-Higgins, introducing the concept to the computer vision community. Richard Hartley and Andrew Zisserman's book reports that an analogous matrix appeared in photogrammetry long before that. Longuet-Higgins' paper includes an algorithm for estimating from a set of corresponding normalized image coordinates as well as an algorithm for determining the relative position and orientation of the two cameras given that E is known. Finally, it shows how the 3D coordinates of the image points can be determined with the aid of the essential matrix.

Use

The essential matrix can be seen as a precursor to the fundamental matrix. Both matrices can be used for establishing constraints between matching image points, but the essential matrix can only be used in relation to calibrated cameras since the inner camera parameters must be known in order to achieve the normalization. If, however, the cameras are calibrated the essential matrix can be useful for determining both the relative position and orientation between the cameras and the 3D position of corresponding image points.

Derivation

Two normalized cameras project the 3D world onto their respective image planes. Let the 3D coordinates of a point P be (x_1, x_2, x_3) and (x'_1, x'_2, x'_3) relative to each camera's coordinate system. Since the cameras are normalized, the corresponding image coordinates are:

$$\begin{pmatrix} y_1 \\ y_2 \end{pmatrix} = \frac{1}{x_3} \begin{pmatrix} x_1 \\ x_2 \end{pmatrix}$$

and

$$\begin{pmatrix} y'_1 \\ y'_2 \end{pmatrix} = \frac{1}{x'_3} \begin{pmatrix} x'_1 \\ x'_2 \end{pmatrix}$$

A homogeneous representation of the two image coordinates is then given by:

$$\begin{pmatrix} y_1 \\ y_2 \\ 1 \end{pmatrix} = \frac{1}{x_3} \begin{pmatrix} x_1 \\ x_2 \\ x_3 \end{pmatrix} \text{ and } E = R[t]_\times$$

which also can be written more compactly as:

$$y = \frac{1}{x_3}\tilde{x} \qquad \text{and} \qquad y' = \frac{1}{x'_3}\tilde{x}'$$

where y and y' are homogeneous representations of the 2D image coordinates and $\tilde{x}$ and $\tilde{x}'$ are proper 3D coordinates but in two different coordinate systems.

Another consequence of the normalized cameras is that their respective coordinate systems are related by means of a translation and rotation. This implies that the two sets of 3D coordinates are related as:

$$\tilde{x}' = R(\tilde{x} - t)$$

where R is a 3×3 rotation matrix and t is a 3-dimensional translation vector.

The essential matrix is then defined as:

$$E = R[t]_\times$$

where $[t]_\times$ is the matrix representation of the cross product with t.

To see that this definition of the essential matrix describes a constraint on corresponding image coordinates multiply E from left and right with the 3D coordinates of point P in the two different coordinate systems:

$$(\tilde{x}')^T E\tilde{x} \overset{(1)}{=} (\tilde{x}-t)^T R^T R[t]_\times \tilde{x} \overset{(2)}{=} (\tilde{x}-t)^T [t]_\times \tilde{x} \overset{(3)}{=} 0$$

- Insert the above relations between and (x') and $\tilde{x}$ the definition of E in terms of R and t.

- $R^T R = I$ since R is a rotation matrix.

- Properties of the matrix representation of the cross product.

Finally, it can be assumed that both x_3 and x'_3 are > 0, otherwise they are not visible in both cameras. This gives:

$$0 = (\tilde{x}')^T E\tilde{x} = \frac{1}{x'_3}(\tilde{x}')^T E\frac{1}{x_3}\tilde{x} = (y')^T Ey$$

which is the constraint that the essential matrix defines between corresponding image points.

Properties of the Essential Matrix

Not every arbitrary 3×3 matrix can be an essential matrix for some stereo cameras. To see this notice that it is defined as the matrix product of one rotation matrix and one skew-symmetric matrix, both 3×3. The skew-symmetric matrix must have two singular values which are equal and another which is zero. The multiplication of the rotation matrix does not change the singular values which means that also the essential matrix has two singular values which are equal and one which is zero. The properties described here are sometimes referred to as *internal constraints* of the essential matrix.

If the essential matrix E is multiplied by a non-zero scalar, the result is again an essential matrix which defines exactly the same constraint as E does. This means that E can be seen as an element of a projective space, that is, two such matrices are considered equivalent if one is a non-zero scalar multiplication of the other. This is a relevant position, for example, if E is estimated from image data. However, it is also possible to take the position that E is defined as:

$$E = [\tilde{t}]_\times R$$

where $\tilde{t} = -Rt,$, and then E has a well-defined "scaling". It depends on the application which position is the more relevant.

The constraints can also be expressed as:

$$\det E = 0$$

and

$$2EE^T E - \mathrm{tr}(EE^T)E = 0.$$

Here the last equation is matrix constraint, which can be seen as 9 constraints, one for each matrix element. These constraints are often used for determining the essential matrix from five corresponding point pairs.

The essential matrix has five or six degrees of freedom, depending on whether or not it is seen as a projective element. The rotation matrix R and the translation vector t have three degrees of freedom each, in total six. If the essential matrix is considered as a projective element, however, one degree of freedom related to scalar multiplication must be subtracted leaving five degrees of freedom in total.

Estimation of the Essential Matrix

Given a set of corresponding image points it is possible to estimate an essential matrix which satisfies the defining epipolar constraint for all the points in the set. However, if the image points are subject to noise, which is the common case in any practical situation, it is not possible to find an essential matrix which satisfies all constraints exactly.

Depending on how the error related to each constraint is measured, it is possible to determine or estimate an essential matrix which optimally satisfies the constraints for a given set of corresponding image points. The most straightforward approach is to set up a total least squares problem, commonly known as the eight-point algorithm.

Determining R and t from E

Given that the essential matrix has been determined for a stereo camera pair, for example, using the estimation method above this information can be used for determining also the rotation and translation (up to a scaling) between the two camera's coordinate systems. In these derivations E is seen as a projective element rather than having a well-determined scaling.

Finding One Solution

An SVD of E gives

where U and V are orthogonal 3×3 matrices and Σ is a 3×3 diagonal matrix with:

$$\Sigma = \begin{pmatrix} s & 0 & 0 \\ 0 & s & 0 \\ 0 & 0 & 0 \end{pmatrix}$$

The diagonal entries of Σ are the singular values of E which, according to the internal constraints of the essential matrix, must consist of two identical and one zero value. Define:

$$W = \begin{pmatrix} 0 & -1 & 0 \\ 1 & 0 & 0 \\ 0 & 0 & 1 \end{pmatrix} \quad \text{with} \quad W^{-1} = W^{T} = \begin{pmatrix} 0 & 1 & 0 \\ -1 & 0 & 0 \\ 0 & 0 & 1 \end{pmatrix}$$

and make the following ansatz:

$$[t]_x = UW£U^{T}$$

$$R = UW^{-1}V^{T}$$

Since Σ may not completely fulfill the constraints when dealing with real world data (f.e. camera images), the alternative:

$$[t]_x = UZU^{T} \quad \text{with} \quad Z = \begin{pmatrix} 0 & 1 & 0 \\ -1 & 0 & 0 \\ 0 & 0 & 0 \end{pmatrix}$$

may help.

Proof

First, these expressions for R and $[t]_x$ do satisfy the defining equation for the essential matrix:

$$[t]_x R = UW\Sigma U^{T}UW^{-1}V^{T} = U\Sigma V^{T} = E$$

Second, it must be shown that this $[t]_x$ is a matrix representation of the cross product for some t.Since:

$$W\Sigma = \begin{pmatrix} 0 & -s & 0 \\ s & 0 & 0 \\ 0 & 0 & 0 \end{pmatrix}$$

it is the case that $W\Sigma$ is skew-symmetric, i.e., $(W\Sigma)^T = -W\Sigma$. This is also the case for our $[t]_x$, since:

$$([t]_x)^T = U(W\Sigma)^T U^T = -UW\Sigma U^T = -[t]_x$$

According to the general properties of the matrix representation of the cross product it then follows that $[t]_x$ must be the cross product operator of exactly one vector t.

Third, it must also need to be shown that the above expression for R is a rotation matrix. It is the product of three matrices which all are orthogonal which means that R, too, is orthogonal or $\det(R) = \pm 1$. To be a proper rotation matrix it must also satisfy $\det(R) = 1$. Since, in this case, E is seen as a projective element this can be accomplished by reversing the sign of E if necessary.

Finding All Solutions

So far one possible solution for R and t has been established given E. It is, however, not the only possible solution and it may not even be a valid solution from a practical point of view. To begin with, since the scaling of E is undefined, the scaling of E is also undefined. It must lie in the null space of E since:

$$Et = R[t]_x t = 0$$

For the subsequent analysis of the solutions, however, the exact scaling of t is not so important as its "sign", i.e., in which direction it points. Let $\hat{t}$ be normalized vector in the null space of E. It is then the case that both $\hat{t}$ and $-\hat{t}$ are valid translation vectors relative E. It is also possible to change W into W^{-1} in the derivations of R and t above. For the translation vector this only causes a change of sign, which has already been described as a possibility. For the rotation, on the other hand, this will produce a different transformation, at least in the general case.

To summarize, given E there are two opposite directions which are possible for t and two different rotations which are compatible with this essential matrix. In total this gives four classes of solutions for the rotation and translation between the two camera coordinate systems. On top of that, there is also an unknown scaling $s > 0$ for the chosen translation direction.

It turns out, however, that only one of the four classes of solutions can be realized in practice. Given a pair of corresponding image coordinates, three of the solutions will always produce a 3D point which lies *behind* at least one of the two cameras and therefore cannot be seen. Only one of the four classes will consistently produce 3D points which are in front of both cameras. This must then be the correct solution. Still, however, it has an undetermined positive scaling related to the translation component.

The above determination of R and t assumes that E satisfy the internal constraints of the essential matrix. If this is not the case which, for example, typically is the case if E has been estimated from real (and noisy) image data, it has to be assumed that it approximately satisfy the internal constraints. The vector $\hat{t}$ is then chosen as right singular vector of E corresponding to the smallest singular value.

3D Points from Corresponding Image Points

The problem to be solved there is how to compute (x_1, x_2, x_3) given corresponding normalized image coordinates (y_1, y_2) and (y_1', y_2'). If the essential matrix is known and the corresponding rotation and translation transformations have been determined, this algorithm provides a solution.

Let r_k denote row k of the rotation matrix R:

$$R = \begin{pmatrix} -r_1 - \\ -r_2 - \\ -r_3 - \end{pmatrix}$$

Combining the above relations between 3D coordinates in the two coordinate systems and the mapping between 3D and 2D points gives:

$$y_1' = \frac{x_1'}{x_3'} = \frac{r_1 \cdot (\tilde{x} - t)}{r_3 \cdot (\tilde{x} - t)} = \frac{r_1 \cdot (y - t/x_3)}{r_3 \cdot (y - t/x_3)}$$

or

$$x_3 = \frac{(r_1 - y_1' r_3) \times t}{(r_1 - y_1' r_3) \times y}$$

Once x_3 is determined, the other two coordinates can be computed as:

$$\begin{pmatrix} x_1 \\ x_2 \end{pmatrix} = x_3 \begin{pmatrix} y_1 \\ y_2 \end{pmatrix}$$

The above derivation is not unique. It is also possible to start with an expression for y_2' and derive an expression for x_3 according to:

$$x_3 = \frac{(r_2 - y_2' r_3) \cdot t}{(r_2 - y_2' r_3) \cdot y}$$

In the ideal case, when the camera maps the 3D points according to a perfect pinhole camera and the resulting 2D points can be detected without any noise, the two expressions for x_3 are equal. In practice, however, they are not and it may be advantageous to combine the two estimates of x_3, for example, in terms of some sort of average.

There are also other types of extensions of the above computations which are possible. They started with an expression of the primed image coordinates and derived 3D coordinates in the unprimed system. It is also possible to start with unprimed image coordinates and obtain primed 3D coordinates, which finally can be transformed into unprimed 3D coordinates. Again, in the ideal case the result should be equal to the above expressions, but in practice they may deviate.

A final remark relates to the fact that if the essential matrix is determined from corresponding image coordinate, which often is the case when 3D points are determined in this way, the translation vector t is known only up to an unknown positive scaling. As a consequence, the reconstructed 3D points, too, are undetermined with respect to a positive scaling.

CAMERA MATRIX

In computer vision a camera matrix or (camera) projection matrix is a 3×4 matrix which describes the mapping of a pinhole camera from 3D points in the world to 2D points in an image.

Let x be a representation of a 3D point in homogeneous coordinates (a 4-dimensional vector), and let y be a representation of the image of this point in the pinhole camera (a 3-dimensional vector). Then the following relation holds:

$$y \sim Cx$$

where C is the camera matrix and the $\sim$ sign implies that the left and right hand sides are equal up to a non-zero scalar multiplication.

Since the camera matrix C is involved in the mapping between elements of two projective spaces, it too can be regarded as a projective element. This means that it has only 11 degrees of freedom since any multiplication by a non-zero scalar results in an equivalent camera matrix.

Derivation

The mapping from the coordinates of a 3D point P to the 2D image coordinates of the point's projection onto the image plane, according to the pinhole camera model is given by:

$$\begin{pmatrix} y_1 \\ y_2 \end{pmatrix} = \frac{f}{x_3} \begin{pmatrix} x_1 \\ x_2 \end{pmatrix}$$

where (x_1, x_2, x_3) are the 3D coordinates of P relative to a camera centered coordinate system, (y_1, y_2) are the resulting image coordinates, and f is the camera's focal length for which we assume $f > 0$. Furthermore, we also assume that $x_3 > 0$.

To derive the camera matrix this expression is rewritten in terms of homogeneous coordinates. Instead of the 2D vector (y_1, y_2) we consider the projective element (a 3D vector) $y = (y_1, y_2, 1)$ and instead of equality we consider equality up to scaling by a non-zero number, denoted $\sim$. First, we write the homogeneous image coordinates as expressions in the usual 3D coordinates.

$$\begin{pmatrix} y_1 \\ y_2 \\ 1 \end{pmatrix} = \frac{f}{x_3} \begin{pmatrix} x_1 \\ x_2 \\ \dfrac{x_3}{f} \end{pmatrix} \sim \begin{pmatrix} x_1 \\ x_2 \\ \dfrac{x_3}{f} \end{pmatrix}$$

Finally, also the 3D coordinates are expressed in a homogeneous representation x and this is how the camera matrix appears:

$$\begin{pmatrix} y_1 \\ y_2 \\ 1 \end{pmatrix} \sim \begin{pmatrix} 1 & 0 & 0 & 0 \\ 0 & 1 & 0 & 0 \\ 0 & 0 & \dfrac{1}{f} & 0 \end{pmatrix} \begin{pmatrix} x_1 \\ x_2 \\ x_3 \\ 1 \end{pmatrix} \quad \text{or } y \sim Cx$$

where C is the camera matrix, which here is given by:

$$C = \begin{pmatrix} 1 & 0 & 0 & 0 \\ 0 & 1 & 0 & 0 \\ 0 & 0 & \dfrac{1}{f} & 0 \end{pmatrix}$$

and the corresponding camera matrix now becomes:

$$C = \begin{pmatrix} 1 & 0 & 0 & 0 \\ 0 & 1 & 0 & 0 \\ 0 & 0 & \dfrac{1}{f} & 0 \end{pmatrix} \sim \begin{pmatrix} f & 0 & 0 & 0 \\ 0 & f & 0 & 0 \\ 0 & 0 & 1 & 0 \end{pmatrix}$$

The last step is a consequence of C itself being a projective element.

The camera matrix derived here may appear trivial in the sense that it contains very few non-zero elements. This depends to a large extent on the particular coordinate systems which have been chosen for the 3D and 2D points. In practice, however, other forms of camera matrices are common.

Camera Position

The camera matrix C derived previously has a null space which is spanned by the vector:

$$n = \begin{pmatrix} 0 \\ 0 \\ 0 \\ 1 \end{pmatrix}$$

This is also the homogeneous representation of the 3D point which has coordinates (0,0,0), that is, the "camera center" (aka the entrance pupil; the position of the pinhole of a pinhole camera) is at O. This means that the camera center (and only this point) cannot be mapped to a point in the image plane by the camera (or equivalently, it maps to all points on the image as every ray on the image goes through this point).

For any other 3D point with $x_3 = 0$, the result y ~ Cx is well-defined and has the for $y = (y_1 y_2 0)^T$ This corresponds to a point at infinity in the projective image plane (even though, if the image plane is taken to be a Euclidean plane, no corresponding intersection point exists).

Normalized Camera Matrix and Normalized Image Coordinates

The camera matrix derived above can be simplified even further if we assume that $f = 1$:

$$C_0 = \begin{pmatrix} 1 & 0 & 0 & 0 \\ 0 & 1 & 0 & 0 \\ 0 & 0 & 1 & 0 \end{pmatrix} = (I \mid 0)$$

where I here denotes a 3×3 identity matrix. Note that 3×4 matrix C here is divided into a concatenation of a 3×3 matrix and a 3-dimensional vector. The camera matrix C_0 is sometimes referred to as a *canonical form*.

So far all points in the 3D world have been represented in a *camera centered* coordinate system, that is, a coordinate system which has its origin at the camera center (the location of the pinhole of a pinhole camera). In practice however, the 3D points may be represented in terms of coordinates relative to an arbitrary coordinate system (X1',X2',X3'). Assuming that the camera coordinate axes (X1,X2,X3) and the axes (X1',X2',X3') are of Euclidean type (orthogonal and isotropic), there is a unique Euclidean 3D transformation (rotation and translation) between the two coordinate systems. In other words, the camera is not necessarily at the origin looking along the z axis.

The two operations of rotation and translation of 3D coordinates can be represented as the two 4×4 matrices:

$$\left(\begin{array}{c|c} R & 0 \\ \hline 0 & 1 \end{array} \right) \text{ and } \left(\begin{array}{c|c} I & t \\ \hline 0 & 1 \end{array} \right)$$

where R is a 3×3 rotation matrix and t is a 3-dimensional translation vector. When the first matrix is multiplied onto the homogeneous representation of a 3D point, the result is the homogeneous representation of the rotated point, and the second matrix performs instead a translation. Performing the two operations in sequence, i.e. first the rotation and then the translation (with translation vector given in the already rotated coordinate system), gives a combined rotation and translation matrix:

$$\left(\begin{array}{c|c} R & t \\ \hline 0 & 1 \end{array} \right)$$

Assuming that R and t are precisely the rotation and translations which relate the two coordinate system (X1,X2,X3) and (X1',X2',X3') above, this implies that:

$$x = \left(\begin{array}{c|c} R & t \\ \hline 0 & 1 \end{array}\right) x'$$

Where X' is the homogeneous representation of the point P in the coordinate system (X1',X2',X3').

Assuming also that the camera matrix is given by C_0, the mapping from the coordinates in the (X1,X2,X3) system to homogeneous image coordinates becomes:

$$y \sim C_0 x = (I|0)\left(\begin{array}{c|c} R & t \\ \hline 0 & 1 \end{array}\right) x' = (R|t)x'$$

Consequently, the camera matrix which relates points in the coordinate system (X1',X2',X3') to image coordinates is:

$$C_N = (R|t)$$

a concatenation of a 3D rotation matrix and a 3-dimensional translation vector.

This type of camera matrix is referred to as a *normalized camera matrix*, it assumes focal length = 1 and that image coordinates are measured in a coordinate system where the origin is located at the intersection between axis X3 and the image plane and has the same units as the 3D coordinate system. The resulting image coordinates are referred to as *normalized image coordinates*.

The Camera Position

Again, the null space of the normalized camera matrix, C_N described above, is spanned by the 4-dimensional vector:

$$n = \left(\begin{array}{c} -R^{-1}t \\ 1 \end{array}\right) = \left(\begin{array}{c} \tilde{n} \\ 1 \end{array}\right)$$

This is also, again, the coordinates of the camera center, now relative to the (X1',X2',X3') system. This can be seen by applying first the rotation and then the translation to the 3-dimensional vector $\tilde{n}$ and the result is the homogeneous representation of 3D coordinates (0,0,0).

This implies that the camera center (in its homogeneous representation) lies in the null space of the camera matrix, provided that it is represented in terms of 3D coordinates relative to the same coordinate system as the camera matrix refers to.

The normalized camera matrix C_N can now be written as:

$$C_N = R(I|R^{-1}t) = R(I|-\tilde{n})$$

where $\tilde{n}$ is the 3D coordinates of the camera relative to the (X1',X2',X3') system.

General Camera Matrix

Given the mapping produced by a normalized camera matrix, the resulting normalized image coordinates can be transformed by means of an arbitrary 2D homography. This includes 2D translations and rotations as well as scaling (isotropic and anisotropic) but also general 2D perspective transformations. Such a transformation can be represented as a 3×3 matrix H which maps the homogeneous normalized image coordinates y to the homogeneous transformed image coordinates y':

$$y' = Hy$$

Inserting the above expression for the normalized image coordinates in terms of the 3D coordinates gives:

$$y' = HC_N x'$$

This produces the most general form of camera matrix:

$$C = HC_N = H(R \,|\, t)$$

CAMERA RESECTIONING

Camera resectioning is the process of estimating the parameters of a pinhole camera model approximating the camera that produced a given photograph or video. Usually, the pinhole camera parameters are represented in a 3×4 matrix called the camera matrix.

This process is often called camera calibration, although that term can also refer to photometric camera calibration.

Parameters of Camera Model

Often, we use $[u \; v \; 1]^T$ to represent a 2D point position in pixel coordinates. Here $[x_w \; y_w \; z_w \; 1]^T$ is used to represent a 3D point position in World coordinates. Note: they were expressed in augmented notation of homogeneous coordinates which is the most common notation in robotics and rigid body transforms. Referring to the pinhole camera model, a camera matrix is used to denote a projective mapping from World coordinates to Pixel coordinates.

$$z_c \begin{bmatrix} u \\ v \\ 1 \end{bmatrix} = K \begin{bmatrix} R & T \end{bmatrix} \begin{bmatrix} x_w \\ y_w \\ z_w \\ 1 \end{bmatrix}$$

Intrinsic Parameters

$$K = \begin{bmatrix} \alpha_x & \gamma & u_0 & 0 \\ 0 & \alpha_y & v_0 & 0 \\ 0 & 0 & 1 & 0 \end{bmatrix}$$

The intrinsic matrix K contains 5 intrinsic parameters. These parameters encompass focal length, image sensor format, and principal point. The parameters $\alpha_x = f \cdot m_x$ and $\alpha_y = f \cdot m_y$ represent focal length in terms of pixels, where m_x and m_y are the scale factors relating pixels to distance and f is the focal length in terms of distance. γ represents the skew coefficient between the x and the y axis, and is often 0. u_0 and v_0 represent the principal point, which would be ideally in the center of the image.

Nonlinear intrinsic parameters such as lens distortion are also important although they cannot be included in the linear camera model described by the intrinsic parameter matrix. Many modern camera calibration algorithms estimate these intrinsic parameters as well in the form of non-linear optimisation techniques. This is done in the form of optimising the camera and distortion parameters in the form of what is generally known as bundle adjustment.

Extrinsic Parameters

$$\begin{bmatrix} R_{3x3} & T_{3x1} \\ 0_{1x3} & 1 \end{bmatrix}_{4x4}$$

R,T are the extrinsic parameters which denote the coordinate system transformations from 3D world coordinates to 3D camera coordinates. Equivalently, the extrinsic parameters define the position of the camera center and the camera's heading in world coordinates. T is the position of the origin of the world coordinate system expressed in coordinates of the camera-centered coordinate system. T is often mistakenly considered the position of the camera. The position, C, of the camera expressed in world coordinates is $C = -R^{-1}T = -R^T T$ (since R is a rotation matrix).

Camera calibration is often used as an early stage in computer vision.

When a camera is used, light from the environment is focused on an image plane and captured. This process reduces the dimensions of the data taken in by the camera from three to two (light from a 3D scene is stored on a 2D image). Each pixel on the image plane therefore corresponds to a shaft of light from the original scene. Camera resectioning determines which incoming light is associated with each pixel on the resulting image. In an ideal pinhole camera, a simple projection matrix is enough to do this. With more complex camera systems, errors resulting from misaligned lenses and deformations in their structures can result in more complex distortions in the final image. The camera projection matrix is derived from the intrinsic and extrinsic parameters of the camera, and is often represented by the series of transformations; e.g., a matrix of camera intrinsic parameters, a 3 × 3 rotation matrix, and a translation vector. The camera projection matrix can be used to associate points in a camera's image space with locations in 3D world space.

Camera resectioning is often used in the application of stereo vision where the camera projection matrices of two cameras are used to calculate the 3D world coordinates of a point viewed by both cameras.

Some people call this camera calibration, but many restrict the term camera calibration for the estimation of internal or intrinsic parameters only.

Algorithms

There are many different approaches to calculate the intrinsic and extrinsic parameters for a specific camera setup. The most common ones are:

- Direct linear transformation (DLT) method.

- Zhang's method.

- Tsai's method.

- Selby's method (for X-ray cameras).

Zhang's Method

Zhang model is a camera calibration method that uses traditional calibration techniques (known calibration points) and self-calibration techniques (correspondence between the calibration points when they are in different positions). To perform a full calibration by the Zhang method at least three different images of the calibration target/gauge are required, either by moving the gauge or the camera itself. If some of the intrinsic parameters are given as data (orthogonality of the image or optical center coordinates) the number of images required can be reduced to two.

In a first step, an approximation of the estimated projection matrix H between the calibration target and the image plane is determined using DLT method. Subsequently, applying self-calibration techniques to obtained the image of the absolute conic matrix. The main contribution of Zhang method is how to extract a constrained instrinsic K and n numbers of R and T calibration parameters n from pose of the calibration target.

Derivation

Assume we have a homography H that maps points x_π on a "probe plane" π to points x on the image.

The circular points $I, J = [1 \quad \pm j \quad 0]^T$ lie on both our probe plane π and on the absolute conic Ω_∞. Lying on Ω_∞ of course means they are also projected onto the *image* of the absolute conic (IAC)$_w$, thus $x_1^T \omega x_1 = 0$ and $x_2^T \omega x_2 = 0$. The circular points project as:

$$x_1 = HI = \begin{bmatrix} h_1 & h_2 & h_3 \end{bmatrix} \begin{bmatrix} 1 \\ j \\ 0 \end{bmatrix} = h_1 + jh_2$$

$$x_2 = HJ = \begin{bmatrix} h_1 & h_2 & h_3 \end{bmatrix} \begin{bmatrix} 1 \\ -j \\ 0 \end{bmatrix} = h_1 - jh_2$$

We can actually ignore x_2 while substituting our new expression for x_1 as follows:

$$
\begin{aligned}
x_1^T \omega x_1 &= \left(h_1 + jh_2\right)^T \omega \left(h_1 + jh_2\right) \\
&= \left(h_1^T + jh_2^T\right) \omega \left(h_1 + jh_2\right) \\
&= h_1^T \omega h_1 + j\left(h_2^T \omega h_2\right) \\
&= 0
\end{aligned}
$$

Tsai's Algorithm

It is a 2-stage algorithm, calculating the pose (3D Orientation, and x-axis and y-axis translation) in first stage. In second stage it computes the focal length, distortion coefficients and the z-axis translation.

Selby's Method (for X-ray Cameras)

Selby's camera calibration method addresses the auto-calibration of X-ray camera systems. X-ray camera systems, consisting of the X-ray generating tube and a solid state detector can be modelled as pinhole camera systems, comprising 9 intrinsic and extrinsic camera parameters. Intensity based registration based on an arbitrary X-ray image and a reference model (as a tomographic dataset) can then be used to determine the relative camera parameters without the need of a special calibration body or any ground-truth data.

STRUCTURE FROM MOTION

Structure from motion (SfM) is a photogrammetric range imaging technique for estimating three-dimensional structures from two-dimensional image sequences that may be coupled with local motion signals. It is studied in the fields of computer vision and visual perception. In biological vision, SfM refers to the phenomenon by which humans (and other living creatures) can recover 3D structure from the projected 2D (retinal) motion field of a moving object or scene.

Principle

Digital surface model of motorway interchange construction site.

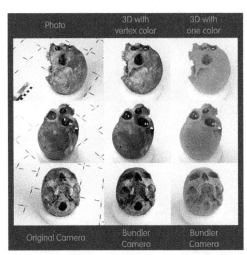

Real photo x SfM with texture color x SfM with simple shader. Made with
Python Photogrammetry Toolbox GUI and rendered in Blender with Cycles.

Humans perceive a lot of information about the three-dimensional structure in their environment by moving around it. When the observer moves, objects around them move different amounts depending on their distance from the observer. This is known as motion parallax, and from this depth information can be used to generate an accurate 3D representation of the world around them.

Finding structure from motion presents a similar problem to finding structure from stereo vision. In both instances, the correspondence between images and the reconstruction of 3D object needs to be found.

To find correspondence between images, features such as corner points (edges with gradients in multiple directions) are tracked from one image to the next. One of the most widely used feature detectors is the scale-invariant feature transform (SIFT). It uses the maxima from a difference-of-Gaussians (DOG) pyramid as features. The first step in SIFT is finding a dominant gradient direction. To make it rotation-invariant, the descriptor is rotated to fit this orientation. Another common feature detector is the SURF (*speeded-up robust features*). In SURF, the DOG is replaced with a Hessian matrix-based blob detector. Also, instead of evaluating the gradient histograms, SURF computes for the sums of gradient components and the sums of their absolute values. Another type of feature recently made practical for structure from motion are general curves (e.g., locally an edge with gradients in one direction), part of a technology known as "Pointless" SfM, useful when point features are insufficient, common in man-made environments.

The features detected from all the images will then be matched. One of the matching algorithms that track features from one image to another is the Lukas–Kanade tracker.

Sometimes some of the matched features are incorrectly matched. This is why the matches should also be filtered. RANSAC (random sample consensus) is the algorithm that is usually used to remove the outlier correspondences. In the paper of Fischler and Bolles, RANSAC is used to solve the *location determination problem* (LDP), where the objective is to determine the points in space that project onto an image into a set of landmarks with known locations.

The feature trajectories over time are then used to reconstruct their 3D positions and the camera's motion. An alternative is given by so-called direct approaches, where geometric information (3D structure and camera motion) is directly estimated from the images, without intermediate abstraction to features or corners.

There are several approaches to structure from motion. In incremental SFM, camera poses are solved for and added one by one to the collection. In global SFM, the poses of all cameras are solved for at the same time. A somewhat intermediate approach is out-of-core SFM, where several partial reconstructions are computed that are then integrated into a global solution.

Applications

Geosciences

Structure from Motion photogrammetry with multi-view stereo provides hyperscale landform models using images acquired from a range of digital cameras and optionally a network of ground control points. The technique is not limited in temporal frequency and can provide point cloud data comparable in density and accuracy to those generated by terrestrial and airborne laser scanning at a fraction of the cost. Structure from motion is also useful in remote or rugged environments where terrestrial laser scanning is limited by equipment portability and airborne laser scanning is limited by terrain roughness causing loss of data and image foreshortening. The technique has been applied in many settings such as rivers, badlands, sandy coastlines, fault zones, landslides, and coral reef settings. SfM has been also successfully applied for the assessment of large wood accumulation volume and porosity in fluvial systems, as well as for the characterization of rock masses through the determination of some properties as the orientation, persistence, etc. of discontinuities. A full range of digital cameras can be utilized, including digital SLR's, compact digital cameras and even smart phones. Generally though, higher accuracy data will be achieved with more expensive cameras, which include lenses of higher optical quality. The technique therefore offers exciting opportunities to characterize surface topography in unprecedented detail and, with multi-temporal data, to detect elevation, position and volumetric changes that are symptomatic of earth surface processes. Structure from Motion can be placed in the context of other digital surveying methods.

Cultural Heritage

Cultural heritage is present everywhere. Its structural control, documentation and conservation is one of humanity's main duties (UNESCO). Under this point of view, SfM is used in order to properly estimate situations as well as planning and maintenance efforts and costs, control and restoration. Because serious constraints often exist connected to the accessibility of the site and impossibility to install invasive surveying pillars that did not permit the use of traditional surveying routines (like total stations), SfM provides a non-invasive approach for the structure, without the direct interaction between the structure and any operator. The use is accurate as only qualitative considerations are needed. It is fast enough to respond to the monument's immediate management needs. The first operational phase is an accurate preparation of the photogrammetric surveying where is established the relation between best distance from the object, focal length, the ground sampling distance (GSD) and the sensor's resolution. With this information the programmed photographic acquisitions must be made using vertical overlapping of at least 60%.

TRIANGULATION

In computer vision triangulation refers to the process of determining a point in 3D space given its projections onto two, or more, images. In order to solve this problem it is necessary to know the parameters of the camera projection function from 3D to 2D for the cameras involved, in the simplest case represented by the camera matrices. Triangulation is sometimes also referred to as reconstruction.

The triangulation problem is in theory trivial. Since each point in an image corresponds to a line in 3D space, all points on the line in 3D are projected to the point in the image. If a pair of corresponding points in two, or more images, can be found it must be the case that they are the projection of a common 3D point x. The set of lines generated by the image points must intersect at x (3D point) and the algebraic formulation of the coordinates of x (3D point) can be computed in a variety of ways.

In practice, however, the coordinates of image points cannot be measured with arbitrary accuracy. Instead, various types of noise, such as geometric noise from lens distortion or interest point detection error, lead to inaccuracies in the measured image coordinates. As a consequence, the lines generated by the corresponding image points do not always intersect in 3D space. The problem, then, is to find a 3D point which optimally fits the measured image points. In the literature there are multiple proposals for how to define optimality and how to find the optimal 3D point. Since they are based on different optimality criteria, the various methods produce different estimates of the 3D point x when noise is involved.

In the following, it is assumed that triangulation is made on corresponding image points from two views generated by pinhole cameras.

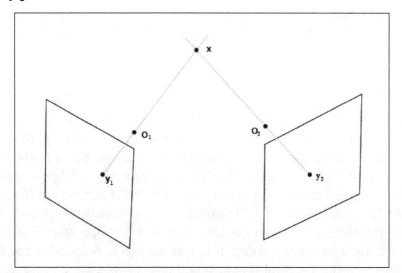

The ideal case of epipolar geometry. A 3D point x is projected onto two camera images through lines (green) which intersect with each camera's focal point, O_1 and O_2. The resulting image points are y_1 and y_2. The green lines intersect at x.

The image above illustrates the epipolar geometry of a pair of stereo cameras of pinhole model. A point x (3D point) in 3D space is projected onto the respective image plane along a line (green) which goes through the camera's focal point, O_1 and O_2, resulting in the two corresponding image points y_1 and y_2. If y_1 and y_2 are given and the geometry of the two cameras are known, the two projection lines (green lines) can be determined and it must be the case that they intersect at point x (3D point).Using basic linear algebra that intersection point can be determined in a straightforward way.

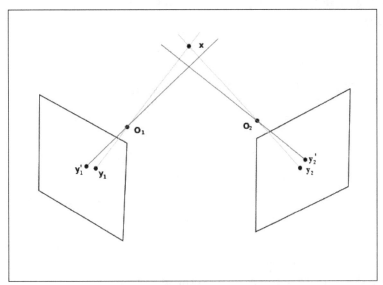

In practice, the image points y_1 and y_2 cannot be measured with arbitrary accuracy. Instead points y'_1 and y'_2 are detected and used for the triangulation. The corresponding projection lines (blue) do not, in general, intersect in 3D space and may also not intersect with point x.

The image above shows the real case. The position of the image points y_1 and y_2 cannot be measured exactly. The reason is a combination of factors such as:

- Geometric distortion, for example lens distortion, which means that the 3D to 2D mapping of the camera deviates from the pinhole camera model. To some extent these errors can be compensated for, leaving a residual geometric error.

- A single ray of light from x (3D point) is dispersed in the lens system of the cameras according to a point spread function. The recovery of the corresponding image point from measurements of the dispersed intensity function in the images gives errors.

- In digital camera the image intensity function is only measured in discrete sensor elements. Inexact interpolation of the discrete intensity function have to be used to recover the true one.

- The image points y'_1 and y'_2 used for triangulation are often found using various types of feature extractors, for example of corners or interest points in general. There is an inherent localization error for any type of feature extraction based on neighborhood operations.

As a consequence, the measured image points are y'_1 and y'_2 instead of y_1 and y_2. However, their projection lines (blue) do not have to intersect in 3D space or come close to x. In fact, these lines intersect if and only if y'_1 and y'_2 satisfy the epipolar constraint defined by the fundamental matrix. Given the measurement noise in y'_1 and y'_2 it is rather likely that the epipolar constraint is not satisfied and the projection lines do not intersect.

This observation leads to the problem which is solved in triangulation. Which 3D point x_{est} is the best estimate of x given y_1' and y_2' and the geometry of the cameras? The answer is often found by defining an error measure which depends on x_{est} and then minimize this error.

All triangulation methods produce $x_{est} = x$ in the case that $y_1 = y_1'$ and $y_2 = y_2'$, that is, when the epipolar constraint is satisfied. It is what happens when the constraint is not satisfied which differs between the methods.

Properties of Triangulation Methods

A triangulation method can be described in terms of a function $ô$ such that:

$$x \sim \tau(y_1', y_2', C_1, C_2)$$

where y_1', y_2' are the homogeneous coordinates of the detected image points and C_1, C_2 are the camera matrices. x (3D point) is the homogeneous representation of the resulting 3D point. The ~ sign implies that τ is only required to produce a vector which is equal to x up to a multiplication by a non-zero scalar since homogeneous vectors are involved.

Before looking at the specific methods, that is, specific functions τ, there are some general concepts related to the methods that need to be explained. Which triangulation method is chosen for a particular problem depends to some extent on these characteristics.

Singularities

Some of the methods fail to correctly compute an estimate of x (3D point) if it lies in a certain subset of the 3D space, corresponding to some combination of y_1', y_2', C_1, C_2. A point in this subset is then a *singularity* of the triangulation method. The reason for the failure can be that some equation system to be solved is under-determined or that the projective representation of x_{est} becomes the zero vector for the singular points.

Invariance

In some applications, it is desirable that the triangulation is independent of the coordinate system used to represent 3D points; if the triangulation problem is formulated in one coordinate system and then transformed into another the resulting estimate x_{est} should transform in the same way. This property is commonly referred to as *invariance*. Not every triangulation method assures invariance, at least not for general types of coordinate transformations.

For a homogeneous representation of 3D coordinates, the most general transformation is a projective transformation, represented by a 4×4 matrix T. If the homogeneous coordinates are transformed according to:

$$\bar{x} \sim Tx$$

then the camera matrices must transform as (C_k):

$$\bar{C}_k \sim C_k T^{-1}$$

to produce the same homogeneous image coordinates (y_k):

$$y_k \sim \overline{C}_k \overline{x} = C_k x$$

If the triangulation function τ is invariant to T then the following relation must be valid:

$$\overline{x}_{est} \sim T x_{est}$$

from which follows that:

$$\tau(y'_1, y'_2, C_1, C_2) \sim T^{-1} \tau(y'_1, y'_2, C_1 T^{-1}, C_2 T^{-1}), \text{ for all } y'_1, y'_2$$

For each triangulation method, it can be determined if this last relation is valid. If it is, it may be satisfied only for a subset of the projective transformations, for example, rigid or affine transformations.

Computational Complexity

The function τ is only an abstract representation of a computation which, in practice, may be relatively complex. Some methods result in a τ which is a closed-form continuous function while others need to be decomposed into a series of computational steps involving, for example, SVD or finding the roots of a polynomial. Yet another class of methods results in τ which must rely on iterative estimation of some parameters. This means that both the computation time and the complexity of the operations involved may vary between the different methods.

IMAGE RECTIFICATION

Computer stereo vision takes two or more images with known relative camera positions that show an object from different viewpoints. For each pixel it then determines the corresponding scene point's depth (i.e. distance from the camera) by first finding matching pixels (i.e. pixels showing the same scene point) in the other image(s) and then applying triangulation to the found matches to determine their depth. Finding matches in stereo vision is restricted by epipolar geometry: Each pixel's match in another image can only be found on a line called the epipolar line. If two images are coplanar, i.e. they were taken such that the right camera is only offset horizontally compared to the left camera (not being moved towards the object or rotated), then each pixel's epipolar line is horizontal and at the same vertical position as that pixel. However, in general settings (the camera did move towards the object or rotate) the epipolar lines are slanted. Image rectification warps both images such that they appear as if they have been taken with only a horizontal displacement and as a consequence all epipolar lines are horizontal, which slightly simplifies the stereo matching process. Note however, that rectification does not fundamentally change the stereo matching process: It searches on lines, slanted ones before and horizontal ones after rectification.

Image rectification is also an equivalent (and more often used) alternative to perfect camera coplanarity. Even with high-precision equipment, image rectification is usually performed because it may be impractical to maintain perfect coplanarity between cameras.

Image rectification can only be performed with two images at a time and simultaneous rectification of more than two images is generally impossible.

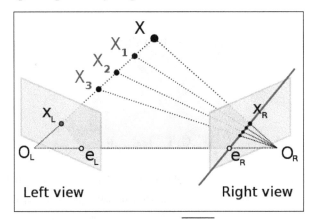

The search for point x_L's match is restricted to the line $\overline{e_R \, x_R}$ in the right image. Since the images are not rectified, the line $e_R \, x_R$ is slanted. After rectification it would be horizontal.

Transformation

If the images to be rectified are taken from camera pairs without geometric distortion, this calculation can easily be made with a linear transformation. X & Y rotation puts the images on the same plane, scaling makes the image frames be the same size and Z rotation & skew adjustments make the image pixel rows directly line up. The rigid alignment of the cameras needs to be known (by calibration) and the calibration coefficients are used by the transform.

In performing the transform, if the cameras themselves are calibrated for internal parameters, an essential matrix provides the relationship between the cameras. The more general case (without camera calibration) is represented by the fundamental matrix. If the fundamental matrix is not known, it is necessary to find preliminary point correspondences between stereo images to facilitate its extraction.

Algorithms

There are three main categories for image rectification algorithms: planar rectification, cylindrical rectification and polar rectification.

Implementation Details

All rectified images satisfy the following two properties:

- All epipolar lines are parallel to the horizontal axis.

- Corresponding points have identical vertical coordinates.

In order to transform the original image pair into a rectified image pair, it is necessary to find a projective transformation H. Constraints are placed on H to satisfy the two properties above. For example, constraining the epipolar lines to be parallel with the horizontal axis means that epipoles must be mapped to the infinite point $[1,0,0]^T$ in homogeneous coordinates. Even with these constraints, H still has four degrees of freedom. It is also necessary to find a matching H' to rectify the second image of an image pair. Poor choices of H and H' can result in rectified images that are dramatically changed in scale or severely distorted.

There are many different strategies for choosing a projective transform H for each image from all possible solutions. One advanced method is minimizing the disparity or least-square difference of corresponding points on the horizontal axis of the rectified image pair. Another method is separating H into a specialized projective transform, similarity transform, and shearing transform to minimize image distortion. One simple method is to rotate both images to look perpendicular to the line joining their collective optical centers, twist the optical axes so the horizontal axis of each image points in the direction of the other image's optical center, and finally scale the smaller image to match for line-to-line correspondence. This process is demonstrated in the following example.

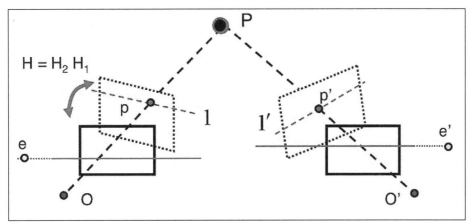

Model used for image rectification example.

Our model for this example is based on a pair of images that observe a 3D point P, which corresponds to p and p' in the pixel coordinates of each image. O and O' represent the optical centers of each camera, with known camera matrices $M = K[I\,0]$ and $M' = K'[RT]$ (we assume the world origin is at the first camera). We will briefly outline and depict the results for a simple approach to find a H and H' projective transformation that rectify the image pair from the example scene.

First, we compute the epipoles, e and e' in each image:

$$e = M\begin{bmatrix} O' \\ 1 \end{bmatrix} = M\begin{bmatrix} -R^T T \\ 1 \end{bmatrix} = K[I\,0]\begin{bmatrix} -R^T T \\ 1 \end{bmatrix} = -KR^T T$$

$$e' = M'\begin{bmatrix} O \\ 1 \end{bmatrix} = M'\begin{bmatrix} 0 \\ 1 \end{bmatrix} = K'[R\,T]\begin{bmatrix} 0 \\ 1 \end{bmatrix} = K'T$$

Second, we find a projective transformation H_1 that rotates our first image to be perpendicular to the baseline connecting O and O' (row 2, column 1 of 2D image set). This rotation can be found by using the cross product between the original and the desired optical axes. Next, we find the projective transformation H_2 that takes the rotated image and twists it so that the horizontal axis aligns with the baseline. If calculated correctly, this second transformation should map the e to infinity on the x axis (row 3, column 1 of 2D image set). Finally, define $H = H_2 H_1$ as the projective transformation for rectifying the first image.

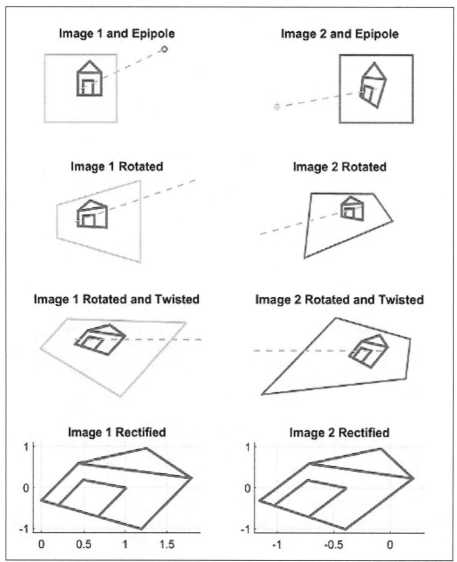

Set of 2D images from example. The original images are taken from different perspectives (row 1). Using systematic transformations from the example (rows 2 and 3), we are able to transform both images such that corresponding points are on the same horizontal scan lines (row 4).

Third, through an equivalent operation, we can find H' to rectify the second image (column 2 of 2D image set). Note that H'_1 should rotate the second image's optical axis to be parallel with the transformed optical axis of the first image. One strategy is to pick a plane parallel to the line where the two original optical axes intersect to minimize distortion from the reprojection process. In this example, we simply define H' using the rotation matrix R and initial projective transformation H as $H' = HR^T$.

Finally, we scale both images to the same approximate resolution and align the now horizontal epipoles for easier horizontal scanning for correspondences (row 4 of 2D image set).

Note that it is possible to perform this and similar algorithms without having the camera parameter matrices M and M'. All that is required is a set of seven or more image to image correspondences to compute the fundamental matrices and epipoles.

VISUAL HULL

The Visual hull is a concept of a 3D reconstruction by a Shape-From-Silhouette (SFS) technique. Since then there have been several different variations of the Shape-From-Silhouette method. The basic principle is to create a 3D representation of an object by its silhouettes within several images from different viewpoints. Each of these silhouettes by different camera views form in their projection a cone, called visual cone and an intersection of all these cones form a description of the real object's shape.

This figure shows a 2D example of the visual cone. (a) shows different viewpoints $C^1, C^2, ...C^4$, which all have a different view at the object O and therefore different silhouettes S^1_1; S^2_1,...,S^4_1. The intersection of the projected silhouettes form the Visual Hull H_1. (b) clarify the difference between the Visual Hull of an object and its approximation by a certain algorithm.

By using this basic idea there are many advantages in using Shape-From-Silhouette techniques. First of all the calculation of the silhouettes is easily to implement, when we assume an indoor environment with special conditions, like static light and static cameras. Without these assumptions it can become difficult to calculate an accurate silhouette out of the images, because of shadows or moving backgrounds. On the other hand are the implementations of the SFS-algorithm straight forward and especially compared to other techniques for shape estimations, like multi-baseline stereo far less complex. The result of the SFS construction is an upper bound of the real object's shape in contrast to a lower bound, which is a big advantage for obstacle avoidance in the field of robotic or visibility analysis in navigation. Another application for SFS estimations are for instance the field of motion capturing.

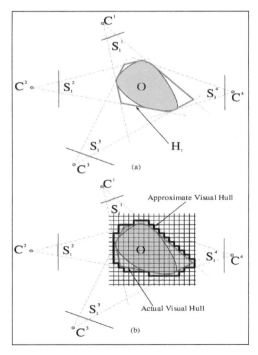

On the other hand there are also disadvantages for these techniques. So there are time consuming testing steps, which are a bottleneck for real-time applications or the silhouette calculations, which are relative sensitive for errors, like noise or wrong camera calibrations. These ends up in problems for the intersection of the visual cones and therefore bad results for the resulting 3D shapes.

Furthermore is the result of each SFS algorithm just an approximation of the actual object's shape, especially if there are only a limited number of cameras and therefore is this approach not practical for applications like detailed shape recognition or realistic rerendering of objects.

The main problem of the SFS-based algorithms are that they are not able to perform an accurate reconstruction of concave objects, like figure below (as long as we assume that the camera views are not too near to the object). An obvious question, which occurs in this context is which parts of an object can be reconstructed by standard SFS techniques, or what are the limits of these approaches?

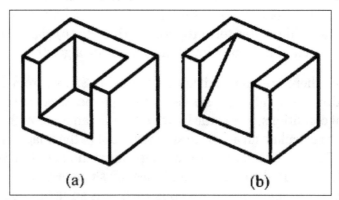

This figure shows different object shapes. (a) is a real world object, whereas
(b) represents its reconstruction by a SFS-approach.

To denote this difference Laurentini introduced the term of the Visual Hull in 1991. His formal definition of the Visual Hull is the following:

> "The visual hull V H(S,R) of an object S relative to a viewing region R is a region of E^3 such that, for each point $P \in V$ H(S,R) and each viewpoint $V \in R$, the half-line starting at V and passing through P contains at least a point of S."

Two more informal definitions given by Laurentini are the following ones:

> "...the visual hull of an object S is the envelope of all the possible circumscribed cones of S. An equivalent intuition is that the visual hull is the maximal object that gives the same silhouette of S from any possible viewpoint."

If we consider these definitions it is easy to see, that $S \le V$ H(S). The proof for this statement is rather forward: First of all we show that V H(S,R) includes the object's silhouettes with respect to R. According to the first definition, each projection of any point $P \in V$ H(S,R) belongs to the silhouette of S, otherwise it would not be a part of the Visual Hull, therefore is $S \le V$ H(S). The reason, why V H(S,R) is the maximum silhouette equivalent is that, if there would be a point $P' \in$ V H(S,R) and we would go along a line starting from V' |in R and passing P', then this line would not intersect S. Therefore P' would not belong to the silhouette of S, according to V' and P' does not belong to the shape of the object.

Other interesting propositions by Laureneti are that V H(S,R) is the closest approximation of S, that can be archived by using volume intersection techniques. Furthermore we can see that if we choose our R that way that R > R', then V H(S,R) > V H(S,R'), so if we want to have a higher precision we need more different viewpoints and so more visual cones. A general conclusion of Laureneti is the following: V H(S,R) <= CH(S), so that the Visual Hull is always smaller or equal to the convex hull.

These accurate definition of the resulting shape of a SFS technique helps us to describe the resulting approximation of the real object.

The direct way of the actual construction of the visual hull would be by intersecting the visual cones. A 2D example of this is given in figure. The problem of this approach is that the visual hull in general consists of a curved and irregular surface and therefore requires a complex geometrical representation for its cones. This leads to a higher complexity and numerical instability, which encourage scientists to choose approximate representation by using a polyhedral shape instead, while intersecting the visual cones.

As we know from the previous definition, the voxelbased SFS computation uses the same principles like the visual cone intersection, just that in this version the final shape representation is done by 3D volume elements (voxels). So we have deviant the room into sections, which we have declared as inside and sections which we have declared as outside, according if they are in the visual cones.

Even though this technique is very easy and fast, it has a big disadvantage. The resulting shape is significantly larger then the true object shape, which makes it only of those applications feasible, in which only an approximation is used.

The modern approaches use surface-based representations instead of the volumetric representation of the scene, which allows to use regularization in a energy minimization framework. These techniques results in a higher robustness to outliers and erroneous camera calibration. Furthermore these approaches try to overcome the inability to reconstruct concavities, due to the fact that they do not affect the silhouettes by using in addition stereo-based methods. They are used to repeatedly inrode inconsistent voxels and so result in smoother reconstruction. So that in addition the aim is to archive a photoconsistency.

At all SFS-approaches gives us a good approximation of the object's shape, which can been used for further calculations. The Visual Hull on the other side gives us a tool to describe the limitations of SFS-techniques and therefore their use in certain applications.

References

- ProjectiveGeometry, PinholeCamera: staff.fnwi.uva.nl, Retrieved 28 April, 2019

- Srimal Jayawardena and Di Yang and Marcus Hutter (2011). "3D Model Assisted Image Segmentation". 2011 International Conference on Digital Image Computing: Techniques and Applications. pp. 51–58. CiteSeerX 10.1.1.751.8774. doi:10.1109/DICTA.2011.17. ISBN 978-1-4577-2006-2. Retrieved 2013-06-01

- Nurollah Tatar (2019). "Stereo rectification of pushbroom satellite images by robustly estimating the fundamental matrix". International Journal of Remote Sensing. 40 (20): 1–19. doi:10.1080/01431161.2019.1624862

- Richard Hartley and Andrew Zisserman (2003). Multiple View Geometry in computer vision. Cambridge University Press. ISBN 978-0-521-54051-3

- Westoby, M. J.; Brasington, J.; Glasser, N. F.; Hambrey, M. J.; Reynolds, J. M. (2012-12-15). "'Structure-from-Motion' photogrammetry: A low-cost, effective tool for geoscience applications". Geomorphology. 179: 300–314.Bibcode:2012Geomo.179..300W.doi:10.1016/j.geomorph.2012.08.021

Applications

Computer vision is a vast subject that has an array of applications. Some of them are facial recognition system, gesture recognition, 3D single-object recognition, face detection, handwriting recognition, machine vision, self-driving car, remote sensing, etc. This chapter closely examines these applications of computer vision to provide an extensive understanding of the subject.

Computer vision, an AI technology that allows computers to understand and label images, is now used in convenience stores, driverless car testing, daily medical diagnostics, and in monitoring the health of crops and livestock.

OBJECT RECOGNITION

Object detection is a computer technology related to computer vision and image processing that deals with detecting instances of semantic objects of a certain class (such as humans, buildings, or cars) in digital images and videos. Well-researched domains of object detection include face detection and pedestrian detection. Object detection has applications in many areas of computer vision, including image retrieval and video surveillance.

Objects detected with OpenCV's Deep Neural Network module (dnn) by using a YOLOv3 model trained on COCO dataset capable to detect objects of 80 common classes.

Uses

It is widely used in computer vision tasks such as activity recognition, face detection, face recognition, video object co-segmentation. It is also used in tracking objects, for example tracking a ball during a football match, tracking movement of a cricket bat, or tracking a person in a video.

Concept

Every object class has its own special feature that helps in classifying the class – for example all circles are round. Object class detection uses these special features. For example, when looking for circles, objects that are at a particular distance from a point (i.e. the center) are sought. Similarly, when looking for squares, objects that are perpendicular at corners and have equal side lengths are needed. A similar approach is used for face identification where eyes, nose, and lips can be found and features like skin color and distance between eyes can be found.

Facial Recognition System

A facial recognition system is a technology capable of identifying or verifying a person from a digital image or a video frame from a video source. There are multiple methods in which facial recognition systems work, but in general, they work by comparing selected facial features from given image with faces within a database. It is also described as a Biometric Artificial Intelligence based application that can uniquely identify a person by analysing patterns based on the person's facial textures and shape.

Swiss European surveillance: face recognition and vehicle make, model, color and license plate reader.

While initially a form of computer application, it has seen wider uses in recent times on mobile platforms and in other forms of technology, such as robotics. It is typically used as access control in security systems and can be compared to other biometrics such as fingerprint or eye iris recognition systems. Although the accuracy of facial recognition system as a biometric technology is lower than iris recognition and fingerprint recognition, it is widely adopted due to its contactless and non-invasive process. Recently, it has also become popular as a commercial identification and marketing tool. Other applications include advanced human-computer interaction, video surveillance, automatic indexing of images, and video database, among others.

Close-up of the infrared illuminator. The light is invisible to the human eye, but creates
a day-like environment for the surveillance cameras.

Techniques for Face Acquisition

Essentially, the process of face recognition is performed in two steps. The first involves feature extraction and selection and the second is the classification of objects. Later developments introduced varying technologies to the procedure. Some of the most notable include the following techniques:

Traditional

Some face recognition algorithms identify facial features by extracting landmarks, or features, from an image of the subject's face. For example, an algorithm may analyze the relative position, size, and shape of the eyes, nose, cheekbones, and jaw. These features are then used to search for other images with matching features.

Other algorithms normalize a gallery of face images and then compress the face data, only saving the data in the image that is useful for face recognition. A probe image is then compared with the face data. One of the earliest successful systems is based on template matching techniques applied to a set of salient facial features, providing a sort of compressed face representation.

Recognition algorithms can be divided into two main approaches: geometric, which looks at distinguishing features, or photometric, which is a statistical approach that distills an image into values and compares the values with templates to eliminate variances. Some classify these algorithms into two broad categories: holistic and feature-based models. The former attempts to recognize the face in its entirety while the feature-based subdivide into components such as according to features and analyze each as well as its spatial location with respect to other features.

Popular recognition algorithms include principal component analysis using eigenfaces, linear discriminant analysis, elastic bunch graph matching using the Fisherface algorithm, the hidden Markov model, the multilinear subspace learning using tensor representation, and the neuronal motivated dynamic link matching.

3-Dimensional Recognition

Three-dimensional face recognition technique uses 3D sensors to capture information about the shape of a face. This information is then used to identify distinctive features on the surface of a face, such as the contour of the eye sockets, nose, and chin.

One advantage of 3D face recognition is that it is not affected by changes in lighting like other techniques. It can also identify a face from a range of viewing angles, including a profile view. Three-dimensional data points from a face vastly improve the precision of face recognition. 3D research is enhanced by the development of sophisticated sensors that do a better job of capturing 3D face imagery. The sensors work by projecting structured light onto the face. Up to a dozen or more of these image sensors can be placed on the same CMOS chip—each sensor captures a different part of the spectrum.

Even a perfect 3D matching technique could be sensitive to expressions. For that goal a group at the Technion applied tools from metric geometry to treat expressions as isometries.

A new method is to introduce a way to capture a 3D picture by using three tracking cameras that point at different angles; one camera will be pointing at the front of the subject, second one to the side, and third one at an angle. All these cameras will work together so it can track a subject's face in real time and be able to face detect and recognize.

Skin Texture Analysis

Another emerging trend uses the visual details of the skin, as captured in standard digital or scanned images. This technique, called Skin Texture Analysis, turns the unique lines, patterns, and spots apparent in a person's skin into a mathematical space.

Surface Texture Analysis works much the same way facial recognition does. A picture is taken of a patch of skin, called a skinprint. That patch is then broken up into smaller blocks. Using algorithms to turn the patch into a mathematical, measurable space, the system will then distinguish any lines, pores and the actual skin texture. It can identify the contrast between identical pairs, which are not yet possible using facial recognition software alone.

Tests have shown that with the addition of skin texture analysis, performance in recognizing faces can increase 20 to 25 percent.

Facial Recognition Combining Different Techniques

As every method has its advantages and disadvantages, technology companies have amalgamated the traditional, 3D recognition and Skin Textual Analysis, to create recognition systems that have higher rates of success.

Combined techniques have an advantage over other systems. It is relatively insensitive to changes in expression, including blinking, frowning or smiling and has the ability to compensate for mustache or beard growth and the appearance of eyeglasses. The system is also uniform with respect to race and gender.

Thermal Cameras

A different form of taking input data for face recognition is by using thermal cameras, by this procedure the cameras will only detect the shape of the head and it will ignore the subject accessories such as glasses, hats, or makeup. Unlike conventional cameras, thermal cameras can capture facial imagery even in low-light and nighttime conditions without using a flash and exposing the position of the camera. However, a problem with using thermal pictures for face recognition is that the databases for face recognition is limited. Diego Socolinsky and Andrea Selinger research the use of thermal face recognition in real life and operation sceneries, and at the same time build a new database of thermal face images. The research uses low-sensitive, low-resolution ferroelectric electrics sensors that are capable of acquiring long-wave thermal infrared (LWIR). The results show that a fusion of LWIR and regular visual cameras has greater results in outdoor probes. Indoor results show that visual has a 97.05% accuracy, while LWIR has 93.93%, and the fusion has 98.40%, however on the outdoor proves visual has 67.06%, LWIR 83.03%, and fusion has 89.02%. The study used 240 subjects over a period of 10 weeks to create a new database. The data was collected on sunny, rainy, and cloudy days.

In 2018, researchers from the U.S. Army Research Laboratory (ARL) developed a technique that would allow them to match facial imagery obtained using a thermal camera with those in databases that were captured using a conventional camera. This approach utilized artificial intelligence and machine learning to allow researchers to visibly compare conventional and thermal facial imagery. Known as a cross-spectrum synthesis method due to how it bridges facial recognition from two different imaging modalities, this method synthesize a single image by analyzing multiple facial regions and details. It consists of a non-linear regression model that maps a specific thermal image into a corresponding visible facial image and an optimization issue that projects the latent projection back into the image space.

ARL scientists have noted that the approach works by combining global information (i.e. features across the entire face) with local information (i.e. features regarding the eyes, nose, and mouth). In addition to enhancing the discriminability of the synthesized image, the facial recognition system can be used to transform a thermal face signature into a refined visible image of a face. According to performance tests conducted at ARL, researchers found that the multi-region cross-spectrum synthesis model demonstrated a performance improvement of about 30% over baseline methods and about 5% over state-of-the-art methods. It has also been tested for landmark detection for thermal images.

Application

Mobile Platforms

1. Social media

Social media platforms have adopted facial recognition capabilities to diversify their functionalities in order to attract a wider user base amidst stiff competition from different applications.

Founded in 2013, Looksery went on to raise money for its face modification app on Kickstarter. After successful crowdfunding, Looksery launched in October 2014. The application allows video chat with others through a special filter for faces that modifies the look of users. While there is image augmenting applications such as FaceTune and Perfect365, they are limited to static images, whereas Looksery allowed augmented reality to live videos. In late 2015, SnapChat purchased Looksery, which would then become its landmark lenses function.

SnapChat's animated lenses, which used facial recognition technology, revolutionized and redefined the selfie, by allowing users to add filters to change the way they look. The selection of filters changes every day, some examples include one that makes users look like an old and wrinkled version of themselves, one that airbrushes their skin, and one that places a virtual flower crown on top of their head. The dog filter is the most popular filter that helped propel the continual success of SnapChat, with popular celebrities such as Gigi Hadid, Kim Kardashian and the likes regularly posting videos of themselves with the dog filter.

DeepFace is a deep learning facial recognition system created by a research group at Facebook. It identifies human faces in digital images. It employs a nine-layer neural net with over 120 million connection weights, and was trained on four million images uploaded by Facebook users. The system is said to be 97% accurate, compared to 85% for the FBI's Next Generation Identification system. One of the creators of the software, Yaniv Taigman, came to Facebook via their acquisition of Face.com.

2. ID verification

The emerging use of facial recognition is in the use of ID verification services. Many companies and others are working in the market now to provide these services to banks, ICOs, and other e-businesses. In 2017, Time & Attendance company ClockedIn released facial recognition as a form of attendance tracking for businesses and organizations looking to have a more automated system of keeping track of hours worked as well as for security and health and safety control.

3. Face ID

Apple introduced Face ID on the flagship iPhone X as a biometric authentication successor to the Touch ID, a fingerprint based system. Face ID has a facial recognition sensor that consists of two parts: a "Romeo" module that projects more than 30,000 infrared dots onto the user's face, and a "Juliet" module that reads the pattern. The pattern is sent to a local "Secure Enclave" in the device's central processing unit (CPU) to confirm a match with the phone owner's face. The facial pattern is not accessible by Apple. The system will not work with eyes closed, in an effort to prevent unauthorized access.

The technology learns from changes in a user's appearance, and therefore works with hats, scarves, glasses, and many sunglasses, beard and makeup.

It also works in the dark. This is done by using a "Flood Illuminator", which is a dedicated infrared flash that throws out invisible infrared light onto the user's face to properly read the 30,000 facial points.

Deployment in Security Services

The Australian Border Force and New Zealand Customs Service have set up an automated border processing system called SmartGate that uses face recognition, which compares the face of the traveller with the data in the e-passport microchip. All Canadian international airports use facial recognition as part of the Primary Inspection Kiosk program that compares a traveler face to their photo stored on the ePassport. This program first came to Vancouver International Airport in early 2017 and was rolled up to all remaining international airports in 2018-2019. The Tocumen International Airport in Panama operates an airport-wide surveillance system using hundreds of live face recognition cameras to identify wanted individuals passing through the airport.

Police forces in the United Kingdom have been trialling live facial recognition technology at public events since 2015. However, a recent report and investigation by Big Brother Watch found that these systems were up to 98% inaccurate.

In May 2017, a man was arrested using an automatic facial recognition (AFR) system mounted on a van operated by the South Wales Police. Ars Technica reported that "this appears to be the first time [AFR] has led to an arrest".

The U.S. Department of State operates one of the largest face recognition systems in the world with a database of 117 million American adults, with photos typically drawn from driver's license photos. Although it is still far from completion, it is being put to use in certain cities to give clues as to who was in the photo. The FBI uses the photos as an investigative tool, not for positive identification. As of 2016, facial recognition was being used to identify people in photos taken by police in San Diego and Los Angeles (not on real-time video, and only against booking photos) and use was planned in West Virginia and Dallas.

In recent years Maryland has used face recognition by comparing people's faces to their driver's license photos. The system drew controversy when it was used in Baltimore to arrest unruly protesters after the death of Freddie Gray in police custody. Many other states are using or developing a similar system however some states have laws prohibiting its use.

The FBI has also instituted its Next Generation Identification program to include face recognition, as well as more traditional biometrics like fingerprints and iris scans, which can pull from both criminal and civil databases. The federal General Accountability Office criticized the FBI for not addressing various concerns related to privacy and accuracy.

In 2019, researchers reported that Immigration and Customs Enforcement uses facial recognition software against state driver's license databases, including for some states that provide licenses to undocumented immigrants.

As of late 2017, China has deployed facial recognition and artificial intelligence technology in Xinjiang. Reporters visiting the region found surveillance cameras installed every hundred meters or so in several cities, as well as facial recognition checkpoints at areas like gas stations, shopping centers, and mosque entrances.

Like China, but a year earlier, The Netherlands has deployed facial recognition and artificial intelligence technology since 2016. The database of the Dutch police currently contains over 2.2 million pictures of 1.3 million Dutch citizens. This accounts for about 8% of the population. Hundreds of cameras have been deployed in the city of Amsterdam alone.

Automatic Facial Recognition systems resemble other mobile CCTV systems.

Additional Uses

In addition to being used for security systems, authorities have found a number of other applications for face recognition systems. While earlier post-9/11 deployments were well-publicized trials, more recent deployments are rarely written about due to their covert nature.

At Super Bowl XXXV in January 2001, police in Tampa Bay, Florida used Viisage face recognition software to search for potential criminals and terrorists in attendance at the event. 19 people with minor criminal records were potentially identified.

In the 2000 Mexican presidential election, the Mexican government employed face recognition software to prevent voter fraud. Some individuals had been registering to vote under several different names, in an attempt to place multiple votes. By comparing new face images to those already in the voter database, authorities were able to reduce duplicate registrations. Similar technologies are being used in the United States to prevent people from obtaining fake identification cards and driver's licenses.

Face recognition has been leveraged as a form of biometric authentication for various computing platforms and devices; Android 4.0 "Ice Cream Sandwich" added facial recognition using a smartphone's front camera as a means of unlocking devices, while Microsoft introduced face recognition login to its Xbox 360 video game console through its Kinect accessory, as well as Windows 10 via its "Windows Hello" platform (which requires an infrared-illuminated camera). Apple's iPhone X smartphone introduced facial recognition to the product line with its "Face ID" platform, which uses an infrared illumination system.

Face recognition systems have also been used by photo management software to identify the subjects of photographs, enabling features such as searching images by person, as well as suggesting photos to be shared with a specific contact if their presence were detected in a photo.

Facial recognition is used as added security in certain websites, phone applications, and payment methods.

The United States' popular music and country music celebrity Taylor Swift surreptitiously employed facial recognition technology at a concert in 2018. The camera was embedded in a kiosk near a ticket booth and scanned concert-goers as they entered the facility for known stalkers.

On August 18, 2019, The Times reported that the UAE-owned Manchester City hired a Texas-based firm, Blink Identity, to deploy facial recognition systems in a driver program. The club has planned a single super-fast lane for the supporters at the Etihad stadium. However, civil rights groups cautioned the club against the introduction of this technology, saying that it would risk "normalising a mass surveillance tool". The policy and campaigns officer at Liberty, Hannah Couchman said that Man City's move is alarming, since the fans will be obliged to share deeply sensitive personal information with a private company, where they could be tracked and monitored in their everyday lives.

Advantages and Disadvantages

Compared to other Biometric Systems

One key advantage of a facial recognition system that it is able to person mass identification as it does not require the cooperation of the test subject to work. Properly designed systems installed in airports, multiplexes, and other public places can identify individuals among the crowd, without passers-by even being aware of the system.

However, as compared to other biometric techniques, face recognition may not be most reliable and efficient. Quality measures are very important in facial recognition systems as large degrees of variations are possible in face images. Factors such as illumination, expression, pose and noise during face capture can affect the performance of facial recognition systems. Among all biometric systems, facial recognition has the highest false acceptance and rejection rates, thus questions have been raised on the effectiveness of face recognition software in cases of railway and airport security.

Weaknesses

Ralph Gross, a researcher at the Carnegie Mellon Robotics Institute in 2008, describes one obstacle related to the viewing angle of the face: "Face recognition has been getting pretty good at full frontal faces and 20 degrees off, but as soon as you go towards profile, there've been problems." Besides the pose variations, low-resolution face images are also very hard to recognize. This is one of the main obstacles of face recognition in surveillance systems.

Face recognition is less effective if facial expressions vary. A big smile can render the system less effective. For instance: Canada, in 2009, allowed only neutral facial expressions in passport photos.

There is also inconstancy in the datasets used by researchers. Researchers may use anywhere from several subjects to scores of subjects and a few hundred images to thousands of images. It is important for researchers to make available the datasets they used to each other, or have at least a standard dataset.

Data privacy is the main concern when it comes to storing biometrics data in companies. Data stores about face or biometrics can be accessed by the third party if not stored properly or hacked. In the Techworld, Parris adds (2017), "Hackers will already be looking to replicate people's faces to trick facial recognition systems, but the technology has proved harder to hack than fingerprint or voice recognition technology in the past."

Ineffectiveness

Critics of the technology complain that the London Borough of Newham scheme has, as of 2004, never recognized a single criminal, despite several criminals in the system's database living in the Borough and the system has been running for several years. "Not once, as far as the police know, has Newham's automatic face recognition system spotted a live target." This information seems to conflict with claims that the system was credited with a 34% reduction in crime (hence why it was rolled out to Birmingham also). However it can be explained by the notion that when the public is regularly told that they are under constant video surveillance with advanced face recognition technology, this fear alone can reduce the crime rate, whether the face recognition system technically works or does not. This has been the basis for several other face recognition based security systems, where the technology itself does not work particularly well but the user's perception of the technology does.

An experiment in 2002 by the local police department in Tampa, Florida, had similarly disappointing results.

A system at Boston's Logan Airport was shut down in 2003 after failing to make any matches during a two-year test period.

In 2014, Facebook stated that in a standardized two-option facial recognition test, its online system scored 97.25% accuracy, compared to the human benchmark of 97.5%.

In 2018, a report by the civil liberties and rights campaigning organisation Big Brother Watch revealed that two UK police forces, South Wales Police and the Metropolitan Police, were using live facial recognition at public events and in public spaces, in September 2019, South Wales Police use of facial recognition was ruled lawful.

Systems are often advertised as having accuracy near 100%; this is misleading as the studies often use much smaller sample sizes than would be necessary for large scale applications. Because facial recognition is not completely accurate, it creates a list of potential matches. A human operator must then look through these potential matches and studies show the operators pick the correct match out of the list only about half the time. This causes the issue of targeting the wrong suspect.

Anti-Facial Recognition Systems

In January 2013 Japanese researchers from the National Institute of Informatics created 'privacy visor' glasses that use nearly infrared light to make the face underneath it unrecognizable to face recognition software. The latest version uses a titanium frame, light-reflective material and a mask which uses angles and patterns to disrupt facial recognition technology through both absorbing and bouncing back light sources. In December 2016 a form of anti-CCTV and facial recognition sunglasses called 'reflectacles' were invented by a custom-spectacle-craftsman based in Chicago named Scott Urban. They reflect infrared and, optionally, visible light which makes the users face a white blur to cameras.

Another method to protect from facial recognition systems is specific haircuts and make-up patterns that prevent the used algorithms to detect a face, known as computer vision dazzle. Incidentally, the makeup styles popular with Juggalos can also protect against facial recognition.

Gesture Recognition

A child being sensed by a simple gesture recognition algorithm detecting hand location and movement.

Gesture recognition is a topic in computer science and language technology with the goal of interpreting human gestures via mathematical algorithms. Gestures can originate from any bodily motion or state but commonly originate from the face or hand. Current focuses in the field include emotion recognition from face and hand gesture recognition. Users can use simple gestures to control or interact with devices without physically touching them. Many approaches have been made using cameras and computer vision algorithms to interpret sign language. However, the identification and recognition of posture, gait, proxemics, and human behaviors is also the subject of gesture recognition techniques. Gesture recognition can be seen as a way for computers to begin to understand human body language, thus building a richer bridge between machines and humans than primitive text user interfaces or even GUIs (graphical user interfaces), which still limit the majority of input to keyboard and mouse and interact naturally without any mechanical devices. Using the concept of gesture recognition, it is possible to point a finger at this point will move accordingly. This could make conventional input on devices such and even redundant.

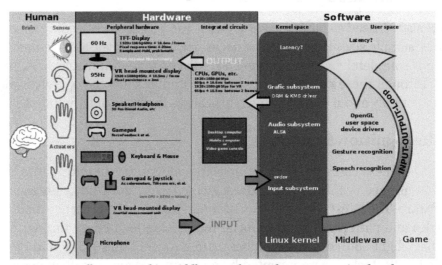

Gesture recognition is usually processed in middleware, the results are transmitted to the user applications.

Gesture recognition features:

- More accurate,

- High stability,

- Time saving to unlock a device.

The major application areas of gesture recognition in the current scenario are:

- Automotive sector,

- Consumer electronics sector,

- Transit sector,

- Gaming sector,

- To unlock smartphones,

- Defence,

- Home automation,

- Automated sign language translation.

Gesture recognition can be conducted with techniques from computer vision and image processing.

Gesture recognition and pen computing: Pen computing reduces the hardware impact of a system and also increases the range of physical world objects usable for control beyond traditional digital objects like keyboards and mice. Such implementations could enable a new range of hardware that does not require monitors. This idea may lead to the creation of holographic display. The term gesture recognition has been used to refer more narrowly to non-text-input handwriting symbols, such as inking on a graphics tablet, multi-touch gestures, and mouse gesture recognition. This is computer interaction through the drawing of symbols with a pointing device cursor.

Gesture Types

In computer interfaces, two types of gestures are distinguished: We consider online gestures, which can also be regarded as direct manipulations like scaling and rotating. In contrast, offline gestures are usually processed after the interaction is finished; e. g. a circle is drawn to activate a context menu.

- Offline gestures: Those gestures that are processed after the user interaction with the object. An example is the gesture to activate a menu.

- Online gestures: Direct manipulation gestures. They are used to scale or rotate a tangible object.

Touchless Interface

Touchless user interface is an emerging type of technology in relation to gesture control. Touchless user interface (TUI) is the process of commanding the computer via body motion and gestures without touching a keyboard, mouse, or screen. For example, Microsoft's Kinect is a touchless game interface; however, products such as the Wii are not considered entirely touchless because they are tethered to controllers. Touchless interface in addition to gesture controls are becoming widely popular as they provide the abilities to interact with devices without physically touching them.

Types of Touchless Technology

There are a number of devices utilizing this type of interface such as, smartphones, laptops, games, television, and music equipment.

Future of Touchless Technology

Companies who are producing or exploring gesture recognition technology include:

Intel Corp.

White Paper: Explore Intel's user experience research, which shows how touchless multifactor authentication (MFA) can help healthcare organizations mitigate security risks while improving clinician efficiency, convenience, and patient care. This touchless MFA solution combines facial recognition and device recognition capabilities for two-factor user authentication.

Microsoft Corp. in the U.S.

The aim of the project then is to explore the use of touchless interaction within surgical settings, allowing images to be viewed, controlled and manipulated without contact through the use of camera-based gesture recognition technology. In particular, the project seeks to understand the challenges of these environments for the design and deployment of such systems, as well as articulate the ways in which these technologies may alter surgical practice. While our primary concerns here are with maintaining conditions of asepsis, the use of these touchless gesture-based technologies offers other potential uses.

Other examples:

- Tobii Rex: eye-tracking device from Sweden,

- Airwriting: technology that allows messages and texts to be written in the air,

- eyeSight: allows for navigation of a screen without physically touching the device,

- Leap Motion: motion sensor device,

- Myoelectric Armband: allows for communication of bluetooth devices.

Input Devices

The ability to track a person's movements and determine what gestures they may be performing can be achieved through various tools. The kinetic user interfaces (KUIs) are an emerging type of user interfaces that allow users to interact with computing devices through the motion of objects and bodies. Examples of KUIs include tangible user interfaces and motion-aware games such as Wii and Microsoft's Kinect, and other interactive projects.

Although there is a large amount of research done in image/video based gesture recognition, there is some variation within the tools and environments used between implementations.

- Wired gloves: These can provide input to the computer about the position and rotation of the hands using magnetic or inertial tracking devices. Furthermore, some gloves can detect finger bending with a high degree of accuracy (5-10 degrees), or even provide haptic feedback to the user, which is a simulation of the sense of touch. The first commercially available hand-tracking glove-type device was the DataGlove, a glove-type device which could detect hand position, movement and finger bending. This uses fiber optic cables running down the back of the hand. Light pulses are created and when the fingers are bent, light leaks through small cracks and the loss is registered, giving an approximation of the hand pose.

- Depth-aware cameras: Using specialized cameras such as structured light or time-of-flight cameras, one can generate a depth map of what is being seen through the camera at a short range, and use this data to approximate a 3d representation of what is being seen. These can be effective for detection of hand gestures due to their short range capabilities.

- Stereo cameras: Using two cameras whose relations to one another are known, a 3d representation can be approximated by the output of the cameras. To get the cameras' relations, one can use a positioning reference such as a lexian-stripe or infrared emitters. In combination with direct motion measurement (6D-Vision) gestures can directly be detected.

- Gesture-based controllers: These controllers act as an extension of the body so that when gestures are performed, some of their motion can be conveniently captured by software. An example of emerging gesture-based motion capture is through skeletal hand tracking, which is being developed for virtual reality and augmented reality applications. An example of this technology is shown by tracking companies uSens and Gestigon, which allow users to interact with their surrounding without controllers.

  Another example of this is mouse gesture trackings, where the motion of the mouse is correlated to a symbol being drawn by a person's hand, as is the Wii Remote or the Myo armband or the mForce Wizard wristband, which can study changes in acceleration over time to represent gestures. Devices such as the LG Electronics Magic Wand, the Loop and the Scoop use Hillcrest Labs' Freespace technology, which uses MEMS accelerometers, gyroscopes and other sensors to translate gestures into cursor movement. The software also compensates for human tremor and inadvertent movement. AudioCubes are another example. The sensors of these smart light emitting cubes can be used to sense hands and fingers as well as other objects nearby, and can be used to process data. Most applications are in music and sound synthesis, but can be applied to other fields.

- Single camera: A standard 2D camera can be used for gesture recognition where the resources/environment would not be convenient for other forms of image-based recognition. Earlier it was thought that single camera may not be as effective as stereo or depth aware cameras, but some companies are challenging this theory. Software-based gesture recognition technology using a standard 2D camera that can detect robust hand gestures.

Algorithms

Depending on the type of the input data, the approach for interpreting a gesture could be done in different ways. However, most of the techniques rely on key pointers represented in a 3D coordinate system. Based on the relative motion of these, the gesture can be detected with a high accuracy, depending on the quality of the input and the algorithm's approach.

In order to interpret movements of the body, one has to classify them according to common properties and the message the movements may express. For example, in sign language each gesture represents a word or phrase. The taxonomy that seems very appropriate for Human-Computer Interaction has been proposed by Quek in "Toward a Vision-Based Hand Gesture Interface". He presents several interactive gesture systems in order to capture the whole space of the gestures:

- Manipulative
- Semaphoric
- Conversational

Different ways of tracking and analyzing gestures exist, and some basic layout is given is in the diagram above. For example, volumetric models convey the necessary information required for an elaborate analysis, however they prove to be very intensive in terms of computational power and require further technological developments in order to be implemented for real-time analysis.

On the other hand, appearance-based models are easier to process but usually lack the generality required for Human-Computer Interaction.

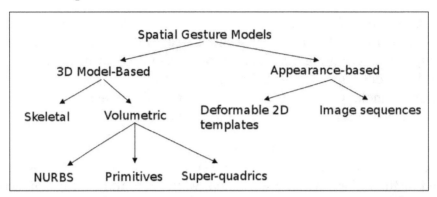

Some literature differentiates 2 different approaches in gesture recognition: a 3D model based and an appearance-based. The foremost method makes use of 3D information of key elements of the body parts in order to obtain several important parameters, like palm position or joint angles. On the other hand, Appearance-based systems use images or videos for direct interpretation.

3D Model-based Algorithms

The 3D model approach can use volumetric or skeletal models, or even a combination of the two. Volumetric approaches have been heavily used in computer animation industry and for computer vision purposes. The models are generally created from complicated 3D surfaces, like NURBS or polygon meshes.

The drawback of this method is that it is very computational intensive, and systems for real time analysis are still to be developed. For the moment, a more interesting approach would be to map simple primitive objects to the person's most important body parts (for example cylinders for the arms and neck, sphere for the head) and analyse the way these interact with each other. Furthermore, some abstract structures like super-quadrics and generalised cylinders may be even more suitable for approximating the body parts.

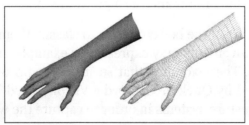

A real hand (left) is interpreted as a collection of vertices and lines in the 3D mesh version (right), and the software uses their relative position and interaction in order to infer the gesture.

Skeletal-based Algorithms

Instead of using intensive processing of the 3D models and dealing with a lot of parameters, one can just use a simplified version of joint angle parameters along with segment lengths. This is known as a skeletal representation of the body, where a virtual skeleton of the person is computed and parts of the body are mapped to certain segments. The analysis here is done using the position and orientation of these segments and the relation between each one of them (for example the angle between the joints and the relative position or orientation).

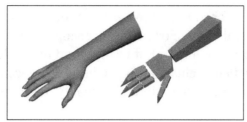

The skeletal version (right) is effectively modeling the hand (left). This has fewer parameters than the volumetric version and it's easier to compute, making it suitable for real-time gesture analysis systems.

Advantages of using skeletal models:

- Algorithms are faster because only key parameters are analyzed.

- Pattern matching against a template database is possible.

- Using key points allows the detection program to focus on the significant parts of the body.

Appearance-based Models

These models don't use a spatial representation of the body anymore, because they derive the parameters directly from the images or videos using a template database. Some are based on the deformable 2D templates of the human parts of the body, particularly hands. Deformable templates are sets of points on the outline of an object, used as interpolation nodes for the object's outline approximation. One of the simplest interpolation functions is linear, which performs an average shape from point sets, point variability parameters and external deformators. These template-based models are mostly used for hand-tracking, but could also be of use for simple gesture classification.

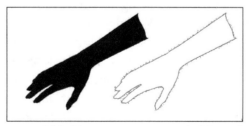

These binary silhouette(left) or contour(right) images represent typical input for appearance-based algorithms. They are compared with different hand templates and if they match, the correspondent gesture is inferred.

A second approach in gesture detecting using appearance-based models uses image sequences as gesture templates. Parameters for this method are either the images themselves, or certain features derived from these. Most of the time, only one (monoscopic) or two (stereoscopic) views are used.

Challenges

There are many challenges associated with the accuracy and usefulness of gesture recognition software. For image-based gesture recognition there are limitations on the equipment used and image noise. Images or video may not be under consistent lighting, or in the same location. Items in the background or distinct features of the users may make recognition more difficult.

The variety of implementations for image-based gesture recognition may also cause issue for viability of the technology to general usage. For example, an algorithm calibrated for one camera may not work for a different camera. The amount of background noise also causes tracking and recognition difficulties, especially when occlusions (partial and full) occur. Furthermore, the distance from the camera, and the camera's resolution and quality, also cause variations in recognition accuracy.

In order to capture human gestures by visual sensors, robust computer vision methods are also required, for example for hand tracking and hand posture recognition or for capturing movements of the head, facial expressions or gaze direction.

Social Acceptability

One significant challenge to the adoption of gesture interfaces on consumer mobile devices such as smartphones and smart watches stems from the social acceptability implications of gestural input. While gestures can facilitate fast and accurate input on many novel form-factor computers, their adoption and usefulness is often limited by social factors rather than technical ones. To this end, designers of gesture input methods may seek to balance both technical considerations and user willingness to perform gestures in different social contexts. In addition, different device hardware and sensing mechanisms support different kinds of recognizable gestures.

Mobile Device

Gesture interfaces on mobile and small form-factor devices are often supported by the presence of motion sensors such as inertial measurement units (IMUs). On these devices, gesture sensing relies on users performing movement-based gestures capable of being recognized by these motion sensors. This can potentially make capturing signal from subtle or low-motion gestures challenging, as they may become difficult to distinguish from natural movements or noise. Through a survey and study of gesture usability, researchers found that gestures that incorporate subtle movement, which appear similar to existing technology, look or feel similar to every actions, and which are enjoyable were more likely to be accepted by users, while gestures that look strange, are uncomfortable to perform, interferes with communication, or involves uncommon movement caused users more likely to reject their usage. The social acceptability of mobile device gestures rely heavily on the naturalness of the gesture and social context.

On-Body and Wearable Computers

Wearable computers typically differ from traditional mobile devices in that their usage and interaction location takes place on the user's body. In these contexts, gesture interfaces may become preferred over traditional input methods, as their small size renders touch-screens or keyboards less appealing. Nevertheless, they share many of the same social acceptability obstacles as mobile devices when it comes to gestural interaction. However, the possibility of wearable computers to be hidden from sight or integrated in other everyday objects, such as clothing, allow gesture input to mimic common clothing interactions, such as adjusting a shirt collar or rubbing one's front pant pocket. A major consideration for wearable computer interaction is the location for device placement and interaction. A study exploring third-party attitudes towards wearable device interaction conducted across the United States and South Korea found differences in the perception of wearable computing use of males and females, in part due to different areas of the body considered as socially sensitive. Another study investigating the social acceptability of on-body projected interfaces found similar results, with both studies labelling areas around the waist, groin, and upper body (for women) to be least acceptable while areas around the forearm and wrist to be most acceptable.

Public Installations

Public Installations, such as interactive public displays, allow access to information and displaying interactive media in public settings such as museums, galleries, and theaters. While touch screens are a frequent form of input for public displays, gesture interfaces provide additional benefits such as improved hygiene, interaction from a distance, improved discoverability, and may favor performative interaction. An important consideration for gestural interaction with public displays is the high probability or expectation of a spectator audience.

Gorilla Arm

Gorilla arm was a side-effect of vertically oriented touch-screen or light-pen use. In periods of prolonged use, users' arms began to feel fatigue and discomfort. This effect contributed to the decline of touch-screen input despite initial popularity in the 1980s.

In order to measure arm fatigue and the gorilla arm side effect, researchers developed a technique called Consumed Endurance.

3D Single-object Recognition

In computer vision, 3D single-object recognition involves recognizing and determining the pose of user-chosen 3D object in a photograph or range scan. Typically, an example of the object to be recognized is presented to a vision system in a controlled environment, and then for an arbitrary input such as a video stream, the system locates the previously presented object. This can be done either off-line, or in real-time. The algorithms for solving this problem are specialized for locating a single pre-identified object, and can be contrasted with algorithms which operate on general classes of objects, such as face recognition systems or 3D generic object recognition. Due to the low cost and ease of acquiring photographs, a significant amount of research has been devoted to 3D object recognition in photographs.

3D Single-object Recognition in Photographs

The method of recognizing a 3D object depends on the properties of an object. For simplicity, many existing algorithms have focused on recognizing rigid objects consisting of a single part, that is, objects whose spatial transformation is a Euclidean motion. Two general approaches have been taken to the problem: pattern recognition approaches use low-level image appearance information to locate an object, while feature-based geometric approaches construct a model for the object to be recognized, and match the model against the photograph.

Pattern Recognition Approaches

These methods use appearance information gathered from pre-captured or pre-computed projections of an object to match the object in the potentially cluttered scene. However, they do not take the 3D geometric constraints of the object into consideration during matching, and typically also do not handle occlusion as well as feature-based approaches.

Feature-based Geometric Approaches

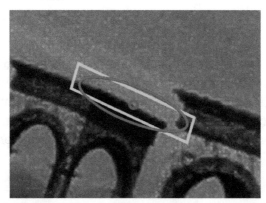

An example of a detected feature in an image. Blue indicates the center of the feature, the red ellipse indicates the characteristic scale identified by the feature detector, and the green parallelogram is constructed from the coordinates of the ellipse as per.

Feature-based approaches work well for objects which have distinctive features. Thus far, objects which have good edge features or blob features have been successfully recognized; for example detection algorithms. Due to lack of the appropriate feature detectors, objects without textured, smooth surfaces cannot currently be handled by this approach.

Feature-based object recognizers generally work by pre-capturing a number of fixed views of the object to be recognized, extracting features from these views, and then in the recognition process, matching these features to the scene and enforcing geometric constraints.

As an example of a prototypical system taking this approach, we will present an outline of the method used by, with some detail elided. The method starts by assuming that objects undergo globally rigid transformations. Because smooth surfaces are locally planar, affine invariant features are appropriate for matching: the paper detects ellipse-shaped regions of interest using both edge-like and blob-like features, and as per [Lowe 2004], finds the dominant gradient direction of the ellipse, converts the ellipse into a parallelogram, and takes a SIFT descriptor on the resulting parallelogram. Color information is used also to improve discrimination over SIFT features alone.

Partial models of features, projected into 3D, constructed from nearby views of a teddy-bear.

Next, given a number of camera views of the object, the method constructs a 3D model for the object, containing the 3D spatial position and orientation of each feature. Because the number of views of the object is large, typically each feature is present in several adjacent views. The center points of such matching features correspond, and detected features are aligned along the dominant gradient direction, so the points at (1, 0) in the local coordinate system of the feature parallelogram also correspond, as do the points (0, 1) in the parallelogram's local coordinates. Thus for every pair of matching features in nearby views, three point pair correspondences are known. Given at least two matching features, a multi-view affine structure from motion algorithm can be used to construct an estimate of points positions (up to an arbitrary affine transformation). The paper of Rothganger et al. therefore selects two adjacent views, uses a RANSAC-like method to select two corresponding pairs of features, and adds new features to the partial model built by RANSAC so long as they are under an error term. Thus for any given pair of adjacent views, the algorithm creates a partial model of all features visible in both views.

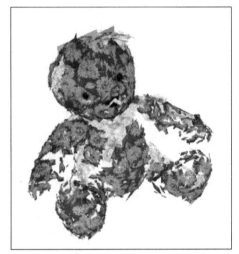

Final merged model of features for the teddy bear, after Euclidean upgrade. For recognition, this model is matched against a photograph of the scene using RANSAC.

To produce a unified model, the paper takes the largest partial model, and incrementally aligns all smaller partial models to it. Global minimization is used to reduce the error, and then a Euclidean upgrade is used to change the model's feature positions from 3D coordinates unique up to affine transformation to 3D coordinates that are unique up to Euclidean motion. At the end of this step, one has a model of the target object, consisting of features projected into a common 3D space.

To recognize an object in an arbitrary input image, the paper detects features, and then uses RANSAC to find the affine projection matrix which best fits the unified object model to the 2D scene. If this RANSAC approach has sufficiently low error, then on success, the algorithm both recognizes the object and gives the object's pose in terms of an affine projection. Under the assumed conditions, the method typically achieves recognition rates of around 95%.

Face Detection

Face detection is a computer technology being used in a variety of applications that identifies human faces in digital images. Face detection also refers to the psychological process by which humans locate and attend to faces in a visual scene.

Automatic face detection with OpenCV.

Related Algorithms

Face detection can be regarded as a specific case of object-class detection. In object-class detection, the task is to find the locations and sizes of all objects in an image that belong to a given class. Examples include upper torsos, pedestrians, and cars.

Face-detection algorithms focus on the detection of frontal human faces. It is analogous to image detection in which the image of a person is matched bit by bit. Image matches with the image stores in database. Any facial feature changes in the database will invalidate the matching process.

A reliable face-detection approach based on the genetic algorithm and the eigen-face technique:

Firstly, the possible human eye regions are detected by testing all the valley regions in the gray-level image. Then the genetic algorithm is used to generate all the possible face regions which include the eyebrows, the iris, the nostril and the mouth corners.

Each possible face candidate is normalized to reduce both the lighting effect, which is caused by uneven illumination; and the shirring effect, which is due to head movement. The fitness value of each candidate is measured based on its projection on the eigen-faces. After a number of iterations, all the face candidates with a high fitness value are selected for further verification. At this stage, the face symmetry is measured and the existence of the different facial features is verified for each face candidate.

Applications

Facial Recognition

Face detection is used in biometrics, often as a part of (or together with) a facial recognition system. It is also used in video surveillance, human computer interface and image database management.

Photography

Some recent digital cameras use face detection for autofocus. Face detection is also useful for selecting regions of interest in photo slideshows that use a pan-and-scale Ken Burns effect.

Modern appliances also use smile detection to take a photograph at an appropriate time.

Marketing

Face detection is gaining the interest of marketers. A webcam can be integrated into a television and detect any face that walks by. The system then calculates the race, gender, and age range of the face. Once the information is collected, a series of advertisements can be played that is specific toward the detected race/gender/age.

An example of such a system is OptimEyes and is integrated into the Amscreen digital signage system.

Emotional Inference

Face detection can be used as part of a software implementation of emotional inference. Emotional inference can be used to help people with autism understand the feelings of people around them.

Lip Reading

Face detection is essential for the process of language inference from visual queues. Lip reading has applications in help computers determine who is speaking which is needed when security is important.

HANDWRITING RECOGNITION

Handwriting recognition (HWR), also known as Handwritten Text Recognition (HTR), is the ability of a computer to receive and interpret intelligible handwritten input from sources such as paper documents, photographs, touch-screens and other devices. The image of the written text may be sensed "off line" from a piece of paper by optical scanning (optical character recognition) or intelligent word recognition. Alternatively, the movements of the pen tip may be sensed "on line", for example by a pen-based computer screen surface, a generally easier task as there are more clues available. A handwriting recognition system handles formatting, performs correct segmentation into characters, and finds the most plausible words.

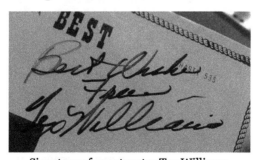
Signature of country star Tex Williams.

Off-line Recognition

Off-line handwriting recognition involves the automatic conversion of text in an image into letter codes which are usable within computer and text-processing applications. The data obtained by this form is regarded as a static representation of handwriting. Off-line handwriting recognition is comparatively difficult, as different people have different handwriting styles. And, as of today, OCR engines are primarily focused on machine printed text and ICR for hand "printed" (written in capital letters) text.

Traditional Techniques

Character Extraction

Off-line character recognition often involves scanning a form or document written sometime in the past. This means the individual characters contained in the scanned image will need to be extracted. Tools exist that are capable of performing this step. However, there are several common imperfections in this step. The most common is when characters that are connected are returned as a single sub-image containing both characters. This causes a major problem in the recognition stage. Yet many algorithms are available that reduce the risk of connected characters.

Character Recognition

After the extraction of individual characters occurs, a recognition engine is used to identify the corresponding computer character. Several different recognition techniques are currently available.

Feature Extraction

Feature extraction works in a similar fashion to neural network recognizers. However, programmers must manually determine the properties they feel are important.

- Is reflected x axisThis approach gives the recognizer more control over the properties used in identification. Yet any system using this approach requires substantially more development time than a neural network because the properties are not learned automatically.

Modern Techniques

Where traditional techniques focus on segmenting individual characters for recognition, modern techniques focus on recognizing all the characters in a segmented line of text. Particularly they focus on machine learning techniques which are able to learn visual features, avoiding the limiting feature engineering previously used. State-of-the-art methods use convolutional networks to extract visual features over several overlapping windows of a text line image which an RNN uses to produce character probabilities.

On-line Recognition

On-line handwriting recognition involves the automatic conversion of text as it is written on a special digitizer or PDA, where a sensor picks up the pen-tip movements as well as pen-up/pen-down switching. This kind of data is known as digital ink and can be regarded as a digital representation of handwriting. The obtained signal is converted into letter codes which are usable within computer and text-processing applications.

The elements of an on-line handwriting recognition interface typically include:

- A pen or stylus for the user to write with.

- A touch sensitive surface, which may be integrated with, or adjacent to, an output display.

- A software application which interprets the movements of the stylus across the writing surface, translating the resulting strokes into digital text. And an off-line recognition is the problem.

General Process

The process of online handwriting recognition can be broken down into a few general steps:

- Preprocessing

- Feature extraction

- Classification

The purpose of preprocessing is to discard irrelevant information in the input data, that can negatively affect the recognition. This concerns speed and accuracy. Preprocessing usually consists of binarization, normalization, sampling, smoothing and denoising. The second step is feature extraction. Out of the two- or more-dimensional vector field received from the preprocessing algorithms, higher-dimensional data is extracted. The purpose of this step is to highlight important information for the recognition model. This data may include information like pen pressure, velocity or the changes of writing direction. The last big step is classification. In this step various models are used to map the extracted features to different classes and thus identifying the characters or words the features represent.

Hardware

Commercial products incorporating handwriting recognition as a replacement for keyboard input were introduced in the early 1980s. Examples include handwriting terminals such as the Pencept Penpad and the Inforite point-of-sale terminal. With the advent of the large consumer market for personal computers, several commercial products were introduced to replace the keyboard and mouse on a personal computer with a single pointing/handwriting system, such as those from PenCept, CIC and others. The first commercially available tablet-type portable computer was the GRiDPad from GRiD Systems, released in September 1989. Its operating system was based on MS-DOS.

In the early 1990s, hardware makers including NCR, IBM and EO released tablet computers running the PenPoint operating system developed by GO Corp. PenPoint used handwriting recognition and gestures throughout and provided the facilities to third-party software. IBM's tablet computer was the first to use the ThinkPad name and used IBM's handwriting recognition. This recognition system was later ported to Microsoft Windows for Pen Computing, and IBM's Pen for OS/2. None of these were commercially successful.

Advancements in electronics allowed the computing power necessary for handwriting recognition to fit into a smaller form factor than tablet computers, and handwriting recognition is often used as an input method for hand-held PDAs. The first PDA to provide written input was the Apple

Newton, which exposed the public to the advantage of a streamlined user interface. However, the device was not a commercial success, owing to the unreliability of the software, which tried to learn a user's writing patterns. By the time of the release of the Newton OS 2.0, wherein the handwriting recognition was greatly improved, including unique features still not found in current recognition systems such as modeless error correction, the largely negative first impression had been made. After discontinuation of Apple Newton, the feature has been ported to Mac OS X 10.2 or later in form of Inkwell (Macintosh).

Palm later launched a successful series of PDAs based on the Graffiti recognition system. Graffiti improved usability by defining a set of "unistrokes", or one-stroke forms, for each character. This narrowed the possibility for erroneous input, although memorization of the stroke patterns did increase the learning curve for the user. The Graffiti handwriting recognition was found to infringe on a patent held by Xerox, and Palm replaced Graffiti with a licensed version of the CIC handwriting recognition which, while also supporting unistroke forms, pre-dated the Xerox patent. The court finding of infringement was reversed on appeal, and then reversed again on a later appeal. The parties involved subsequently negotiated a settlement concerning this and other patents Graffiti (Palm OS).

A Tablet PC is a special notebook computer that is outfitted with a digitizer tablet and a stylus, and allows a user to handwrite text on the unit's screen. The operating system recognizes the handwriting and converts it into typewritten text. Windows Vista and Windows 7 include personalization features that learn a user's writing patterns or vocabulary for English, Japanese, Chinese Traditional, Chinese Simplified and Korean. The features include a "personalization wizard" that prompts for samples of a user's handwriting and uses them to retrain the system for higher accuracy recognition. This system is distinct from the less advanced handwriting recognition system employed in its Windows Mobile OS for PDAs.

Although handwriting recognition is an input form that the public has become accustomed to, it has not achieved widespread use in either desktop computers or laptops. It is still generally accepted that keyboard input is both faster and more reliable. As of 2006, many PDAs offer handwriting input, sometimes even accepting natural cursive handwriting, but accuracy is still a problem, and some people still find even a simple on-screen keyboard more efficient.

Software

Initial software modules could understand print handwriting where the characters were separated; however, cursive handwriting writing with connected characters presented Sayre's Paradox, a difficulty involving character segmentation. Author of the first applied pattern recognition program in 1962 was Shelia Guberman, then in Moscow. Commercial examples came from companies such as Communications Intelligence Corporation and IBM.

In the early 1990s, two companies, ParaGraph International, and Lexicus came up with systems that could understand cursive handwriting recognition. ParaGraph was based in Russia and founded by computer scientist Stepan Pachikov while Lexicus was founded by Ronjon Nag and Chris Kortge who were students at Stanford University. The ParaGraph CalliGrapher system was deployed in the Apple Newton systems, and Lexicus Longhand system was made available commercially for the PenPoint and Windows operating system. Lexicus was acquired by Motorola in 1993 and went on to develop Chinese handwriting recognition and predictive text systems for Motorola. ParaGraph was acquired in 1997 by SGI and its handwriting recognition team formed a P&I division, later acquired from SGI by Vadem. Microsoft has acquired CalliGrapher handwriting recognition and other digital ink technologies developed by P&I from Vadem in 1999.

Wolfram Mathematica (8.0 or later) also provides a handwriting or text recognition function TextRecognize.

MACHINE VISION

Machine vision (MV) is the technology and methods used to provide imaging-based automatic inspection and analysis for such applications as automatic inspection, process control, and robot guidance, usually in industry. Machine vision refers to many technologies, software and hardware products, integrated systems, actions, methods and expertise. Machine vision as a systems engineering discipline can be considered distinct from computer vision, a form of computer science. It attempts to integrate existing technologies in new ways and apply them to solve real world problems. The term is the prevalent one for these functions in industrial automation environments but is also used for these functions in other environments such as security and vehicle guidance.

Early Automatix (now part of Omron) machine vision system Autovision II from 1983 being demonstrated at a trade show. Camera on tripod is pointing down at a light table to produce backlit image shown on screen, which is then subjected to blob extraction.

The overall machine vision process includes planning the details of the requirements and project, and then creating a solution. During run-time, the process starts with imaging, followed by automated analysis of the image and extraction of the required information.

Definitions of the term "Machine vision" vary, but all include the technology and methods used to extract information from an image on an automated basis, as opposed to image processing, where the output is another image. The information extracted can be a simple good-part/bad-part signal, or more a complex set of data such as the identity, position and orientation of each object in an image. The information can be used for such applications as automatic inspection and robot and process guidance in industry, for security monitoring and vehicle guidance. This field encompasses a large number of technologies, software and hardware products, integrated systems, actions, methods and expertise. Machine vision is practically the only term used for these functions in industrial automation applications; the term is less universal for these functions in other environments such as security and vehicle guidance. Machine vision as a systems engineering discipline can be considered distinct from computer vision, a form of basic computer science; machine vision attempts to integrate existing technologies in new ways and apply them to solve real world problems in a way that meets the requirements of industrial automation and similar application areas. The term is also used in a broader sense by trade shows and trade groups such as the Automated Imaging Association and the European Machine Vision Association. This broader definition also encompasses products and applications most often associated with image processing. The primary uses for machine vision are automatic inspection and industrial robot/process guidance.

Imaging based Automatic Inspection and Sorting

The primary uses for machine vision are imaging-based automatic inspection and sorting and robot guidance. In this topic the former is abbreviated as "automatic inspection". The overall process includes planning the details of the requirements and project, and then creating a solution.

Methods and Sequence of Operation

The first step in the automatic inspection sequence of operation is acquisition of an image, typically using cameras, lenses, and lighting that has been designed to provide the differentiation required by subsequent processing. MV software packages and programs developed in them then employ various digital image processing techniques to extract the required information, and often make decisions (such as pass/fail) based on the extracted information.

Equipment

The components of an automatic inspection system usually include lighting, a camera or other imager, a processor, software, and output devices.

Imaging

The imaging device (e.g. camera) can either be separate from the main image processing unit or combined with it in which case the combination is generally called a smart camera or smart sensor. Inclusion of the full processing function into the same enclosure as the camera is often referred to as embedded processing. When separated, the connection may be made to specialized intermediate hardware, a custom processing appliance, or a frame grabber within a computer using either an analog or standardized digital interface. MV implementations also use digital cameras capable of direct connections (without a framegrabber) to a computer via FireWire, USB or Gigabit Ethernet interfaces.

While conventional (2D visible light) imaging is most commonly used in MV, alternatives include multispectral imaging, hyperspectral imaging, imaging various infrared bands, line scan imaging, 3D imaging of surfaces and X-ray imaging. Key differentiations within MV 2D visible light imaging are monochromatic vs. color, frame rate, resolution, and whether or not the imaging process is simultaneous over the entire image, making it suitable for moving processes.

Though the vast majority of machine vision applications are solved using two-dimensional imaging, machine vision applications utilizing 3D imaging are a growing niche within the industry. The most commonly used method for 3D imaging is scanning based triangulation which utilizes motion of the product or image during the imaging process. A laser is projected onto the surfaces of an object. In machine vision this is accomplished with a scanning motion, either by moving the workpiece, or by moving the camera & laser imaging system. The line is viewed by a camera from a different angle; the deviation of the line represents shape variations. Lines from multiple scans are assembled into a depth map or point cloud. Stereoscopic vision is used in special cases involving unique features present in both views of a pair of cameras. Other 3D methods used for machine vision are time of flight and grid based. One method is grid array based systems using pseudorandom structured light system as employed by the Microsoft Kinect system circa 2012.

Image Processing

After an image is acquired, it is processed. Central processing functions are generally done by a CPU, a GPU, a FPGA or a combination of these. Deep learning training and inference impose higher processing performance requirements. Multiple stages of processing are generally used in a sequence that ends up as a desired result. A typical sequence might start with tools such as filters which modify the image, followed by extraction of objects, then extraction (e.g. measurements, reading of codes) of data from those objects, followed by communicating that data, or comparing it against target values to create and communicate "pass/fail" results. Machine vision image processing methods include:

- Stitching/Registration: Combining of adjacent 2D or 3D images.

- Filtering (e.g. morphological filtering)

- Thresholding: Thresholding starts with setting or determining a gray value that will be useful for the following steps. The value is then used to separate portions of the image, and sometimes to transform each portion of the image to simply black and white based on whether it is below or above that grayscale value.

- Pixel counting: counts the number of light or dark pixels

- Segmentation: Partitioning a digital image into multiple segments to simplify and change the representation of an image into something that is more meaningful and easier to analyze.

- Edge detection: finding object edges

- Color Analysis: Identify parts, products and items using color, assess quality from color, and isolate features using color.

- Blob detection and extraction: inspecting an image for discrete blobs of connected pixels (e.g. a black hole in a grey object) as image landmarks.

- Neural net / deep learning / machine learning processing: weighted and self-training multi-variable decision making Circa 2019 there is a large expansion of this, using deep learning and machine learning to significantly expand machine vision capabilities.

- Pattern recognition including template matching. Finding, matching, and counting specific patterns. This may include location of an object that may be rotated, partially hidden by another object, or varying in size.

- Barcode, Data Matrix and "2D barcode" reading

- Optical character recognition: automated reading of text such as serial numbers

- Gauging/Metrology: measurement of object dimensions (e.g. in pixels, inches or millimeters)

- Comparison against target values to determine a "pass or fail" or "go/no go" result. For example, with code or bar code verification, the read value is compared to the stored target value. For gauging, a measurement is compared against the proper value and tolerances. For verification of alpha-numberic codes, the OCR'd value is compared to the proper or target value. For inspection for blemishes, the measured size of the blemishes may be compared to the maximums allowed by quality standards.

Outputs

A common output from automatic inspection systems is pass/fail decisions. These decisions may in turn trigger mechanisms that reject failed items or sound an alarm. Other common outputs include object position and orientation information for robot guidance systems. Additionally, output types include numerical measurement data, data read from codes and characters, counts and classification of objects, displays of the process or results, stored images, alarms from automated space monitoring MV systems, and process control signals. This also includes user interfaces, interfaces for the integration of multi-component systems and automated data interchange.

Imaging based Robot Guidance

Machine vision commonly provides location and orientation information to a robot to allow the robot to properly grasp the product. This capability is also used to guide motion that is simpler than robots, such as a 1 or 2 axis motion controller. The overall process includes planning the details of the requirements and project, and then creating a solution. This part describes the technical process that occurs during the operation of the solution. Many of the process steps are the same as with automatic inspection except with a focus on providing position and orientation information as the end result.

Market

As recently as 2006, one industry consultant reported that MV represented a $1.5 billion market in North America. However, the editor-in-chief of an MV trade magazine asserted that "machine vision is not an industry per se" but rather "the integration of technologies and products that provide services or applications that benefit true industries such as automotive or consumer goods manufacturing, agriculture, and defense."

SELF-DRIVING CAR

A self-driving car, also known as an autonomous vehicle (AV), connected and autonomous vehicle (CAV), driverless car, robo-car, or robotic car, is a vehicle that is capable of sensing its environment and moving safely with little or no human input.

Waymo Chrysler Pacifica Hybrid undergoing testing in the San Francisco Bay Area.

Self-driving cars combine a variety of sensors to perceive their surroundings, such as radar, lidar, sonar, GPS, odometry and inertial measurement units. Advanced control systems interpret sensory information to identify appropriate navigation paths, as well as obstacles and relevant signage.

Autonomous racing car on display at the 2017 New York City ePrix.

Long distance trucking is seen as being at the forefront of adopting and implementing the technology.

There is some inconsistency in the terminology used in the self-driving car industry. Various organizations have proposed to define an accurate and consistent vocabulary.

Such confusion has been documented in SAE J3016 which states that "Some vernacular usages associate autonomous specifically with full driving automation (Level 5), while other usages apply it to all levels of driving automation, and some state legislation has defined it to correspond approximately to any ADS [automated driving system] at or above Level 3 (or to any vehicle equipped with such an ADS)."

Terminology and Safety Considerations

Modern vehicles provide partly automated features such as keeping the car within its lane, speed controls or emergency braking. Nonetheless, differences remain between a fully autonomous self-driving car on one hand and driver assistance technologies on the other hand. According to the BBC, confusion between those concepts leads to deaths.

The Association of British Insurers considers the usage of the word autonomous in marketing for modern cars to be dangerous because car ads make motorists think 'autonomous' and 'autopilot' means a vehicle can drive itself when they still rely on the driver to ensure safety. Technology alone still is not able to drive the car.

When some car makers suggest or claim vehicles are self-driving, when they are only partly automated, drivers risk becoming excessively confident, leading to crashes, while fully self-driving cars are still a long way off in the UK.

Autonomous vs. Automated

Autonomous means self-governing. Many historical projects related to vehicle automation have been automated (made automatic) subject to a heavy reliance on artificial aids in their environment, such as magnetic strips. Autonomous control implies satisfactory performance under significant uncertainties in the environment and the ability to compensate for system failures without external intervention.

One approach is to implement communication networks both in the immediate vicinity (for collision avoidance) and farther away (for congestion management). Such outside influences in the decision process reduce an individual vehicle's autonomy, while still not requiring human intervention.

Wood et al. wrote, "This Article generally uses the term 'autonomous,' instead of the term 'automated.' "The term "autonomous" was chosen "because it is the term that is currently in more widespread use (and thus is more familiar to the general public). However, the latter term is arguably more accurate. 'Automated' connotes control or operation by a machine, while 'autonomous' connotes acting alone or independently. Most of the vehicle concepts (that we are currently aware of) have a person in the driver's seat, utilize a communication connection to the Cloud or other vehicles, and do not independently select either destinations or routes for reaching them. Thus, the term 'automated' would more accurately describe these vehicle concepts." As of 2017, most commercial projects focused on automated vehicles that did not communicate with other vehicles or with an enveloping management regime. EuroNCAP defines autonomous in "Autonomous Emergency Braking" as: "the system acts independently of the driver to avoid or mitigate the accident." which implies the autonomous system is not the driver.

Autonomous vs. Cooperative

To enable a car to travel without any driver embedded within the vehicle, some companies use a remote driver.

Self-driving Car

PC Magazine defines a self-driving car as "A computer-controlled car that drives it." The Union of Concerned Scientists states that self-driving cars are "cars or trucks in which human drivers are never required to take control to safely operate the vehicle. Also known as autonomous or 'driverless' cars, they combine sensors and software to control, navigate, and drive the vehicle."

Classification

A classification system based on six different levels (ranging from fully manual to fully automated systems) was published in 2014 by SAE International, an automotive standardization body, as J3016, Taxonomy and Definitions for Terms Related to On-Road Motor Vehicle Automated Driving Systems. This classification system is based on the amount of driver intervention and attentiveness required, rather than the vehicle capabilities, although these are very loosely related. In the United States in 2013, the National Highway Traffic Safety Administration (NHTSA) released a formal classification system, but abandoned this system in favor of the SAE standard in 2016. Also in 2016, SAE updated its classification, called J3016_201609.

Tesla Autopilot system is classified as an SAE Level 2 system.

Levels of driving automation

In SAE's automation level definitions, "driving mode" means "a type of driving scenario with characteristic dynamic driving task requirements (e.g., expressway merging, high speed cruising, low speed traffic jam, closed-campus operations, etc.)"

- Level 0: Automated system issues warnings and may momentarily intervene but has no sustained vehicle control.

- Level 1 ("hands on"): The driver and the automated system share control of the vehicle. Examples are systems where the driver controls steering and the automated system controls engine power to maintain a set speed (Cruise Control) or engine and brake power to maintain and vary speed (Adaptive Cruise Control or ACC); and Parking Assistance, where steering is automated while speed is under manual control. The driver must be ready to retake full control at any time. Lane Keeping Assistance (LKA) Type II is a further example of Level 1 self-driving. The Automatic Emergency Braking alerts the driver to a crash and permits full braking capacity is also a Level 1 feature.

- Level 2 ("hands off"): The automated system takes full control of the vehicle (accelerating, braking, and steering). The driver must monitor the driving and be prepared to intervene immediately at any time if the automated system fails to respond properly. The shorthand "hands off" is not meant to be taken literally. In fact, contact between hand and wheel is often mandatory during SAE 2 driving, to confirm that the driver is ready to intervene.

- Level 3 ("eyes off"): The driver can safely turn their attention away from the driving tasks, e.g. the driver can text or watch a movie. The vehicle will handle situations that call for an immediate response, like emergency braking. The driver must still be prepared to intervene within some limited time, specified by the manufacturer, when called upon by the vehicle to do so.

- Level 4 ("mind off"): As level 3, but no driver attention is ever required for safety, e.g. the driver may safely go to sleep or leave the driver's seat. Self-driving is supported only in limited spatial areas (geofenced) or under special circumstances. Outside of these areas or circumstances, the vehicle must be able to safely abort the trip, e.g. park the car, if the driver does not retake control.

- Level 5 ("steering wheel optional"): No human intervention is required at all. An example would be a robotic taxi.

In the formal SAE definition below, note in particular what happens in the shift from SAE 2 to SAE 3: the human driver no longer has to monitor the environment. This is the final aspect of the "dynamic driving task" that is now passed over from the human to the automated system. At SAE 3, the human driver still has the responsibility to intervene when asked to do so by the automated system. At SAE 4 the human driver is relieved of that responsibility and at SAE 5 the automated system will never need to ask for an intervention.

Semi-automated Vehicles

Between manually driven vehicles (SAE Level 0) and fully autonomous vehicles (SAE Level 5), there are a variety of vehicle types that can be described to have some degree of automation. These are collectively known as semi-automated vehicles. As it could be a while before the technology and infrastructure are developed for full automation, it is likely that vehicles will have increasing levels of automation. These semi-automated vehicles could potentially harness many of the advantages of fully automated vehicles, while still keeping the driver in charge of the vehicle.

Technical Challenges

There are different systems that help the self-driving car control the car. Systems that need improvement include the car navigation system, the location system, the electronic map, the map matching, the global path planning, the environment perception, the laser perception, the radar perception, the visual perception, the vehicle control, the perception of vehicle speed and direction, and the vehicle control method.

The challenge for driverless car designers is to produce control systems capable of analyzing sensory data in order to provide accurate detection of other vehicles and the road ahead. Modern self-driving cars generally use Bayesian simultaneous localization and mapping (SLAM) algorithms, which fuse data from multiple sensors and an off-line map into current location estimates and map updates. Waymo has developed a variant of SLAM with detection and tracking of other moving objects (DATMO), which also handles obstacles such as cars and pedestrians. Simpler systems may use roadside real-time locating system (RTLS) technologies to aid localization. Typical sensors include lidar, stereo vision, GPS and IMU. Control systems on automated cars may use Sensor Fusion, which is an approach that integrates information from a variety of sensors on the car to produce a more consistent, accurate, and useful view of the environment. Heavy rainfall, hail, or snow could impede the car sensors.

Driverless vehicles require some form of machine vision for the purpose of visual object recognition. Automated cars are being developed with deep neural networks, a type of deep learning architecture with many computational stages, or levels, in which neurons are simulated from the environment that activate the network. The neural network depends on an extensive amount of data extracted from real-life driving scenarios, enabling the neural network to "learn" how to execute the best course of action.

In May 2018, researchers from the Massachusetts Institute of Technology announced that they had built an automated car that can navigate unmapped roads. Researchers at their Computer Science and Artificial Intelligence Laboratory (CSAIL) have developed a new system, called MapLite, which allows self-driving cars to drive on roads that they have never been on before, without using 3D maps. The system combines the GPS position of the vehicle, a "sparse topological map" such as OpenStreetMap, (i.e. having 2D features of the roads only), and a series of sensors that observe the road conditions.

Nature of the Digital Technology

Autonomous vehicles, as digital technology, have certain characteristics that distinguish them from other types of technologies and vehicles. Due to these characteristics, autonomous vehicles are able to be more transformative and agile to possible changes. The characteristics will be explained based on the following subjects: homogenization and decoupling, connectivity, reprogrammable and smart, digital traces and modularity.

Homogenization and Decoupling

Homogenization comes from the fact that all digital information assumes the same form. During the ongoing evolution of the digital era, certain industry standards have been developed on how to store digital information and in what type of format. This concept of homogenization also applies to autonomous vehicles. In order for autonomous vehicles to perceive their surroundings, they have to use different techniques each with their own accompanying digital information (e.g. radar, GPS, motion sensors and computer vision). Due to homogenization, the digital information from these different techniques is stored in a homogeneous way. This implies that all digital information comes in the same form, which means their differences are decoupled, and digital information can be transmitted, stored and computed in a way that the vehicles and its operating system can better understand and act upon it. Homogenization also helps to exponentially increase the computing power of hard- and software (Moore's law) which also supports the autonomous vehicles to understand and act upon the digital information in a more cost-effective way, therefore lowering the marginal costs.

Connectivity

Connectivity means that users of a certain digital technology can connect easily with other users, other applications or even other enterprises. In the case of autonomous vehicles, it is essential for them to connect with other 'devices' in order to function most effectively. Autonomous vehicles are equipped with communication systems which allow them to communicate with other autonomous vehicles and roadside units to provide them, amongst other things, with information about road work or traffic congestion. In addition, scientists believe that the future will have computer programs that connect and manage each individual autonomous vehicle as it navigates through an intersection. This type of connectivity must replace traffic lights and stop signs. These types of characteristics drive and further develop the ability of autonomous vehicles to understand and cooperate with other products and services (such as intersection computer systems) in the autonomous vehicles market. This could lead to a network of autonomous vehicles all using the same network and information available on that network. Eventually, this can lead to more autonomous vehicles using the network because the information has been validated through the usage of other autonomous vehicles. Such movements will strengthen the value of the network and is called network externalities.

Reprogrammable

Another characteristic of autonomous vehicles is that the core product will have a greater emphasis on the software and its possibilities, instead of the chassis and its engine. This is because autonomous vehicles have software systems that drive the vehicle meaning that updates through reprogramming or editing the software can enhance the benefits of the owner (e.g. update in better distinguishing blind person vs. non-blind person so that the vehicle will take extra caution when approaching a blind person). A characteristic of this reprogrammable part of autonomous vehicles is that the updates need not only to come from the supplier, because through machine learning, smart autonomous vehicles can generate certain updates and install them accordingly (e.g. new navigation maps or new intersection computer systems). These reprogrammable characteristics of the digital technology and the possibility of smart machine learning give manufacturers of autonomous vehicles the opportunity to differentiate themselves on software. This also implies that autonomous vehicles are never finished because the product can continuously be improved.

Digital Traces

Autonomous vehicles are equipped with different sorts of sensors and radars. As said, this allows them to connect and interoperate with computers from other autonomous vehicles and roadside units. This implies that autonomous vehicles leave digital traces when they connect or interoperate. The data that comes from these digital traces can be used to develop new (to be determined) products or updates to enhance autonomous vehicles' driving ability or safety.

Modularity

Traditional vehicles and their accompanying technologies are manufactured as a product that will be complete, and unlike autonomous vehicles, they can only be improved if they are redesigned or reproduced. As said, autonomous vehicles are produced but due to their digital characteristics never finished. This is because autonomous vehicles are more modular since they are made up out of several modules which will be explained hereafter through a Layered Modular Architecture. The Layered Modular Architecture extends the architecture of purely physical vehicles by incorporating four loosely coupled layers of devices, networks, services and contents into Autonomous

Vehicles. These loosely coupled layers can interact through certain standardized interfaces:

- The first layer of this architecture consists of the device layer. This layer consists of the following two parts: logical capability and physical machinery. The physical machinery refers to the actual vehicle itself (e.g. chassis and carrosserie). When it comes to digital technologies, the physical machinery is accompanied by a logical capability layer in the form of operating systems that helps to guide the vehicles itself and make it autonomous. The logical capability provides control over the vehicle and connects it with the other layers.

- On top of the device layer comes the network layer. This layer also consists of two different parts: physical transport and logical transmission. The physical transport layer refers to the radars, sensors and cables of the autonomous vehicles which enable the transmission of digital information. Next to that, the network layer of autonomous vehicles also has a logical transmission which contains communication protocols and network standard to communicate the digital information with other networks and platforms or between layers. This increases the accessibility of the autonomous vehicles and enables the computational power of a network or platform.

- The service layer contains the applications and their functionalities that serves the autonomous vehicle (and its owners) as they extract, create, store and consume content with regards to their own driving history, traffic congestion, roads or parking abilities for example.

- The final layer of the model is the contents layer. This layer contains the sounds, images and videos. The autonomous vehicles store, extract and use to act upon and improve their driving and understanding of the environment. The contents layer also provides metadata and directory information about the content's origin, ownership, copyright, encoding methods, content tags, geo-time stamps, and so on.

The consequence of layered modular architecture of autonomous vehicles (and other digital technologies) is that it enables the emergence and development of platforms and ecosystems around a product and certain modules of that product. Traditionally, automotive vehicles were developed, manufactured and maintained by traditional manufacturers. Nowadays app developers and content creators can help to develop more comprehensive product experience for the consumer which creates a platform around the product of autonomous vehicles.

Human Factor Challenges

Self-driving cars are already exploring the difficulties of determining the intentions of pedestrians, bicyclists, and animals, and models of behavior must be programmed into driving algorithms. Human road users also have the challenge of determining the intentions of autonomous vehicles, where there is no driver with which to make eye contact or exchange hand signals. Drive.ai is testing a solution to this problem that involves LED signs mounted on the outside of the vehicle, announcing status such as "going now, don't cross" vs. "waiting for you to cross".

Two human-factor challenges are important for safety. One is the handoff from automated driving to manual driving, which may become necessary due to unfavorable or unusual road conditions, or if the vehicle has limited capabilities. A sudden handoff could leave a human driver dangerously unprepared in the moment. In the long term, humans who have less practice at driving might have a lower skill level and thus be more dangerous in manual mode. The second challenge is known as risk compensation: as a system is perceived to be safer, instead of benefiting entirely from all of the increased safety, people engage in riskier behavior and enjoy other benefits. Semi-automated cars have been shown to suffer from this problem, for example with users of Tesla Autopilot ignoring the road and using electronic devices or other activities against the advice of the company that the car is not capable of being completely autonomous. In the near future, pedestrians and bicyclists may travel in the street in a riskier fashion if they believe self-driving cars are capable of avoiding them.

In order for people to buy self-driving cars and vote for the government to allow them on roads, the technology must be trusted as safe. Self-driving elevators were invented in 1900, but the high number of people refusing to use them slowed adoption for several decades until operator strikes increased demand and trust was built with advertising and features like the emergency stop button.

Testing

A prototype of Waymo's self-driving car, navigating public streets in Mountain View, California in 2017.

The testing of vehicles with varying degrees of automation can be carried out either physically, in a closed environment or, where permitted, on public roads (typically requiring a license or permit, or adhering to a specific set of operating principles), or in a virtual environment, i.e. using computer simulations. When driven on public roads, automated vehicles require a person to monitor their proper operation and "take over" when needed. For example, New York state has strict requirements for the test driver, such that the vehicle can be corrected at all times by a licensed operator; highlighted by Cardian Cube Company's application and discussions with New York State officials and the NYS DMV.

Apple is testing self-driving cars, and has increased its fleet of test vehicles from three in April 2017, to 27 in January 2018, and 45 by March 2018.

Russian internet-company Yandex started to develop self-driving cars in 2016. In February 2018, they tested the prototype of an unmanned taxi on the streets of Moscow. In June 2018, a Yandex self-driving vehicle completed a 485-mile (780 km) trip on a federal highway from Moscow to Kazan, staying in autonomous mode for 99% of the time. In August 2018, Yandex-taxi began working with self-driving cars in the Russian town of Innopolis, and they plan to operate two unmanned vehicles with five stops within the town. In Las Vegas in January 2019, Yandex tested an unmanned vehicle for the first time outside Russia. Testing continued during the international Consumer Electronics Show between 8 and 11 January. Yandex received permission from the Israeli Ministry of Transport to test the company's unmanned vehicle on the public roads in 2019.

The progress of automated vehicles can be assessed by computing the average distance driven between "disengagements", when the automated system is switched off, typically by the intervention of a human driver. In 2017, Waymo reported 63 disengagements over 352,545 mi (567,366 km) of testing, an average distance of 5,596 mi (9,006 km) between disengagements, the highest among companies reporting such figures. Waymo also traveled a greater total distance than any of the other companies. Their 2017 rate of 0.18 disengagements per 1,000 mi (1,600 km) was an improvement over the 0.2 disengagements per 1,000 mi (1,600 km) in 2016, and 0.8 in 2015. In March 2017, Uber reported an average of just 0.67 mi (1.08 km) per disengagement. In the final three months of 2017, Cruise (now owned by GM) averaged 5,224 mi (8,407 km) per disengagement over a total distance of 62,689 mi (100,888 km). In July 2018, the first electric driverless racing car, "Robocar", completed a 1.8-kilometer track, using its navigation system and artificial intelligence.

Table: Miles per disengagement.

Car maker	2016		2018 (000)	
	Distance between disengagements	Total distance traveled	Distance between disengagements	Total distance traveled
Zoox			1.9 mi (3.1 km)	30.8 mi (49.6 km)
Waymo	5.1 mi (8.2 km)	635.9 mi (1,023.4 km)	11.1 mi (17.9 km)	1,272 mi (2,047 km)
Volkswagen	.006 mi (0.0097 km)	.009 mi (0.014 km)		
Uber			.0004 mi (0.00064 km)	26.9 mi (43.3 km)
Tesla	.003 mi (0.0048 km)	.5 mi (0.80 km)		
Pony.ai			1 mi (1.6 km)	16.3 mi (26.2 km)
Nuro			1 mi (1.6 km)	20.7 mi (33.3 km)
Nissan	2.6 mi (4.2 km)	6.0 mi (9.7 km)	.2 mi (0.32 km)	5.4 mi (8.7 km)
Mercedes-Benz	.002 mi (0.0032 km)	.7 mi (1.1 km)	.002 mi (0.0032 km)	1.7 mi (2.7 km)
General Motors	.05 mi (0.080 km)	8.1 mi (13.0 km)	5.2 mi (8.4 km)	448 mi (721 km)
Ford	.2 mi (0.32 km)	.6 mi (0.97 km)		
Delphi Automotive Systems	.01 mi (0.016 km)	2.7 mi (4.3 km)		
Bosch	0.007 mi (0.011 km)	1.0 mi (1.6 km)		
BMW	.6 mi (0.97 km)	.6 mi (0.97 km)		
Baidu			.2 mi (0.32 km)	18.0 mi (29.0 km)
Aurora			.09 mi (0.14 km)	32.9 mi (52.9 km)
Applie			.001 mi (0.0016 km)	79.7 mi (128.3 km)

Fields of Application

Autonomous Trucks and Vans

Companies such as Otto and Starsky Robotics have focused on autonomous trucks. Automation of trucks is important, not only due to the improved safety aspects of these very heavy vehicles, but also due to the ability of fuel savings through platooning.

Autonomous vans are being used by online grocers such as Ocado.

Transport Systems

In Europe, cities in Belgium, France, Italy and the UK are planning to operate transport systems for automated cars, and Germany, the Netherlands, and Spain have allowed public testing in traffic. In 2015, the UK launched public trials of the LUTZ Pathfinder automated pod in Milton Keynes. Beginning in summer 2015, the French government allowed PSA Peugeot-Citroen to make trials in real conditions in the Paris area. The experiments were planned to be extended to other cities such as Bordeaux and Strasbourg by 2016. The alliance between French companies THALES and Valeo (provider of the first self-parking car system that equips Audi and Mercedes premi) is testing its own system. New Zealand is planning to use automated vehicles for public transport in Tauranga and Christchurch.

In China, Baidu and King Long produce automated minibus, a vehicle with 14 seats, but without driving seat. With 100 vehicles produced, 2018 will be the first year with commercial automated service in China.

Potential Advantages

Safety

Driving safety experts predict that once driverless technology has been fully developed, traffic collisions (and resulting deaths and injuries and costs) caused by human error, such as delayed reaction time, tailgating, rubbernecking, and other forms of distracted or aggressive driving should be substantially reduced. Consulting firm McKinsey & Company estimated that widespread use of autonomous vehicles could "eliminate 90% of all auto accidents in the United States, prevent up to US$190 billion in damages and health-costs annually and save thousands of lives".

According to motorist website "TheDrive.com" operated by Time magazine, none of the driving safety experts they were able to contact were able to rank driving under an autopilot system at the time (2017) as having achieved a greater level of safety than traditional fully hands-on driving, so the degree to which these benefits asserted by proponents will manifest in practice cannot be assessed. Confounding factors that could reduce the net effect on safety may include unexpected interactions between humans and partly or fully automated vehicles, or between different types of vehicle system; complications at the boundaries of functionality at each automation level (such as handover when the vehicle reaches the limit of its capacity); the effect of the bugs and flaws that inevitably occur in complex interdependent software systems; sensor or data shortcomings; and successful compromise by malicious interveners.

To help reduce the possibility of these confounding factors, some companies have begun to open-source parts of their driverless systems. Udacity for instance is developing an open-source software stack, and some companies are having similar approaches.

Welfare

Automated cars could reduce labor costs; relieve travelers from driving and navigation chores, thereby replacing behind-the-wheel commuting hours with more time for leisure or work; and also would lift constraints on occupant ability to drive, distracted and texting while driving, intoxicated, prone to seizures, or otherwise impaired. For the young, the elderly, people with disabilities, and low-income citizens, automated cars could provide enhanced mobility. The removal of the steering wheel—along with the remaining driver interface and the requirement for any occupant to assume a forward-facing position—would give the interior of the cabin greater ergonomic flexibility. Large vehicles, such as motorhomes, would attain appreciably enhanced ease of use.

Traffic

Additional advantages could include higher speed limits; smoother rides; and increased roadway capacity; and minimized traffic congestion, due to decreased need for safety gaps and higher speeds. Currently, maximum controlled-access highway throughput or capacity according to the US Highway Capacity Manual is about 2,200 passenger vehicles per hour per lane, with about 5% of the available road space is taken up by cars. One study estimated that automated cars could increase capacity by 273% ($\approx$8,200 cars per hour per lane). The study also estimated that with 100% connected vehicles using vehicle-to-vehicle communication, capacity could reach 12,000 passenger vehicles per hour (up 545% from 2,200 pc/h per lane) traveling safely at 120 km/h (75 mph) with a following gap of about 6 m (20 ft) of each other. Human drivers at highway speeds keep between 40 to 50 m (130 to 160 ft) away from the vehicle in front. These increases in highway capacity could have a significant impact in traffic congestion, particularly in urban areas, and even effectively end highway congestion in some places. The ability for authorities to manage traffic flow would increase, given the extra data and driving behavior predictability combined with less need for traffic police and even road signage.

Lower Costs

Safer driving is expected to reduce the costs of vehicle insurance.

Energy and Environmental Impacts

Vehicle automation can improve fuel economy of the car by optimizing the drive cycle. Reduced traffic congestion and the improvements in traffic flow due to widespread use of automated cars will translate into higher fuel efficiency. Additionally, self-driving cars will be able to accelerate and brake more efficiently, meaning higher fuel economy from reducing wasted energy typically associated with inefficient changes to speed. However, the improvement in vehicle energy efficiency does not necessarily translate to net reduction in energy consumption and positive environmental outcomes. It is expected that convenience of the automated vehicles encourages the consumers to travel more, and this induced demand may partially or fully offset the fuel efficiency improvement brought by automation. Overall, the consequence of vehicle automation on global energy demand and emissions are highly uncertain, and heavily depends on the combined effect of changes in consumer behavior, policy intervention, technological progress and vehicle technology.

Parking Space

Manually driven vehicles are reported to be used only 4–5% of the time, and being parked and unused for the remaining 95–96% of the time. Autonomous taxis could, on the other hand, be used continuously after it has reached its destination. This could dramatically reduce the need for parking space. For example, in Los Angeles a 2015 study found 14% of the land is used for parking alone, equivalent to some 1,702 hectares (4,210 acres). This combined with the potential reduced need for road space due to improved traffic flow, could free up large amounts of land in urban areas, which could then be used for parks, recreational areas, buildings, among other uses; making cities more livable.

Besides this, privately owned self-driving cars, also capable of self-parking would provide another advantage: the ability to drop off and pick up passengers even in places where parking is prohibited. This would benefit park and ride facilities.

Related Effects

By reducing the labor and other costs of mobility as a service, automated cars could reduce the number of cars that are individually owned, replaced by taxi/pooling and other car-sharing services. This would also dramatically reduce the size of the automotive production industry, with corresponding environmental and economic effects. Assuming the increased efficiency is not fully offset by increases in demand, more efficient traffic flow could free roadway space for other uses such as better support for pedestrians and cyclists.

The vehicles' increased awareness could aid the police by reporting on illegal passenger behavior, while possibly enabling other crimes, such as deliberately crashing into another vehicle or a pedestrian. However, this may also lead to much expanded mass surveillance if there is wide access granted to third parties to the large data sets generated.

Potential Limits or Obstacles

The sort of hoped-for potential benefits from increased vehicle automation described may be limited by foreseeable challenges, such as disputes over liability, the time needed to turn over the existing stock of vehicles from non-automated to automated, and thus a long period of humans and autonomous vehicles sharing the roads, resistance by individuals to having to forfeit control of their cars, concerns about the safety of driverless in practice, and the implementation of a legal framework and consistent global government regulations for self-driving cars.

Other obstacles could include de-skilling and lower levels of driver experience for dealing with potentially dangerous situations and anomalies, ethical problems where an automated vehicle's software is forced during an unavoidable crash to choose between multiple harmful courses of action ('the trolley problem'), concerns about making large numbers of people currently employed as drivers unemployed, the potential for more intrusive mass surveillance of location, association and travel as a result of police and intelligence agency access to large data sets generated by sensors and pattern-recognition AI, and possibly insufficient understanding of verbal sounds, gestures and non-verbal cues by police, other drivers or pedestrians.

Possible technological obstacles for automated cars are:

- Artificial Intelligence is still not able to function properly in chaotic inner-city environments.

- A car's computer could potentially be compromised, as could a communication system between cars.

- Susceptibility of the car's sensing and navigation systems to different types of weather (such as snow) or deliberate interference, including jamming and spoofing.

- Avoidance of large animals requires recognition and tracking, and Volvo found that software suited to caribou, deer, and elk was ineffective with kangaroos.

- Autonomous cars may require very high-quality specialised maps to operate properly. Where these maps may be out of date, they would need to be able to fall back to reasonable behaviors.

- Competition for the radio spectrum desired for the car's communication.

- Field programmability for the systems will require careful evaluation of product development and the component supply chain.

- Current road infrastructure may need changes for automated cars to function optimally.

Social challenges include:

- Government over-regulation, or even uncertainty about potential future regulation, may delay deployment of automated cars on the road.

- Employment – Companies working on the technology have an increasing recruitment problem in that the available talent pool has not grown with demand. As such, education and training by third-party organisations such as providers of online courses and self-taught community-driven projects such as DIY Robocars and Formula Pi have quickly grown in popularity, while university level extra-curricular programmes such as Formula Student Driverless have bolstered graduate experience. Industry is steadily increasing freely available information sources, such as code, datasets and glossaries to widen the recruitment pool.

Potential Disadvantages

A direct impact of widespread adoption of automated vehicles is the loss of driving-related jobs in the road transport industry. There could be resistance from professional drivers and unions who are threatened by job losses. In addition, there could be job losses in public transit services and crash repair shops. The automobile insurance industry might suffer as the technology makes certain aspects of these occupations obsolete. A frequently cited paper by Michael Osborne and Carl Benedikt Frey found that automated cars would make many jobs redundant.

Privacy could be an issue when having the vehicle's location and position integrated into an interface that other people have access to. In addition, there is the risk of automotive hacking through the sharing of information through V2V (Vehicle to Vehicle) and V2I (Vehicle to Infrastructure) protocols. There is also the risk of terrorist attacks. Self-driving cars could potentially be loaded with explosives and used as bombs.

The lack of stressful driving, more productive time during the trip, and the potential savings in travel time and cost could become an incentive to live far away from cities, where housing is cheaper, and work in the city's core, thus increasing travel distances and inducing more urban sprawl, raising energy consumption and enlarging the carbon footprint of urban travel. There is also the risk that traffic congestion might increase, rather than decrease. Appropriate public policies and regulations, such as zoning, pricing, and urban design are required to avoid the negative impacts of increased suburbanization and longer distance travel.

Some believe that once automation in vehicles reaches higher levels and becomes reliable, drivers will pay less attention to the road. Research shows that drivers in automated cars react later when they have to intervene in a critical situation, compared to if they were driving manually. Depending on the capabilities of automated vehicles and the frequency with which human intervention is needed, this may counteract any increase in safety, as compared to all-human driving, that may be delivered by other factors.

Ethical and moral reasoning come into consideration when programming the software that decides what action the car takes in an unavoidable crash; whether the automated car will crash into a bus, potentially killing people inside; or swerve elsewhere, potentially killing its own passengers or nearby pedestrians. A question that programmers of AI systems find difficult to answer is "what decision should the car make that causes the 'smallest' damage to people's lives?" Adding to the challenge of determining machine ethics is the fact that morality is not universal.

The ethics of automated vehicles are still being articulated, and may lead to controversy. They may also require closer consideration of the variability, context-dependency, complexity and non-deterministic nature of human ethics. Different human drivers make various ethical decisions when driving, such as avoiding harm to themselves, or putting themselves at risk to protect others. These decisions range from rare extremes such as self-sacrifice or criminal negligence, to routine decisions good enough to keep the traffic flowing but bad enough to cause accidents, road rage and stress.

Human thought and reaction time may sometimes be too slow to detect the risk of an upcoming fatal crash, think through the ethical implications of the available options, or take an action to implement an ethical choice. Whether a particular automated vehicle's capacity to correctly detect an upcoming risk, analyse the options or choose a 'good' option from among bad choices would be as good or better than a particular human's may be difficult to predict or assess. This difficulty may be in part because the level of automated vehicle system understanding of the ethical issues at play in a given road scenario, sensed for an instant from out of a continuous stream of synthetic physical predictions of the near future, and dependent on layers of pattern recognition and situational intelligence, may be opaque to human inspection because of its origins in probabilistic machine learning rather than a simple, plain English 'human values' logic of parsable rules. The depth of understanding, predictive power and ethical sophistication needed will be hard to implement, and even harder to test or assess.

The scale of this challenge may have other effects. There may be few entities able to marshal the resources and AI capacity necessary to meet it, as well as the capital necessary to take an automated vehicle system to market and sustain it operationally for the life of a vehicle, and the legal capacity to deal with the potential for liability for a significant proportion of traffic accidents. This may have the effect of narrowing the number of different system operators, and eroding the diverse global vehicle market down to a small number of system suppliers.

Potential Changes for Different Industries

The traditional automobile industry is subject to changes driven by technology and market demands. These changes include breakthrough technological advances and when the market demands and adopts new technology quickly. In the rapid advance of both factors, the end of the era of incremental change was recognized. When the transition is made to a new technology, new entrants to the automotive industry present themselves, which can be distinguished as mobility providers such as Uber and Lyft, as well as tech giants such as Google and Nvidia. As new entrants to the industry arise, market uncertainty naturally occurs due to the changing dynamics. For example, the entrance of tech giants, as well as the alliances between them and traditional car manufacturers causes a variation in the innovation and production process of autonomous vehicles. Additionally, the entrance of mobility providers has caused ambiguous user preferences. As a result of the rise of mobility providers, the number of vehicles per capita has flatlined. In addition, the rise of the sharing economy also contributes to market uncertainty and causes forecasters to question whether personal ownership of vehicles is still relevant as new transportation technology and mobility providers are becoming preferred among consumers.

Taxis

With the aforementioned ambiguous user preference regarding the personal ownership of autonomous vehicles, it is possible that the current mobility provider trend will continue as it rises in popularity. Established providers such as Uber and Lyft are already significantly present within the industry, and it is likely that new entrants will enter when business opportunities arise.

Healthcare, Car Repair and Car Insurance

With the increasing reliance of autonomous vehicles on interconnectivity and the availability of big data which is made usable in the form of real-time maps, driving decisions can be made much faster in order to prevent collisions. Numbers made available by the US government state that 94% of the vehicle accidents are due to human failures. As a result, major implications for the healthcare industry become apparent. Numbers from the National Safety Council on killed and injured people on US roads multiplied by the average costs of a single incident reveal that an estimated US$500 billion loss may be imminent for the US healthcare industry when autonomous vehicles are dominating the roads. It is likely the anticipated decrease in traffic accidents will positively contribute to the widespread acceptance of autonomous vehicles, as well as the possibility to better allocate healthcare resources. As collisions are less likely to occur, and the risk for human errors is reduced significantly, the repair industry will face an enormous reduction of work that has to be done on the reparation of car frames. Meanwhile, as the generated data of the autonomous vehicle is likely to predict when certain replaceable parts are in need of maintenance, car owners and the repair industry will be able to proactively replace a part that will fail soon. This "Asset Efficiency Service" would implicate a productivity gain for the automotive repair industry. As fewer collisions implicate less money spent on repair costs, the role of the insurance industry is likely to be altered as well. It can be expected that the increased safety of transport due to autonomous vehicles will lead to a decrease in payouts for the insurers, which is positive for the industry, but fewer payouts may imply a demand drop for insurances in general. The insurance industry may have to create new insurance models in the near future to accommodate the changes. An unexpected disadvantage of the widespread acceptance of autonomous vehicles would be a reduction in organs available for transplant.

Rescue, Emergency Response and Military

The technique used in autonomous driving also ensures life savings in other industries. The implementation of autonomous vehicles with rescue, emergency response, and military applications has already led to a decrease in deaths. Military personnel use autonomous vehicles to reach dangerous and remote places on earth to deliver fuel, food and general supplies, and even rescue people. In addition, a future implication of adopting autonomous vehicles could lead to a reduction in deployed personnel, which will lead to a decrease in injuries, since the technological development allows autonomous vehicles to become more and more autonomous. Another future implication is the reduction of emergency drivers when autonomous vehicles are deployed as fire trucks or ambulances. An advantage could be the use of real-time traffic information and other generated data to determine and execute routes more efficiently than human drivers. The time savings can be invaluable in these situations.

Interior Design and Entertainment

With the driver decreasingly focused on operating a vehicle, the interior design and media-entertainment industry will have to reconsider what passengers of autonomous vehicles are doing when they are on the road. Vehicles need to be redesigned, and possibly even be prepared for multipurpose usage. In practice, it will show that travelers have more time for business and leisure. In both cases, this gives increasing opportunities for the media-entertainment industry to demand attention. Moreover, the advertisement business is able to provide location based ads without risking driver safety.

Telecommunication and Energy

All cars can benefit from information and connections, but autonomous cars "Will be fully capable of operating without C-V2X".

Since many autonomous vehicles are going to rely on electricity to operate, the demand for lithium batteries increases. Similarly, radar, sensors, lidar, and high-speed internet connectivity require higher auxiliary power from vehicles, which manifests as greater power draw from batteries. The larger battery requirement causes a necessary increase in supply of these type of batteries for the chemical industry. On the other hand, with the expected increase of battery powered (autonomous) vehicles, the petroleum industry is expected to undergo a decline in demand. As this implication depends on the adoption rate of autonomous vehicles, it is unsure to what extent this implication will disrupt this particular industry. This transition phase of oil to electricity allows companies to explore whether there are business opportunities for them in the new energy ecosystem.

Restaurant, Hotels and Airlines

Driver interactions with the vehicle will be less common within the near future, and in the more distant future the responsibility will lie entirely with the vehicle. As indicated above, this will have implications for the entertainment- and interior design industry. For roadside restaurants, the implication will be that the need for customers to stop driving and enter the restaurant will vanish, and the autonomous vehicle will have a double function. Moreover, accompanied with the rise of disruptive platforms such as Airbnb that have shaken up the hotel industry, the fast increase of developments within the autonomous vehicle industry might cause another implication for their customer bases. In the more distant future, the implication for motels might be that a decrease in guests will occur, since autonomous vehicles could be redesigned as fully equipped bedrooms. The improvements regarding the interior of the vehicles might additionally have implications for the airline industry. In the case of relatively short-haul flights, waiting times at customs or the gate imply lost time and hassle for customers. With the improved convenience in future car travel, it is possible that customers might go for this option, causing a loss in customer bases for airline industry.

Elderly and Disabled

Autonomous vehicles will have a severe impact on the mobility options of persons that are not able to drive a vehicle themselves. To remain socially engaged with society or even able to do groceries, the elderly people of today are walking, cycling, busing or depending on caretakers to drive them to these places. In addition to the perceived freedom of the elderly people of the future, the demand for human aides will decrease. When we also consider the increased health of the elderly, it is safe to state that care centers will experience a decrease in the number of clients. Not only elderly people face difficulties of their decreased physical abilities, also disabled people will perceive the benefits of autonomous vehicles in the near future, causing their dependency on caretakers to decrease. Both industries are largely depending on informal caregivers, who are mostly relatives of the persons in need. Since there is less of a reliance on their time, employers of informal caregivers or even governments will experience a decrease of costs allocated to this matter.

Children

Children and teens, which are not able to drive a vehicle themselves, are also benefiting of the introduction of autonomous cars. Daycares and schools are able to come up with automated pick up and drop off systems by car in addition to walking, cycling and busing, causing a decrease of reliance on parents and childcare workers. The extent to which human actions are necessary for driving will vanish. Since current vehicles require human actions to some extent, the driving school industry will not be disrupted until the majority of autonomous transportation is switched to the emerged dominant design. It is plausible that in the distant future driving a vehicle will be considered as a luxury, which implies that the structure of the industry is based on new entrants and a new market.

Vehicle Communication Systems

Vehicle networking may be desirable due to difficulty with computer vision being able to recognize brake lights, turn signals, buses, and similar things. However, the usefulness of such systems would be diminished by the fact current cars are equipped with them; they may also pose privacy concerns.

Individual vehicles may benefit from information obtained from other vehicles in the vicinity, especially information relating to traffic congestion and safety hazards. Vehicular communication systems use vehicles and roadside units as the communicating nodes in a peer-to-peer network, providing each other with information. As a cooperative approach, vehicular communication systems can allow all cooperating vehicles to be more effective. According to a 2010 study by the US National Highway Traffic Safety Administration, vehicular communication systems could help avoid up to 79% of all traffic accidents.

There have so far been no complete implementations of peer-to-peer networking on the scale required for traffic: each individual vehicle would have to connect with potentially hundreds of different vehicles that could be going in and out of range.

In 2012, computer scientists at the University of Texas in Austin began developing smart intersections designed for automated cars. The intersections will have no traffic lights and no stop signs, instead using computer programs that will communicate directly with each car on the road.

In 2017, Researchers from Arizona State University developed a 1/10 scale intersection and proposed an intersection management technique called Crossroads. It was shown that Crossroads is very resilient to network delay of both V2I communication and Worst-case Execution time of the intersection manager. In 2018, a robust approach was introduced which is resilient to both model mismatch and external disturbances such as wind and bumps.

Among connected cars, an unconnected one is the weakest link and will be increasingly banned from busy high-speed roads, as predicted by the Helsinki think tank, Nordic Communications Corporation, in January 2016.

REMOTE SENSING AND COMPUTER VISION

Recognition is one of the important aspects of visual perception. For human vision, the recognition and classification of objects is a natural, spontaneous activity. In contrast, general recognition still proves to be beyond the capabilities of current computer systems. The complexity of the vision task forced a shift in research from general purpose vision systems to those operating in a controled environment.

The model based approach is a powerful technique for the recognition of objects in complex real-world images. It performs the explicit representation of knowledge and relational information at different data-abstraction levels. Object models are used to guide the interpretation of a given image by suppressing the influence of image noise and eliminating false hypotheses. Fig. 1 describes the basic principle of model based vision. It consists out of three steps: grouping, indexing, and verification. Grouping comprises the translation of the raw pixel data into a symbolic relational description. This stage involves the extraction of geometric primitives (points, edges, regions) and their characterisation, as well as quantifying the relations that exist between these primitives (e.g. spatial relations). Once a symbolic description is generated, the symbols are used to index into a database of object models which are known to exist within the observations. This indexing phase then generates a set of hypotheses about the object models and their pose within the observed image. The verification phase checks the consistency of the hypotheses and eliminates false and inconsistent results, which are due to image noise. The grouping process can be repeated using the object model information, to redirect the grouping operators and refine the accuracy in this stage. In this way, model based vision allows the integration of bottom-up (i.e. from data to interpretation) and top-down (i.e. from model to extraction) control strategies.

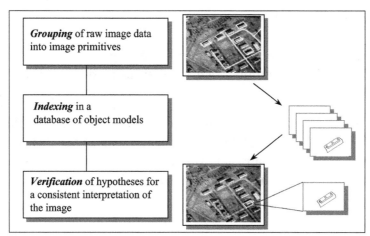

A model based vision system.

Image Primitives for Remote Sensing

Texture Analysis

Textural features are important pattern elements in human interpretation of data. Although no formal definition of texture exists, intuitively this descriptor provides measures of properties such as smoothness, coarseness and regularity. Texture analysis however is far from being a proven technique. The problem is basically two-fold:

- Texture analysis faces the challenge of finding adequate descriptors for a given texture. Higher-order statistics are necessary to describe the tonal variability, and filters of varying sizes are needed to handle the different size and spatial distribution of the tonal features within textures. Processing time and memory space restrict the number of descriptors which can be computed for a given image, so a set of discriminant texture descriptors need to be established for a given problem.

- A set of texture descriptors is computed for each pixel in the image, using the image information contained in a window centered on the pixel. This results in a Ndimensional feature space in which decision boundaries have to be laid to discriminate a number of classes. Depending on the required classes and the texture descriptors chosen, the class clusters are interwoven in the feature space. This, combined with the highdimensionality of the problem, requires dedicated classification techniques to solve the problem.

Gray Level Co-occurrence Matrices

Grey-level co-occurence matrices (GLCM) have been extensively studied in texture analysis. GLCM describe the frequency of one gray tone appearing in a specified spatial linear relationship with another gray tone, within the area under investigation (an LxL averaging window centered around the pixel to be classified). Each element (i,j) of the matrix represents an estimate of the probability that two pixels with a specified separation have grey levels i and j. The separation is usually specified by a displacement d and an angle ϑ:

$$\text{GLCM}, \phi(d, \vartheta) = \left[\hat{f}(i, j | d, \vartheta) \right]$$

$\varphi(d, \vartheta)$ is a square matrix of side equal to the number of grey levels in the image, or to reduce the size of the matrix one can limit the number of grey levels using quantisation.

The dimensionality of these GLCM can achieve large proportions and can lead to computational difficulties. Therefore, several statistical features are derived from the GLCM. Some of these features are related to specific first-order statistical concepts, such as contrast and variance, and have a clear textural meaning (e.g. pixel pair repetition rate, spatial frequencies detection, etc.). Other parameters contain textural information but are associated with more than one specific "textural" meaning.

Examples of GLCM features:

$$\text{energy}\{\phi(d, \vartheta)\} = \sum_{i,j} \hat{f}(i, j | d, \vartheta)^2$$

$$\text{energy}\{\phi(d, \vartheta)\} = \sum_{i,j} \hat{f}(i, j | d, \vartheta) . \log(\hat{f}(i, j | d, \vartheta))$$

$$\text{energy}\{\phi(d, \vartheta)\} = \sum_{i,j} (i - j)^2 . \hat{f}(i, j | d, \vartheta)$$

Gaussian Markov Random Fields

A second method for texture feature extraction is the use of gaussian markov random field models. This gaussian MRF model characterises the statistical relationship of the zero mean intensity I(s) at pixel s and its neighbours within a given neighbourhood structure N_s, with the following difference equation:

$$I(s) = \sum_{r \in N} \theta_r (I(s+r) + I(s-r)) + e(s)$$

Where e(s) is a zero mean stationary Gaussian noise sequence with the following properties:

$$E(e(s)e(r)) = -\theta_r v, \quad r \in (N_s \setminus \{s\})$$
$$= v, \qquad r = s$$
$$= 0 \qquad \text{elsewhere}$$

The neighbourhood N_s is shown in fig.2a where the order needs to be specified. This results in a stochastic model where the unknown weights θ r and v of the model are estimated using the least squares (LS) method, based on the image information in a LxL averaging window centered around the central pixel s. This set of weights $θ_r$, together with the variance v, is then used as a feature vector characterising the texture in the central pixel.

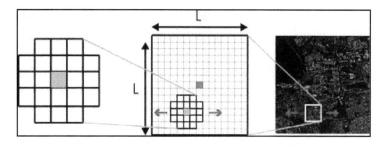

(a) Markov neighbourhood for order 1 to 7, (b) Estimation of markov parameters in LxL window 2.1.3.

Multitemporal Texture Analysis

Texture analysis has been mainly preoccupied with greylevel (i.e. single band) images. The use of multiband textures like in color, multitemporal or multispectral imagery can enhance the differentiation of textured regions. Each surface cover has a characteristic temporal signature, which can be exploited to further discriminate different regions. However, temporal analysis is usually done using point-based techniques (e.g. principal components analysis), discarding any spatial information. By analysing multitemporal textures, both the temporal as the spatial component can be taken into account to characterise a certain cover type.

To analyse multiband textures, the idea of GLCM is extended. Instead of measuring cooccurrence pairs within one single band, co-occurrences are measured between two different bands, where the separation between co-occurrence pixels i and j is specified by a multiband displacement d_{MB} and angle $θ_{MB}$. Using this co-occurrence matrix, the same derived features can be calculated.

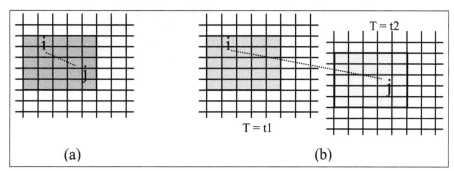

(a) grey level co-occurrence, (b) multitemporal co-occurrence.

A similar extension has been applied to the markov random field model. We estimate a vector value y(s), which denotes a multiband image observation at pixel location s, using the linear estimator:

$$y_i(s) = \sum_{j=1}^{P} \sum_{r \in N_{ij}} θ_{ij}(r) y_j(s \oplus r) + e_i(s), \quad i = 1...P, \ r \in N_{ij}$$

where P is the number of image bands, N_{ij} is the neighbourhood set relating pixels in band i to neighbours in band j, θ_{ij} are the unknown weights and $e_i(s)$ denotes the estimation error, which is modeled as a similar gaussian noise sequence as MRF.

Experimental Results on Texture Analysis for Remote Sensing

Surface texture has been identified as an important interpretative parameter for land use mapping in remote sensing. Texture allows the description of the spatial distribution of pixel intensities within a certain land use class. In the case of human settlements, this description gives a much finer characterisation of the different urban land use classes that can be observed. E.g. as the bright double-bounce backscatter in radar images gives evidence of possible human settlements within the image, the spatial distribution of these bright responses allows refining this analysis to a more detailed classification like e.g. the commercial city (geometrically ordered street patterns) vs. the old city center (disordered patterns). As a prospective technique, texture becomes more important as spatial detail increases. With the new very high resolution sensors with their meter-resolution accuracy, traditional point techniques will be inadequate as observation tool and the spatial variance of a land use class will take a much more prominent role.

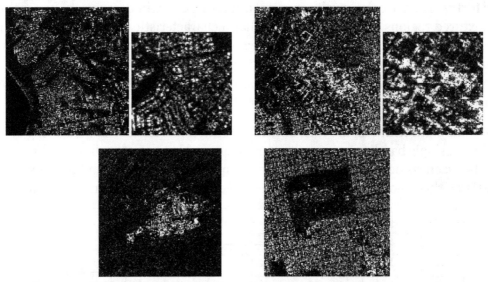

Examples of urban textures in Radarsat SAR imagery.

Urban SAR texture classes were examined with GLCM and MRF. Both techniques are able to distinguish several classes. It is found that directional patterns of streets make good texture descriptors. Important parameters are the size of the averaging window and the Markov neighbourhood mask, and the scale. Choosing a small averaging window leads to a good localization of area boundaries, but a fragmented image. Increasing the window results in a less fragmented image but with a decrease in spatial accuracy. The classification result can be cleaned up in post-processing (median, morphological filtering) depending on the desired output. An important remark is that each texture has a spatial scale at which it is best described, and these specific scales do not necessarily correspond for the different texture classes one wishes to distinguish (e.g. a mountain range and a suburb). A multi-scale approach should be used to solve this problem.

left to right - Composite Radarsat image; ground truth classes; MRF result.

  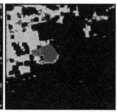 

(a)Averaging window 9x9, (b) 21x21, (c) 45x45.

Characterisation of multitemporal textures were also investigated. The dataset used in these experiments consists of two ERS SAR images, acquired above Louvain on Jan.1997 and Nov.1997. Four textures of interest have been identified within the scene, corresponding with city, agricultural field, forest and water. "City" and "water" are relatively easy to identify, due to the characteristic backscatter respons of the radar signal. The "field" and "forest" textures are difficult to distinguish on a singleband image. Comparing these textures within one single band shows that to visually distinguish the textures is not trivial. Forming a false-color composite with the multidate set, shows a more clear separation. The temporal signature of each texture class provides important information in the characterisation of the texture. It is important to note that this temporal signature in our example is not spatially invariant and point based characterisation of this signature would be inadequate. The spatial distribution of the temporal signature should also be taken into account, leading to the characterisation of multitemporal textures. Figure (a) shows a comparison between the co-occurrence matrices recorded within two distinct textured regions. The left column of figure (a) shows the co-occurrence matrices for field texture, the right column for forest texture. While the grey-level co-occurrence matrices show little difference between the two textures, the multitemporal co-occurrence matrix characterises the difference between the field and forest texture much more clearly.

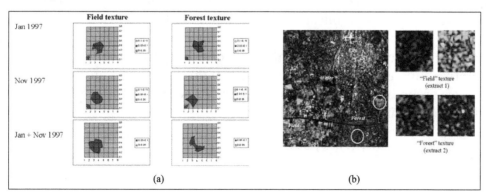

(a) Co-occurrence matrices for field and forest textures, (b) false color composite with a multi-temporal set.

Line Detection

Historically the Hough Transform (HT) has been the main means for detecting straight edges and since the method was originally introduced it has been developed and refined for that purpose. The basic concept involved in locating lines or edges with the HT is point-line duality: a point can be defined as a pair of coordinates or in terms of a set of lines passing through it. This concept starts to make sense if we consider a set of colinear points and the sets of lines passing through each of them and note that there is only one line common to all these sets. Therefore it is possible to find the line containing all the points simply by eliminating the lines that are not multiple hits.

In practical terms, the HT maps an edge or line pixel with coordinates (x,y) into a parametric space. The Duda and Hart's equation is commonly used to perform this transformation:

$\rho = x.\cos(\theta) + y.\sin(\theta)$

The parametric space coordinates, θ and ρ, are respectively the orientation and the distance from the origin to the line. The set of lines passing through each point is represented as a set of sine curves in the parametric space. Multiple hits, i.e. clusters, in the (θ, ρ)-space indicate the presence of lines in the original image. One of the main features of the HT is that a line will be detected regardless of possible fragmentation along it.

The primary requirement of the HT is a binary image as input (an edge map) and therefore thresholding will have to be used at some stage in pre-processing. In order to improve the performance of the HT we studied the use of the following pre-processing techniques:

- Nonlinear diffusion: A smoothing technique with edge enhancement or preserving properties; interior regions are easily flattened while boundaries are kept as sharp as possible;

- Gradient model for automatic threshold: Determines the threshold value of the magnitude of the gradient, yielding the binary image that is used in the HT step. 2.2.1.

Image Filtering

An extract of an aerial image of a residential zone is shown in figure. In this image, due to the large size and resolution, a considerable amount of detail is available. Typically, these high resolution aerial photographs show a small amount of noise and consequently it would not interfere too much in the later stages of a line extraction method. However, the large amount of detail available often leads to the extraction of artificial or irrelevant line features. Hence, to avoid the extraction of these features, the image must be simplified, i.e. smoothed. Simple gaussian blurring can be used. However, as figure clearly illustrates, this kind of smoothing has the major drawback of blurring significant features, essential at the later stages of this line extraction method. To circumvent this problem, we propose the use of nonlinear diffusion which is able to introduce the required smoothing while preserving the relevant edges:

$$\text{div}(c(\vec{r},t)\nabla I(\vec{r},t)) = \frac{\partial I(\vec{r},t)}{\partial t}$$

In this equation, I represent the image, r G is a vector with spatial pixel coordinates and t is the time or scale parameter. The diffusion coefficient $c(\vec{r},t)$ (commonly known as diffusivity), is a smoothly varying function of the magnitude of the gradient of the image, assuming large values for low gradients (i.e. interior regions), and low values in the vicinity of object boundaries, with high gradient magnitude:

$$c(\vec{r},t)=\frac{1}{1+\dfrac{\left\|\nabla I(\vec{r},t)\right\|^{2}}{\theta}}$$

The result is that diffusion takes place in interior regions but is inhibited in the neighborhood of edges, preserving the edge sharpness. The parameter θ also controls the amount of smoothing introduced. In this paper we set θ equal to the average value of the squared gradient magnitude. Additionally, a morphological close-open filter could be applied before the calculation of the image gradient on each diffusion iteration, thus more easily removing high contrast small scale details. A smoothed version of the aerial image is shown in figure (c). A flattening effect on uniform regions is perceptible but the sharpness of relevant edges is clearly preserved. Small scale details also appear simplified.

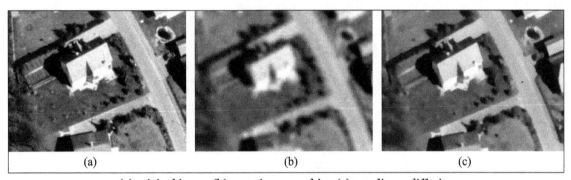

(a)   (b)   (c)

(a) original image (b) gaussian smoothing (c) non-linear diffusion

Gradient Threshold

A statistical method is introduced to automatically determine a threshold value for the magnitude of the gradient of a grayscale image, separating edge and nonedge pixels. This method models the histogram (H) of the gradient magnitude into the weighted sum of two Gamma distributions, $f(\alpha, \beta)$, each representing the distribution of either edge or nonedge pixels:

$$H=p_{0}.f(\alpha_{0},\beta_{0})+(1-p_{0}).f(\alpha_{1},\beta_{1})$$

The weighting factor p_{0} represents the probability of a certain pixel being a nonedge pixel. The parameters of this model, p_{0} and the characteristic parameters of the Gamma densities α and β, are estimated using an iterative process. The parameters estimation problem is divided into two steps. The first step attempts to find the α and β parameters of both the edge and nonedge density functions. The second step calculates the percentage of nonedge pixels, p_{0}. These two steps are performed alternately until the parameters converge or no progress is made.

Once convergence is achieved and all five parameters are known, a minimum value for the threshold is determined such that it satisfies the MAP (maximum a posteriori) criterion:

$$p_{0}.f(\alpha_{0},\beta_{0})<(1-p_{0}).f(\alpha_{1},\beta_{1})$$

Typically aerial photographs have a reasonably large size. Hence, a single threshold value for the gradient magnitude common to the whole image might not always be appropriate. Instead, we propose to divide this image into smaller partitions (square non-overlapping tiles) and then calculate local gradient histograms. Applying the gradient histogram modeling mentioned before to each of these histograms yields a distinct threshold value for each of the selected partitions. This approach is naturally slower as one need to determine as many gradient threshold values as the number of different tiles. However, these calculations can easily be carried out in parallel. Figure shows the resulting edge map once we apply this model on the histograms of the gradient of the aerial image. The image was divided in 16 equal size tiles (256x256). This binary edge map serves as input of the HT.

Hierarchical Hough Transform

The primary requirement of the hough transform is a binary edge image as input. Each edge pixel maps into a curve in the (ρ, θ) parameter space domain. Edge pixels lying on a straight line generate a family of curves that intersect in the same point of the parameter space. To extract the lines, one just needs to find these peaks in the parameter space.

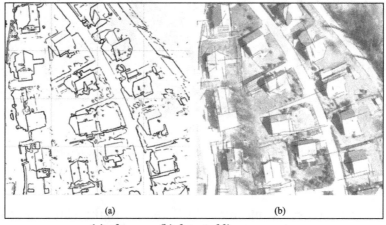

(a) edge map (b) detected line segments.

Traditional implementations of the HT use a parameter space that considers the whole edge image. We use a multi-resolution hierarchical scheme that considers several parameter spaces. It starts with large tiles of the binary input image, performs the HT and looks for line features on the parameter spaces concerning these tiles. Line features found are then removed from the (input) data, the tile size is halved and the HT proceeds in the same way with the smaller tiles. Both the minimum and maximum tile sizes can easily be adjusted, yielding different accuracies, with a more either local or global view of the input image. A typical result obtainable with this method is shown in figure. In this case, the minimum and maximum tile sizes were set to, respectively, 64x64 and 256x256.

Shape Description using Spatial Models

Probabilistic Hypergraph Representations

The recognition of objects in complex real-world images requires the use of powerful techniques for representing knowledge and relational information. As the techniques for detecting image primitives described in the previous chapter are not sufficient for the recognition of real-world objects, by using these primitives and taking into account the relations between them more complex objects can be described. The representation that is chosen to model these objects should meet two important criteria. On the one hand it should be able to characterise a whole class of objects (i.e. an object model), thereby accurately describing the variety in shape, color and texture that can occur. On the other hand, the representation should allow for fast recognition techniques. We consider graph theoretic representation formalism. An object is described as an assembly of parts, each represented as nodes in a graph carrying information that characterizes the part. Relationships among the parts are as arcs in the graph, but can also be represented by nodes (hypergraphs). The latter representation allows for higher-order relations instead of just binary relations. Recognition involves finding a subgraph isomorphism between the scene graph and each of the model graphs. A fast heuristic graph matching technique that exploits local context information is presented and compared with probabilistic relaxation approaches to structural matching.

Basic Representation Principles

Objects are represented using parametric structural hypergraphs (PSH) and object models are represented as random parametric structural hypergraphs (RPSH). The parts as well as the relationships between the parts are represented as nodes in the graph. Relationships can be Nary but have to be decomposable into binary relationships. A hypergraph contains several levels of nodes. The zero-level nodes represent object parts. The nodes at the first level represent binary relationships between pairs of object parts. Each relationship node is connected with the pair of nodes that participate in the relationship. The nodes at level n represent N-ary relationships between object parts. Since all relationships with arity higher than two are decomposable into binary relationships, the relationship nodes at level n are only connected with the pairs of nodes at level n-1 into which the relationship can be decomposed.

Nodes that represent object parts are characterized using attribute specifications. Object parts typically represent image primitives such as line-segments, region-segments. Characteristics of line-segment are: length, orientation, position of the center. Characteristics of region segments are: shape, color, texture, centroid position, orientation. In object graphs, specific values are assigned to the node attributes. In model graphs, likelihood distributions are specified for the attributes.

Nodes that represent binary relationships are characterised by a set of attributes and a pair of references to the child nodes that participate in the relationship. The relational attributes can be metrical or logical. Examples of metric relational attributes are: distance between the centers of a pair of line segments, angle between a pair of line segments. Examples of binary logical relational attributes are predicates like: "is parallel to", "is neighbour of". Logical attributes are assigned truth values. The relational attributes have specific values in object graphs. In model graphs, likelihood distributions are assigned to the relational attributes.

For notational simplicity, the sets of attributes (attribute vectors) are assumed to be vector quantised, such that they can be represented by discrete labels. As such, nodes in object graphs have specific labels and nodes in object models have label distributions which describe the likelihood of the labels for object instances of the models.

Graph Matching

Definitions and mathematics are introduced that form the base of the recognition process. Attributed hypergraphs are used as representation for higher-order structural patterns. An attributed hypergraph I, defined on a set of labels Ω, consists out of two parts: 1) H which denotes the structure of hyperedges, and 2) λ: H$\rightarrow\Omega$ which describes the attribute values of the hyperedge set. A hyperedge of order v with index k is denoted as I^v_k. Object parts in the hypergraph correspond to hyperedges of order 0 and are notated by I_k, dropping the superscript to ease the notation.

A random hypergraph M represents a random family of attributed hypergraphs, thereby serving as a model description which captures the variability present within a class. It consists out of two parts: 1) H which denotes its structure, and 2) P: H x $\Omega\rightarrow$ [0, 1] which describes the random elements. Associated with each possible outcome I of M and graph correspondence T: I$\rightarrow$M there is a probability P (I<MT) of I being an instance of M through T.

Correspondence between a scene primitive I_k and a model primitive M_{Tk} proceeds by comparing the support set of both primitives. The support set S of a primitve I_k is defined as the set of hyperedges that contain I_k in their argument list:

$$S(I_k) = \{I^v_l \mid I_k \in Arg(I^v_l)\},$$

Where, $Arg(I^v_l)$ denotes the argument list of the hyperedge I^v_l. Built over the support set is the context histogram, which is used to characterize scene and model primitive. For a scene primitive Ik and label α, the context histogram gathers the occurrence frequencies of a label α in the support set of I_k and is defined as:

$$C\left(I_k,\alpha\right)=\frac{\sum\limits_{I^v_l \in S(I_k)} \partial\left(\lambda\left(I^v_l\right)-\alpha\right)}{\left|S(I_k)\right|}$$

The denominator normalises the total mass of the contex histogram to unity.

Calculated on a random hypergraph, a context histogram is defined as containing the expected occurrence frequencies of the labels, modified by a hedge function F which encodes prior knowledge of the correspondence between scene and model primitive:

$$C\left(I_k \prec M_{T_k},\alpha\right)=\frac{\sum\limits_{M^v_l \in S(M_{T_k})} P\left(\lambda\left(M^v_l\right)=\alpha\right).F\left(I_k \prec M_{T_k}, \alpha, M^v_l\right)}{\left|S(M_{T_k})\right|}$$

The hedge function weights the contribution of each hyperedge within the support set of the model primitive, by taking into account the support that the primitives in the argument list of the hyperedge receive. This is modeled after the Q-coefficient in probabilistic relaxation. For binary relations this coefficient is expressed as:

$$Q\left(I_k \prec M_{T_k}\right)= \prod\limits_{I^1_{k,1} \in S(I_k) M^1_{Tk,Tl} \in S(M_{Tk})} p\left(\lambda\left(M^1_{T_k,T_l}\right)=\lambda\left(I^1_{k,1}\right)\right).P\left(I_l \prec M_{T_l}\right)$$

Where, the subscript in the first order hyperedges $I^1_{k,l}$ denotes its arguments.

For first order hypergraphs, the hedge function F is taken as:

$$F\left(I_k \prec M_{T_k}, \alpha, M^1_{T_k, T_l}\right) = \max_{I^1_{k,l} \in S(I_k)} p\left(I_l \prec M_{T_l}\right)$$

Similarity between a scene primitive I_k and a model primitive M_{Tk} is defined as:

$$S\left(I_k, M_{T_k}\right) = \sum_{\alpha \in \Omega} \min\left(C\left(I_k, \alpha\right), C\left(I_k \prec M_{T_k}, \alpha\right)\right)$$

Which can be used again as prior estimation, thereby establishing an iterative recognition scheme.

Experiments

We applied the theory in an experimental setup making a comparison between probabilistic re-laxation and context histogram matching (CHM). The aim is to detect structural objects within a image given a model of the object. This extends simple detection of an object within a scene, since each object part has to be correctly identified within the model.

Figure presents an artificial scene containing a number of building structures. This image consists out of line segments which form the basic primitives of the representation. Binary relations are gen-erated using the relative angle between line segments, resulting in a first order hypergraph. On top of this layer, a second layer of hyperedges is constructed by attaching to each binary hyperedge a virtual line segment, linking the midpositions of its arguments. With these virtual line segments the same angle relations can be constructed. First and second order relations for a segment are gener-ated within a neighbourhood radius of resp. 30 and 10 pixels to restrict the number of hyperedges to a manageable size. The quantisation level is set to eight resulting into 8 discrete relation labels. No use is made of unary measurements to characterize a line segment as the matching process relies solely on the information offered by the angle relation. The model is an extract from the scene which has to be localized. Model and scene hypergraph representations are generated independently from each other. A threshold of 50% is placed on the match probability to suppress scene noise and the best model match is retained. Figures shows highlighted the scene segments that pass the threshold for CHM and relaxation. Both methods show good structural matching results. Relaxation however, compared to CHM, shows an inferior noise suppressing ability which deteriorates as the match-ing results converge. This is again shown in the second example. Figure presents part of the city of Ghent. After initial segmentation the scene image contains 205 line segments. A crossroad structure needs to be identified in the image, containing 43 segments. Using a neighbourhood radius of 30 and 1st order relations, which shows the recognized scene segments for CHM and relaxation.

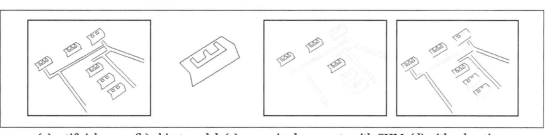

(a) artificial scene, (b) object model, (c) recognized segments with CHM, (d) with relaxation.

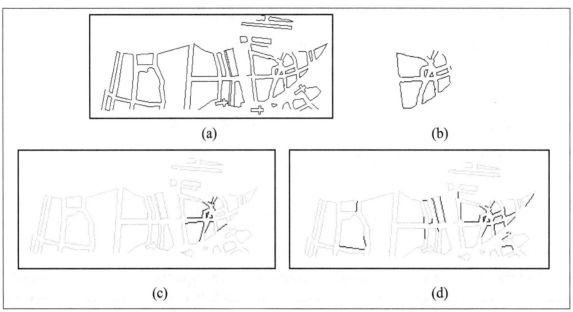

(a) original image, (b) model, (c) recognized segments with CHM, (d) with relaxation.

Description of Contours Using Curvature Scale Space

The scale of an observation is an important aspect in the description of an object. The appearance of an object depends on the scale at which it is observed and is only meaningful within a specific interval. Multi-scale representations have been developed within the computer vision community as a method for the automatic analysis and extraction of information from observations. This extraction is performed through a low-level analysis of the image with operators like edge detectors. The information that is extracted depends on the relation between the size of the objects in the image and the size of the operators. A scale space representation captures the scale aspect of objects by representing the input data on different scales. Thus the original signal is extended to a one-parameter family of derived signals that gradually supresses high detail structures. An important requirement in generating derived signals is that structures on a rough scale form a simplification of structures on a fine scale and are not formed by the transformation from fine to rough. Convolution with a gaussian kernel and its derivatives fulfills this requirement and forms the basis for scale space theory.

Basic Principles

We examine the use of curvature scale space (CSS) to represent object shapes extracted from a multisensor dataset. In CSS, contour evolution is studied by smoothing the shape with a gaussian kernel and computing the curvature at varying levels of detail. Consider a parametric vector equation for a contour)) $\bar{r}(u) = (x(u), y(u))$, where u is an arbitrary parameter. If g (u,σ) is a 1-D gaussian kernel of width σ, then X (u,σ) and Y (u,σ) represent the components of the evolved contour:

$$X(u,\sigma) = x(u) * g(u,\sigma)$$
$$Y(u,\sigma) = y(u) * g(u,\sigma)$$

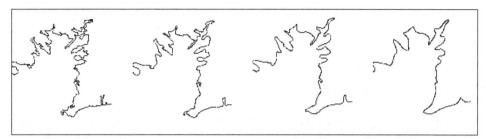

Smoothing with increasing scale σ = 1.0, 2.0, 4.0 and 8.0.

According to the properties of convolution, the derivatives of every component can be calculated as:

$$X_u(u,\sigma)=x(u) * g_u(u,\sigma)$$
$$X_{uu}(u,\sigma)=y(u) * g_{uu}(u,\sigma)$$

The curvature of an evolved digital contour can be computed by:

$$\kappa(u,\sigma)=\frac{X_u(u,\sigma)Y_{uu}(u,\sigma)-X_{uu}(u,\sigma)Y_u(u,\sigma)}{\left(X_u^2(u,\sigma)Y_u^2(u,\sigma)\right)^{3/2}}$$

A CSS image is generated by locating the zero crossings of the curvature κ (u, σ) for every smoothed contour. The resulting points can be displayed in a (u, σ) plane, where u is the curve parameter and σ is the width of the gaussian kernel. The result of this process represents a binary image called the CSS image of the contour. The information in the CSS image can be used to characterize the shape of a curve. Useful information is the contour points corresponding with zero-crossings which persist at a high scale. Since at a high scale (i.e. after smoothing with high σ) irrelevant shape deformations will be smoothed out, one can expect that the curvature zero-crossings which remain will mark important features.

Applications

In computer vision, analysis of image content is performed through the recognition of objects. As opposed to a pixel based analysis, objects allow for a more meaningful interpretation of the image which is closer to human perception. Dealing with objects also allows for an easier integration of context knowledge (given by an application expert) to make the application more robust and advanced.

Automatic Spatial Registration

Registration is a fundamental task in image processing used to match two or more images taken at different times, from different sensors or from different viewpoints. Problems that can occur are change over time, occlusion, image noise and differences in image geometry. Instead of performing registration on a set of control points, we have introduced the notion of control objects. The location and shape of these objects (e.g. coastlines, roads, and rivers) are used for automatic registation of multisensor imagery. The technique of curvature scale space can be used to represent the shape of objects. A representation can be constructed that is robust to image noise and is scale invariant, allowing the extraction of shape features which characterise a control object regardless of its original scale. Based on these features, images can be registered going from Resurs to Landsat TM.

Change Detection for Monitoring

The localisation and identification of significant changes in image sequences is an important task within the exploitation of satellite image data for monitoring purposes. With the growing availability of high resolution satellite imagery, the need for sophisticated automatic or semiautomatic aids for data processing is significant. The available change detection methods in temporal image sequences use difference images and as a result are highly sensitive to registration errors as well as photometric or radiometric conditions. Even if techniques would be developed for the elimination of all the differences due to image creation, there would still be differences of which the significance can only be measured by image processing specialists familiar with the observed scene. Computer vision allows for the development of more advanced techniques for the detection of changes in image sequences, where semantic information in the form of reference images will be used. Instead of detecting changes on the level of the individual pixels, changes can be detected on a higher semantic level. The detection process is guided by the use of image models describing expected changes. This allows the filtering of irrelevant image noise and results in a detection scheme which is more robust. Examples of an image model are regions of homogeneous spectral or textural characteristics, where the model consists out of spectral, textural as well as shape information.

APPLICATIONS OF COMPUTER VISION IN HEALTHCARE

Artificial Intelligence has already been implemented in the healthcare sector. Now the use of computer vision in this field is making surface and can support the rise to various applications that can prove to be life-saving for patients. This AI-powered technology is assisting more doctors to better diagnose their patients, prescribe the right treatments and monitor the evolution of several diseases.

Computer vision not only helps medical professionals in saving their valuable time on basic tasks but also saving patients' life. The applications of the technology for medical use has to perform by extending current ways that it's already being used and adding a layer of creativity and imagination.

Currently, there are several areas in healthcare where computer vision is being utilized and benefiting medical professionals to better diagnose patients, including medical imaging analysis, predictive analysis, health monitoring, among others. Below the benefits computer vision technology can assist health systems.

Precise Diagnoses

Computer vision systems offer precise diagnoses minimizing false positives. The technology can potentially obliterate the requirement for redundant surgical procedures and expensive therapies.

Computer vision algorithms trained using a huge amount of training data can detect the slightest presence of a condition which may typically be missed out by human doctors because of their sensory limitations. The use of computer vision in healthcare diagnosis can provide significantly high levels of precision which may in coming days go up to 100 percent.

Timely Detection of Illness

There are most fatal illnesses that need to be diagnosed in their early stages, such as cancer. Computer vision enables the detection of early symptoms with high certainty owing to its finely tuned pattern-recognition capability. This can be useful in timely treatment and saving countless lives for the long term.

Heightened Medical Process

The use of computer vision in healthcare can considerably lessen the time doctors usually take in analysing reports and images. It frees and offers them more time to spend with patients and provide personalized and constructive advice. By enhancing the quality of physician-patient interactions, it can also assist medical professionals to give consultation to more and more patients.

The use of computer vision in healthcare supports caregivers to deliver efficient and accurate healthcare services through its life-saving applications.

Medical Imaging

For the last decades, computer-supported medical imaging application has been a trustworthy help for physicians. It doesn't only create and analyse images, but also becomes an assistant and helps doctors with their interpretation. The application is used to read and convert 2D scan images into interactive 3D models that enable medical professionals to gain a detailed understanding of a patient's health condition.

Computer Vision for Health Monitoring

By leveraging computer vision technology doctors can analyse health and fitness metrics to assist patients to make faster and better medical decisions. Today, it is being utilized by healthcare centers to measure the blood lost during surgeries, majorly during c-section procedures. This can assist in taking emergency measures if the quantity of blood lost reaches the last stage. Additionally, the technology can also be leveraged to measure the body fat percentage of people using images taken from regular cameras.

Nuclear Medicine

As a section of clinical medicine, nuclear medicine deals with the use of radionuclide pharmaceuticals in diagnosis. Sometimes computer vision techniques of remote radiation therapy are also referred to nuclear medicine. In diagnostics, it mainly utilizes single-photon emission computed tomography and positron emission tomography.

References

- Computer-vision-applications-shopping-driving-and-more, ai-sector-overviews: emerj.com, Retrieved 14 March, 2019

- Ross, Girshick (2014). "Rich feature hierarchies for accurate object detection and semantic segmentation" (PDF). Proceedings of the IEEE Conference on Computer Vision and Pattern Recognition. IEEE: 580–587. arXiv:1311.2524. doi:10.1109/CVPR.2014.81. ISBN 978-1-4799-5118-5

- Zhang, Jian, Yan, Ke, He, Zhen-Yu, and Xu, Yong (2014). "A Collaborative Linear Discriminative Representation Classification Method for Face Recognition. In 2014 International Conference on Artificial Intelligence and Software Engineering (AISE2014). Lancaster, PA: DEStech Publications, Inc. p.21 ISBN 9781605951508

- Xia Liu Fujimura, K., "Hand gesture recognition using depth data", Proceedings of the Sixth IEEE International Conference on Automatic Face and Gesture Recognition, May 17–19, 2004 pages 529- 534, ISBN 0-7695-2122-3, doi:10.1109/AFGR.2004.1301587

- Steger, Carsten; Markus Ulrich; Christian Wiedemann (2018). Machine Vision Algorithms and Applications (2nd ed.). Weinheim: Wiley-VCH. p. 1. ISBN 978-3-527-41365-2. Retrieved 2018-01-30

- Thrun, Sebastian (2010). "Toward Robotic Cars". Communications of the ACM. 53 (4): 99–106. doi:10.1145/1721654.1721679

- The-role-of-computer-vision-in-healthcare: analyticsinsight.net, Retrieved 04 April, 2019

INDEX